DISCREET INDISCRETIONS

COMMUNICATION AND SOCIAL ORDER

An Aldine de Gruyter Series of Texts and Monographs

Series Editor

David R. Maines, Wayne State University

Advisory Editors

Bruce Gronbeck • Peter K. Manning • William K. Rawlins

David L. Altheide and Robert Snow, **Media Worlds in the Postjournalism Era**

Joseph Bensman and Robert Lilienfeld, **Craft and Consciousness: Occupational Technique and the Development of World Images** (*Second Edition*)

Valerie Malhotra Bentz, **Becoming Mature: Childhood Ghosts and Spirits in Adult Life**

Jörg R. Bergmann, **Discreet Indiscretions**

Herbert Blumer, **Industrialization as an Agent of Social Change: A Critical Analysis** (*Edited with an Introduction by David R. Maines and Thomas J. Morrione*)

Dennis Brissett and Charles Edgley (*editors*), **Life as Theater: A Dramaturgical Sourcebook** (*Second Edition*)

Richard Harvey Brown (*editor*), **Writing the Social Text: Poetics and Politics in Social Science Discourse**

Norman K. Denzin, **Hollywood Shot by Shot: Alcoholism in American Cinema**

Irwin Deutscher, Fred P. Pestello, and H. Frances G. Pestello, **Sentiments and Acts**

Bryan S. Green, **Gerontology and the Construction of Old Age: A Study in Discourse Analysis**

Pasquale Gagliardi (ed), **Symbols and Artifacts: Views of the Corporate Landscape** (paperback)

J. T. Hansen, A. Susan Owen, and Michael Patrick Madden, **Parallels: The Soldiers' Knowledge and the Oral History of Contemporary Warfare**

Emmanuel Lazega, **The Micropolitics of Knowledge: Communication and Indirect Control in Workgroups**

Niklas Luhmann, **Risk: A Sociological Theory**

David R. Maines (*editor*), **Social Organization and Social Process: Essays in Honor of Anselm Strauss**

Peter K. Manning, **Organizational Communication**

Stjepan G. Meštrović, **Durkheim and Postmodernist Culture**

R. S. Perinbanayagam, **Discursive Acts**

William K. Rawlins, **Friendship Matters: Communication, Dialectics, and the Life Course**

Dmitry Shlapentokh and Vladimir Shlapentokh, **Soviet Cinematography, 1918–1991: Ideological Conflict and Social Reality**

Anselm Strauss, **Continual Permutations of Action**

Jim Thomas, **Communicating Prison Culture: The Deconstruction of Social Existence**

Jacqueline P. Wiseman, **The Other Half: Wives of Alcoholics and Their Social-Psychological Situation**

DISCREET INDISCRETIONS

The Social Organization of Gossip

Jörg R. Bergmann

Translated by
John Bednarz, Jr.

(with the assistance of Eva Kafka Barron)

ALDINE DE GRUYTER
New York

About the Author

Jörg R. Bergmann is professor of sociology at the Justus-Liebig-University, Giessen, Germany. He received his advanced doctoral degree from the University of Constance in Baden-Württemberg and has taught at the University of Trier. His research interests, which have yielded a number of journal articles and contributions to edited volumes, include conversation analysis, ethnography and social interaction in institutional settings. He is currently doing research on moral communication in everyday life and the mass media. This is his first book to appear in English.

Originally published as *Klatsch: Zur Sozialform der diskreten Indiscretion*
© Copyright 1987 by Walter de Gruyter & Co., Berlin

ALDINE DE GRUYTER
A division of Walter de Gruyter, Inc.
200 Saw Mill River Road
Hawthorne, New York 10532

This publication is printed on acid-free paper ∞

Library of Congress Cataloging-in-Publication Data
Bergmann, Jörg R.
  [Klatsch, English]
  Discreet indiscretions : the social organization of gossip / Jörg
R. Bergmann : translated by John Bednarz, Jr., with the assistance
of Eva Kafka Barron.
      p.   cm. — (Communication and social order)
  Includes bibliographical references and index.
  ISBN 0-202-30467-1. — ISBN 0-202-30460-4 (pbk.)
  1. Gossip.   I. Title.   II. Series.
HM263.B38913   1993
302.2′24—dc20   93-4263
                                                     CIP

Manufactured in the United States of America

10 9 8 7 6 5 4 3 2 1

FTW
AEH1109

Contents

Preface

A group of people who had been eating lunch together and gossiping about their friends and acquaintances were asked what they had been doing and talking about the entire time. "Nothing," they answered. The following study is concerned with this "nothing," with what it designates and what it conceals. It examines gossip as a specific type of oral communication that everyday consumes a considerable part of the time and attention of millions of people—either in face-to-face encounters or on the telephone. The gossip about prominent figures that occurs in the mass media: in newspaper gossip columns, or on television will be mentioned only in passing. This work concentrates wholly on the everyday, friendly, or unfriendly gossip that can be viewed—before any means of technical reproduction—as a source medium of mass communication.

The goal of the following investigation is to define gossip as an independent genre of everyday communication. According to its scientific classification, it operates within the sociologies of culture, language, and knowledge. This reference to the sociological character of the following text, however, should not be read as a warning. Its intention is not to translate its subject matter into an existing theoretical language and then to perform a brilliant reconstruction of it. Instead, it intends to perform a detailed examination of the internal structures and external social embeddedness of gossip. The investigation is based on recordings of actual gossip-conversations that are partially transcribed in the text. In analyzing this material I have tried to approximate Georg Christoph Lichtenberg's ideal, namely, "to split an idea that everyone views as simple into seven others, just as a prism refracts light into different rays, one more beautiful than the next, and then again to collect an array of these and produce clarity where others see nothing but a dazzling confusion."

The work was written between 1984 and 1986 and presented in a slightly modified form as an Habilitationsschrift to the Faculty of Social Sciences of the University of Constance. I would like to thank Professors H. Baier, Th. Luckmann, and H.-G. Soeffner who advised the work for their advice, instruction, and criticism. I am especially indebted to Professor Th. Luckmann for his uncompromising judgment and his steadfast support during our years of joint teaching and research. Our

DFG-Project, "Strukturen und Funktionen von restriktiven Gattungen der alltäglichen Kommunikation," is thematically and methodologically related to the present investigation. I would like to thank those who cooperated in this project—Angela Keppler, Hubert Knoblauch, Ute Lacher and Bernd Ulmer—for their advice, research findings, and "enthusiasm" during our data analyzing sessions. I owe thanks as well to Harold Garfinkel, Emanuel Schegloff, Paul Drew, Charles and Marjorie Goodwin, John Heritage, Anita Pomerantz and above all to Gail Jefferson, who did not, to be sure, exert a direct influence on the crafting of this text, but through their exemplary work, counsel, and encouragement still played their part in it. Finally, I would like to give special thanks to Gerhard Riemann (Kassel) for generously making available to me a conversational transcript. I would also like to say that my investigation of gossip, that obscure object of desire, would have gotten nowhere without the help of Ska Wiltschek—but what I owe her goes beyond what can be put into words here.

Jörg R. Bergmann
Staufenberg

Foreword

Dear Reader (may I be allowed to address in this antiquated fashion whomever the following lines will reach)!

It would be amusing to introduce the author of this book about gossip by indulging in a little bit of gossip myself. Undeterred by the obviousness of such a simple rhetorical maneuver, I would reminisce about a contretemps which occurred at a meeting to which both Jörg Bergmann and I were invited. He and I listened with interest to the competent contributions and with patience to the indifferent ones. Only when Dr. X (I had better not name him after all) began talking nonsense about a subject close to my friend's mind and heart did our reactions differ. I, fancying myself to be a definitively hardened practitioner of the academic craft, endured unmoved. He, however, turned redder and redder in his face until he could no longer contain himself. He suggested to a perplexed audience that if Dr. X insisted on divagating on the subject under discussion, he would do well to acquaint himself with an introductory text on the topic if, as might be likely, he were to find the pertinent advanced literature too difficult to grasp. Or words to that effect.

Having followed my inclination and told you this little story, I find that I was not gossiping about Jörg Bergmann after all. As you know, and as you will find amply documented in this book, gossip contains a piece of news involving a morally dubious if not outright reprehensible action. But, in fact, I did not consider my friend's outburst morally reprehensible at all, even if it made me doubt his diplomatic aptitude. If the story were to qualify as gossip, it would be gossip about Dr. X—had I dared to lift his incognito. In any case, even if I had named him, I could not have been certain that you would recognize the name. Dr. X is not quite so famous internationally as he would like to be. Again, as you and I know in a general way, and as the book will show with precision, one can certainly tell anecdotes about reprehensible actions even if the actor is not known to the listener. But then the genre of the story will be only a very distant cousin to gossip. My story, then, wasn't gossip about the author of this book; in fact, it wasn't gossip at all.

And more: even if I had named Dr. X and even if you had recognized the name, another element of what Bergmann calls the triad of gossip would be missing: Dear Reader, I do not know *you*. I therefore do not know whether you share my view of what is and what is not morally reprehensible. It is not fortuitous that few things are more embarrassing than starting off on a nice spot of gossip and being rewarded by a stony glare. Which reminds me that a foreword is no place to gossip, and it is just as well that my little story does not qualify for that genre. In any case, gossiping is very much a face-to-face affair in which one must cautiously proceed step by step in order to avoid expressions of cold disapproval by the listener. (Bergmann will tell you all about the whys and hows.) Epistolary gossip is derivative. Once a gossiping relationship is established, one can, of course, continue by letter, in a gossiping network perhaps even by circular letter.

If the subject matter indicated by the title of the book seems frivolous, and if this impression is reinforced by the chatty nature of my observations—be undeceived! Gossip is a genre of moral communication in a twofold sense: it moralizes and it is moralized about. It is human to gossip, and it is human to pretend that one is not a gossiper. The analysis of gossip reveals much about the moral order of a society and even more about the communicative construction and maintenance of that order. Not that studying gossip for its own sake ("because it is there") is not almost as much fun as gossiping *viva voce*! But, in addition, the communicative processes and forms involved in gossiping, which have both a reconstructive (of a past event) and moral (evaluating acts and persons) function, are of great general interest to social theory. Gossiping could be considered a laboratory case for the study of the construction of social relationships, of the drawing of boundaries between a We and a They, of the creation of moral solidarities, and of shifting alignments. It is all the more surprising that almost without exception (such as Georg Simmel's discussion of secrets, which has implications for our topic) gossip was not considered worthy of theoretical interest, and that in the few instances where gossip made its appearance in the literature of the social sciences—mostly in social anthropology—it was more speculated about than studied in detail. Bergmann's is a pioneering study!

Some years ago Bergmann was my assistant (the "my" refers to a peculiarity of the German university system) at the University of Constance. He collaborated with me on a project in which we tried to describe, and analytically *re*construct, the ways in which social science "data" are constructed. This was part of a general ("sociology-of-knowledge") interest in knowing more, and in more concrete detail, about the essentially communicative procedures by which social realities and social relationships are constructed. After some earlier theoretical essays of mine on the structure and functions of communicative genres and the communicative budgets of a society, Bergmann and I were fortunate to gather an excellent team of collaborators (Bergmann lists them in his foreword) around a project on reconstructive communicative genres, and equally fortunate in receiving support from the German Science Foundation. The results of our investigations will be published soon. Bergmann's book, while not part of the project, originated within its context. In fact, the project-linked analyses of gossip helped us to grasp more precisely the links between the reconstructive and moral functions of communicative processes and gave the main impetus for a successor project on moral genres of communication in which we (Bergmann, I and again an excellent team) are studying a wide range of data, from religious TV programs to anti-smoking campaigns, ecological groups, genetic and family counselling, to family "secrets." In a sense, gossip was the link between our old and our new investigations.

The book, already highly acclaimed after its German publication, will make its own way among a readership traditionally more open to the detailed analysis of concrete social phenomena than its German counterpart. I hardly need to praise the book. But if I did not in the beginning succeed in gossiping about Bergmann, I may at least end by praising him. He is a sociologist whom Georg Simmel would have been proud to acknowledge as a descendant.

Thomas Luckmann

Translator's Acknowledgment

Several parties contributed significantly to the publication of this translation. I would like to take this opportunity to express my sincere thanks and gratitude to them for their help. I would like to thank the Rutgers University Computer Services, and in particular Mr. Warren Mayer, for their technical assistance. I would like to thank Prof. Dr. Jörg Bergmann for his help, especially with the bibliography. I would also like to thank Dr. Richard Koffler for his unselfish editorial assistance in particular, and for his encouragement and support in general. And finally, I would like to thank Mrs. Eva Kafka Barron for her invaluable help in translating those difficult parts of the text that were beyond my limited talents.

The contributions of all of these parties only helped to make this a better translation. Its shortcomings are the responsibility of the translator himself.

Transcription Symbols

[	Beginning of an overlap, i.e., two parties speaking simultaneously.
]	End of an overlap.
=	Rapid succession of another utterance, or rapid speaking within an utterance.
(0.8)	Pause; duration in seconds.
(—)	Short break; short pause (ca. ¼ sec.)
yes:::	Extension of a vocable; the number of points indicates the length of the extension.
°yes°	Softly.
°°yes°°	Very softly.
no	Emphatically.
NO	Loudly.
. ;	Strongly or weakly falling intonation.
? ,	Strongly or weakly rising intonation.
perha-	Break off of a word or utterance.
·hh hh	Detectable breathing.
<u>but</u>	Utterance underscored with laughter.
(oh)	Uncertain transcription.
( )	Speaker unknown or the content of the utterance is incomprehensible; the size of the bracket indicates the length of the incomprehensible utterance.
<laughter>	Paraphrase of paralinguistic, gestural, and extraconversational events or information concerning the situation or context of the conversation.
. . .	Omissions from the transcript.

The names of persons as well as the specification of times and places appearing in the transcripts have been changed.

The transcription symbols used in this book to capture the details of conversational material are common to conversation analytic research. They have been developed and elaborated by Gail Jefferson.

Chapter 1

The Everyday Understanding of Gossip as a Social Scientific Resource

ON THE DANGERS OF OBVIOUSNESS FOR THE SOCIAL SCIENTIST

Any sociological attempt to understand gossip must live with the fact that, long before sociology appeared on the scene and made it the subject of scientific investigation, gossip was a social phenomenon of daily life about which actors had their own ideas and made their own judgments. From our everyday experience we know what is meant when a conversation is called a coffee-klatsch. We do not need to resort to a dictionary when a person is called a gossip. We are not puzzled when we come upon a gossip column in a newspaper. Each one of us has already encountered gossip firsthand. Of course, there are those who dismiss gossip as an empty and useless waste of time; who ignore and distance themselves from it. But even these reactions presuppose that they have had experience with gossip. So any sociological investigation of gossip must assume that it is preceded by an everyday-typifying construction of its subject. And, we can add, if a sociological study of gossip starts from a prescientific knowledge of it, then, of course, it also profits from the structure that it helps to explain.

Science and philosophy can take it as a principle that what is familiar is not yet understood. To be sure, wherever scientific investigation is concerned with everyday phenomena this axiom can also be read in the opposite sense: that what is understood is to this extent already familiar. Then the fact that a phenomenon like gossip constitutes a familiar and obvious part of everyday life no longer appears as a mere deficit ("not yet") but as a foundation ("implicit") of methodologically proven knowledge—as a foundation that is significant for scientific access to its subject in different ways.

1

The obviousness with which we encounter something as gossip in our everyday life or participate in it is for a sociology of gossip at the same time the initial capital and an encumbrance. To start from the positive side, gossip for us is something implicit in everyday life. In the words of Alfred Schütz, it is a phenomenon that presents itself in the prescientific social world, "as no longer in need of analysis."[1] This is true of our experience of everyday life, especially for those who gossip. Their activity is obvious to the point of being overlooked. Often, at the end of such a conversation they look at their watches and express real or feigned surprise that so much time has passed. A sociology of gossip can now use this obviousness in the everyday experience of gossip as a given that can be converted into methodological certainty; that gossip is an easily identifiable subject of investigation that merely waits to be awakened from its slumber of the "implicitly familiar." Thus every sociological investigation of gossip draws quite decisively from our daily experience of gossip insofar as this creates a subject of investigation for it—to start with, anyway. For this helpful foundation is burdened with two dangerous encumbrances.

First, we have to realize that all obviousness—including the obviousness of gossip—implies an unexpressed "noli me tangere" and that even the slightest examination would be enough to make it disappear it forever.[2] But any scientific examination has to disregard this proscription, even if it destroys the unavoidable obviousness of its subject. This also means that, in the case of gossip as in that of any other ordinary everyday phenomenon, scientific examination will produce disappointments because it so alienates and distorts its subject—for the everyday understanding—that it becomes hardly recognizable anymore. Attempts to explain what is funny about a joke usually end up in disappointment, no matter how correct and plausible they may be. Scientists—this is their fate—are like little children who take apart their dolls or toy trucks in order to try to find the voice inside or what propels it. In this sense science always produces disappointment wherever it concerns itself with ordinary, everyday phenomena. All knowledge contains a destructive element whenever it goes beyond the familiar. This is the sense of the Hegelian remark that, "The most rational thing a child can do with his toy is to take it apart."[3] The analysis of gossip—and isn't gossip a kind of toy for adults?—will also find it impossible to avoid analyzing its subject to the point of unrecognizability. And, even if it could be put back together again, its character would still be changed: a self-evident practice becomes something that now lives off of its scientific explanation.

Thus, as far as the obviousness of its subject is concerned, any sociological study of gossip is confronted with a dilemma. Science's claim to provide knowledge requires it to analyze the obviousness of ordinary, everyday phenomena. But at the same time it depends on this obviousness because prescientific knowledge provides its subject. We can avoid this dilemma, of course, by emphasizing one of its sides. But this solution is not acceptable for sociologists, no matter which side they declare themselves for. In taking one side they throw out the baby with the bath water; if they take the other they jump into the bath with the child. Less metaphorically speaking, in either case they do not assume an appropriate attitude toward the socially preconstituted quality of their subject, with the result that they do not grasp the subject properly.

Ironically, the danger of losing its subject threatens the sociology of gossip whenever it unreservedly submits itself to its "scientific" ambitions. There can be no obviousness for the imperious glance of science. "I am the Lord of knowledge, thou shalt have no ordinary, everyday knowledge beside me"—runs the First Commandment of scientific belief in itself. For such an attitude the fact that a phenomenon like gossip is a socially preconstituted obviousness of daily life must be a constant irritation. Therefore, as far as it is concerned, sociology stands and falls with the removal of this irritation. Durkheim, the Nestor of this position, conceded—although with a palpable displeasure—that the sociologist, as a rule, always begins with "vulgar concepts." But because these "vulgar concepts" are emotionally charged, ambiguous, and subjectively colored as a rule, the first and foremost task of the sociologist is, "to throw off the yoke of these empirical categories."[4] But in this scientific campaign of liberation, the subject of investigation is also removed with the relentless elimination of all prescientific everyday elements. The subject is not taken seriously as what it really is and ought to be. In its prescientific givenness it appears as a factor of disturbance and therefore should be replaced, right at the start, with a scientifically purified creation. The scientific instrument thereby eliminates the undesired detritus but also its subject at the same time.

The fact that social scientific works often do not get very far when they laboriously strive to be scientific reveals itself in a symptom that is mostly passed over as marginal—in the ridiculousness of scientific prose. Helmut Plessner observed that, "every fact that is analyzed away into nothing without being aware of this is ridiculous."[5] It is quite clear that this danger of ridiculousness confronts those attempts that deal with ordinary, everyday phenomena in the straightforward scientific spirit. If, for example, a scientific text contains remarks about a "device for the proper, standard regulation of specific bodily noises," and if this is a description of nothing more than the well-known handkerchief, then it is hard to tell here whether this is a parody of science or an unintentional comedy about unbridled scientific erudition.[6] Of course, no investigation of gossip is immune to this danger of ridiculousness. Therefore, the fact of ridiculousness should be accepted. But not by making the reticent subject of knowledge sneak away in the face of science's imperious manner.

One encumbrance that burdens the everyday obviousness of gossip resides in the fact that its socially preconstituted mode of givenness provokes a forced scientific approach. But gossip evaporates when subjected to the pressure of the unrestrained and reckless attempt to treat it scientifically. Any sociological attempt to understand it must remain aware of the obviousness of its subject and reflect this in its language, even though it unavoidably effaces it.

A second encumbrance that burdens gossip because of its socially preconstituted character threatens its sociological understanding in the opposite direction. Precisely because gossip—even for the sociologist— is such an obvious cultural practice, scientific understanding can be sacrificed to everyday understanding but not vice versa. Phenomena that present themselves in everyday experience as "no longer in need of analysis" empirically resist attempts at scientific analysis. Over long periods the analytical observation of the scientist melts the phenomenon only on the surface—just like a snowball in one's hand. Its nucleus remains unaffected. That is to say, contrary to their claim to transform what is familiar into knowledge, scientists always rely on their everyday experience.

The difficulty in minutely analyzing an everyday phenomenon like gossip lies not only in the fact that it is an obvious part of our daily practice and, as such, escapes reflection. Max Weber had already warned against this when he remarked, "that the obvious (because it is an immediate part of our experience) tends to be the least 'considered.'"[7] The specific methodological structure of the social scientific process of appropriation and analysis also appears as an obstacle. Everyday phenomena drastically lose their obviousness when they are made the subject of scientific investigation. But their internal structure is not so easily surrendered. The concept that social scientists elicit from their subject must be pulled down by them layer by layer. In this work there is no other choice than to rely once again on an everyday understanding that, then, decomposes as the analysis continues. In this— hermeneutic—process, scientists, strictly speaking, come to no conclusion. Every interpretive acquisition is "burdened" with lasting and newly introduced elements of everyday understanding that advancing cognition has to use to perform its continually penetrating, analyzing function. The process of scientific interpretation is, like that of the interpretation of everyday experience that it follows, in principle open and unending.[8] This is the fact that misleads so many scientists to a kind of interpretive fatalism, that is, that makes them restrict hermeneutic efforts to a minimum in determining their subject and still implicitly to rely on their everyday understanding and its intuition. For if it appears hopeless from the beginning to arrive at a genuinely scientific determination of the subject, free from all elements of everyday understanding, it does not make much sense to try to do this.

If what is known about the ordinary, everyday understanding of gossip is analyzed only on its surface and—as in everyday experience—used directly and immediately as practical knowledge, then sociologists can come to realize the way in which other social processes are reflected or refracted in gossip. But they do not ascertain anything about its internal structure and composition in this way. So a sociology of gossip is threatened with a loss of its so seemingly familiar subject in this case too. To be sure, this time not because gossip is removed by an imperious scientific claim to knowledge but because it is left, so to speak, in a cocoon of everyday understanding.

As it seems, any sociological attempt to understand gossip would do well to remember what botany knows: particularly attractive plants are often the most dangerous ones, because gossip belongs to this species. For those who approach it sociologically—later we will find that this also applies to those who practice it—gossip is an attractive and at the same time dangerous business. Attractive because its everyday mode of givenness allows it to present itself as an "analysis-friendly" subject of investigation. Dangerous because this subject escapes any scientific approach that wants scientifically to purify its everyday ordinariness or to use it unrestrictedly as a scientific source. How then can we reach the phenomenon of gossip in its everyday obviousness? This question invites us to search the existing scientific literature for the concept of gossip.

GOSSIP—METHODOLOGICALLY INSTRUMENTALIZED

Gossip is not unknown to the scientific literature. In many works from different domains such as urban sociology, sociology of communities, sociology of the family, professions, groups, organizations, law, the anthropology of law, social psychology, sociopathology, and, of course, the sociology of language—the list could go on—we can find statements about gossip, or, rather, we detect them. For many of these works only discuss gossip in passing. Gossip has remained, in large part, a typically marginal phenomenon in the sociological literature. It has been acknowledged but has not been able to attract concentrated attention. It is clearly possible that this marginalization expresses the extent to which our everyday understanding of gossip determines its social scientific treatment. For the cliché that there are more important things than gossip is a fixed part of our everyday understanding of it.

Gossip, in accordance with the first observation, is thematized in the social scientific literature as an autonomous, relevant subject of investigation only in a few cases; often as a phenomenon that occurs marginally in the treatment of a sociologically "established" problem. Surprisingly, we find an instructive example of this mode of thematizing gossip in social scientific methodology.

At present there is no textbook on social research that does not contain a chapter on the possibility of treating an empirical question through the collection of information and data "in the field," that is, by using the methods of field research. Whether this method is understood in the tradition of cultural and social anthropology as "ethnography" or sociologically as "participant observation,"[9] its essential characteristic is the attempt, via the long-term participation in the social life of a group, an institution, or an environment, to preserve an authentic depiction of the observed course of social action and the perspectives of the actors. One of the main difficulties that accompany this method revolves around the question, how are social scientists to gain access to their "field," how are they to establish themselves and move about in it? And at this point the literature often refers to gossip. Malinowski, who can be looked upon as the chief witness here because he had founded the modern type of scientific ethnography with his research on the Trobriand Islanders at the time of World War I,[10] repeatedly underscores in his methodological discussions the need for the ethnographer not only sporadically to visit the world of the natives but also to live as intimately as possible among them. And to illustrate this postulate he refers to his own method: "Soon after I established myself in Omarakana (Trobriand Islands) I began to take part, in a way, in the village life, to look forward to the important or festive events, to take personal interest in the gossip and in the development of the small village occurrences; to wake up every morning to a day, presenting itself to me more or less as it does to the native."[11]

Although at no point does Malinowski address the question of the sense it can have for a field researcher to participate in the gossip of the people he observes, an answer to it is not difficult to supply. First of all, the context of his statement reveals that the field researcher, when he participates in gossip, can announce and document his intention to live in the community like "one of the natives." To reject gossip would mean that his life as an ethnographer would not "take a natural course in harmony with his surroundings."[12] In addition to this *integrative effect*, the ethnographer's participation in gossip still has another meaning for Malinowski. The field researcher obtains information about himself naturally, without having to resort to the standard—viewed skeptically by Malinowski[13]—question-and-answer method. To the field researcher who participates in gossip, what the people are gossiping about simply falls in his lap of itself as *acquired information*.

Malinowski did not explicitly reflect upon the methodological functions that gossip can fulfill in the context of field research, nor did he care about its substantive determination. He assumes our everyday understanding of gossip and works with it—just as anyone who uses the interview as a research method clearly assumes that a question will always produce an answer.[14] And although generations of field researchers after Malinowski—following his suggestion—took part in the gossip of those they investigated, for a long time no one thought to make gossip a subject of instruction for students of anthropology and sociology within the framework of scientific training in universities. Obviously, the ability to gossip and to take part in it is so basic that it can be assumed by any competent member of society and does not need to be (or tolerates being) problematized or instructed. In this regard social scientists differ little from other professional groups such as the police[15] or local journalists[16] who use and value the integrative and informative effect of gossip in the same straightforward manner in their work.

Against the background of this unproblematic instrumentalization of gossip it is now clear that some social scientists encountered difficulties in their attempt to use gossip as a means of field research. Accordingly, the anthropologist M.N. Srinivas in his study on Rampura, a caste village in the southern district of Mysore, reports that he often visited the brahman tea shop because, as Srivinas says, "It was part of my work to pick up gossip." But he quickly found out that the village leader, who must have been very helpful to him in the realization of his research, disapproved of these visits because honorable people would avoid the tea shop because of the gossip circulating there. In his visits he would also acquire gossip that he did not need.[17] Karola Elwert-Kretschmer, a sociologist working in developing economies, reports about another difficulty. In her field research in a west Malayan village she had concerned herself expressly with gossip as a source of information but found out that she did not always get access to it. "The peasant women were the ones who did not gossip with me. I was neither asked about third parties nor were third parties spoken about in my presence." She was brought into gossip only about those who—like herself—were outsiders in the village in the eyes of the peasants as well in her own eyes.[18] In another way, Ronald Frankenberg ascertained in his study of a northern Welsh village that because of his position as an outsider a field researcher can almost never participate in the gossip of a community as a member does. Frankenberg had observed that the residents of the village did not hesitate to complain or joke about their friends and acquaintances. But he himself could not participate in this way in these conversations. Even carefully critical statements are blocked by remarks such as "That's my cousin you're talking about." And he depicts a situation in which he was rebuked when he made a disparaging remark about the card playing of the grandmother of his partner's future son-in-law.[19] Finally, Colin Bell's experiences are relevant here. Bell encountered gossip very early in the course of his study of the social mobility of middle-class families in two neighborhoods in West Swansea. As he writes, he could not resist the temptation to participate in this gossip and tell the information that he got about one family to another one. Although this active participation in gossip generated more gossip very rapidly, Bell decided to stop this behavior after some time because "the communicability of my informants began to dwindle when they realized that I would also talk to other people about them."[20]

None of these field researchers substantively or methodologically pursued the problems they encountered in dealing with gossip in the framework of their research activity. Gossip remained for each a means of acquiring data and of promoting the commitment of the researcher to his field of study. The problems of the methodological instrumentalization of gossip initially meant only that this means has limited applicability. But this is where these problems are interesting, because they cast additional light on the phenomenon of gossip and illuminate its multifaceted structure for the first time. Thus we come to realize—contrary to Malinowski's implicit functional attribution—that gossip can also function very well as a *means of social segregation and distancing*, which for those who are excluded from it does not entail the acquisition of information but the denial of it. The experiences of field researchers also clearly demonstrate that gossip is not a purely descriptive category but contains a decidedly *evaluative component*. Of course, these findings hardly go beyond what is known about gossip from our everyday experience. If we "faithfully" repeat gossip in conversation or dismiss information as mere gossip, then we are thereby clearly referring to that segregating and evaluating sense of gossip that caused so much difficulty for the field researchers. The methodological instrumentalization of gossip and the experiences of field researchers in dealing with it disclose only its socially preconstituted quality without even approaching an analytically reconstructive determination of it.

Moreover, there is an early reference in the *Nicomachean Ethics* concerning the irreverent suspicion that anthropologists are people who are not averse to gossip. Aristotle writes about the ideal form of the "great-souled man"—that is, someone who "claims and is worthy of great things and most of all the greatest things"—is no *anthropologos*. In German translations of this we find: the great-souled man is not one who speaks readily or much about others or who likes a conversation to take a personal turn. English translations unanimously prefer a more direct mode of expression: the fact that the high-minded person is not an *anthropologos* means quite briefly and to the point: "He is no gossip."[21]

GOSSIP—ETHNOGRAPHICALLY INVENTORIED

An immeasurably wide range of works containing statements about gossip is formed by all those texts that concern themselves with a claim to provide a complete ethnographic description of the daily life of a social group—a tribe, a village, or an urban neighborhood. We should not be surprised, then, that in these ethnographic studies gossip always appears as only one thematic aspect among others. Their goal is usually much broader and consists of describing the social life of a local group in all its color, stratification, and complexity. However, it appears worthwhile to sweep these scattered remarks about gossip together like chips and fragments of different sizes and to draw conclusions from them about the treatment that gossip received in these works. Ethnographic presentations characteristically do not try immediately to immerse the phenomena grasped by them in an aggressive theoretical acid bath but to preserve them in their concrete, rough form. The basic attitude of being initially interested in details for their own sake allows one to expect that even ethnographic marginal notes and side remarks on gossip have, all things considered, a considerable expressive value.

Because ethnographic studies will subsequently constitute an important foundation of the present investigation, a preliminary clarification seems in order, for the ethnographic literature, in which gossip admittedly does not play a central role but is nonetheless not unknown, provides a very mixed picture. If we consider its history in the discipline and the chosen forms of its presentation, then the following types of ethnographies can be distinguished:

- The largest group by far are the *anthropological ethnographies*, which together describe an enormous spectrum of socially and politically distinct societies. This spectrum extends from small, leaderless communities without a state apparatus and a differentiated system of relationships to ethnic groups with a complex organization of rules of ancestry, age groups, and social institutions to societies organized as states with centralized authority.[22] The fact that the ethnographies of these societies refer so often to gossip has its particular basis in an argument that has been represented in the anthropological literature to this day, the argument that, especially in early societies, gossip is an extraordinarily widespread activity conducted with devotion. It was the Austro-American ethnologist Paul Radin who in 1927, in his well-known book *Primitive Man as Philosopher*, disclosed that "Primitive people are indeed among the most persistent and inveterate of gossips."[23] Even if we do not share Radin's view of the particularly gossipy nature of "primitive" peoples we cannot deny the fact that it is above all anthropological ethnographies that contain information about gossip.

- A second type of ethnographic investigation that pays at least passing attention to gossip are *sociological ethnographies*. Gossip, as a form of communication between villagers or urban neighbors, has been a familiar theme in the sociology of communities whose methodological orientation has been strongly influenced by cultural anthropology ever since the 1920s.[24] But we also find observations and remarks on gossip in the ethnographies of the sociology of the family, which are concerned with the social network of urban families, as well as in the ethnographies of the sociology of organizations that investigate the forms of communicative behavior within formal organizations from a microsociological perspective.

- A further type of ethnographic investigation in which we encounter gossip can be called *historical ethnography*. In this case it is not our own observations that serve as the basic data of description but budget ledgers, court records, inquiry reports, and other source material from which a detailed picture of the daily life—and of the gossip—of a family or a village can be reconstructed. "Montaillou is only a drop in the ocean," writes LeRoy Ladurie in his study of a Pyrenees village at the beginning of the fourteenth century, "but the microscopic investigation of this drop, which we can perform thanks to the exhaustive curiosity of the Inquisitor from Pamiers, provides us, through the cultivation of the infusoria that flourish there, with a survey of world history."[25]

- A final group of ethnographic works can be summarized under the title of *literary ethnographies*. It is clear that ethnographic writing has for some time now been in a state of crisis. In contrast to the stylistically evident self-certainty of earlier ethnographers of the cast of Evans-Pritchard, present-day ethnographers are (in Clifford Geertz's formulation) "harassed by grave inner uncertainties, amounting to almost a sort of epistemological hypochondria, concerning how one can know that anything one says about other forms of life is as a matter of fact so."[26] This crisis is expressed, on one hand, by the sudden spurt of works that view ethnographies as "texts" or even as a separate species of literature and analyze them in respect of their distinctive stylistic and rhetorical characteristics or more exactly, in respect of the implicit conventions of this species of ethnographic realism.[27] On the other hand, the crisis of traditional ethnographic writing expresses itself in the experimental search for new narrative and poetic forms of ethnographic experience and in the accompanying blurring of the boundaries between scientific and literary ethnography.[28] Now gossip is, as some authors—perhaps somewhat overstatedly—have maintained, "neglected by sociologists and left to the brilliance of some social novelists."[29] We cannot simply count social novels, despite the ethnographic details and insights they provide, among literary ethnographies in the sense meant here. Nevertheless, against the background of this remark it is noteworthy that the ethnographies written with an explicit claim to literary validity regularly concern themselves with the phenomenon of gossip.

If we go through the mountain of materiel that ethnographers have assembled on gossip, we will make an astounding discovery. Although the ethnographic approach seems able to distance us from the familiar things of our daily life, so that they can be understood and analyzed, we are forced to the conclusion that ethnographic studies do not really provide access to the socially preconstituted quality of gossip. This does not mean that they cannot tell us anything about gossip but that they notoriously neglect to make gossip a subject of analysis that, as a practice, specifically refers to everyday experience. This will be made clear in the following through the description of two principles of the ethnography of gossip.

One widespread principle of the ethnography of gossip resides in the documentary *reproduction* of gossip conversations and letting them speak more or less for themselves. Let's take as an example a passage from Laurence W. Wylie's study *Village in the Vaucluse*:

> The village women are alone when they are doing their household tasks, but much of their work they can do in the company of other women. When the women stay at home and have only sewing or knitting to keep them busy, they often invite a friend or two to have a cup of coffee with them. The friends bring their sewing or knitting and, after sipping their coffee, they get to their handiwork. If the weather is warm and sunny they carry their chairs out in front of the house to work and talk in the open. There they may be joined by one or two other women, and many of the people passing by stop to chat a moment. These work-and-talk groups are

self-sufficient. Because the conversation in these groups so often centers on village events and especially on village personalities, and because the conversation is usually critical, the men complain about the evil effects of the gossip groups. This complaint is justifiable, although the men also indulge in character assassination. But on the whole, the men are more interested in sports and political argument than in local gossip, while for the women the gossip circles are the most important form of recreation.

The woman's group that I was able to observe most naturally was the one that met in front of Madame Pleindoux's house. On sunny days this group sits in a corner of the Town Hall Square across from the café. This is a strategic spot because anyone who goes anywhere in the village is almost forced to pass this way. One morning I sat with this group, life was dull. The women were knitting and had little to talk about. This conversation was interrupted by the arrival of Madame Peyroux who had just been to Reynard's store to buy yarn. She announced that the price of yarn had been raised another ten francs. This brought forth from all the women protests against those mysterious forces which seemed intent on destroying them. This topic would have been pursued the rest of the morning, as it often was, if Madame Fraysee had not dropped by with news of the latest escapade of Paul Jouvaud.

Paul, the adolescent moronic son of Simon Jouvaud, was feared by everyone in the village, especially by the women. He was strong as an ox and was reputed to have an abnormally large sexual organ. Madame Fraysee reported that a few minutes before, her husband had been passing an abandoned house up on the top of the hill. He heard shouts and when he went to investigate, he found that Paul had made twelve-year-old Suzanne Canazzi go in the house with him and wouldn't let her leave. Fraysee slapped Paul, hoping it might teach him a lesson.

Everyone in the group was outraged. The expected catastrophe had almost taken place. The women expressed pity for the Jouvauds, but, they said, "What can you expect from such people?" Simon and Marcelle were first cousins. They had always been in love with each other, but their parents would not let them marry. Confronted by the menace of Paul Jouvaud, the women agreed that if no satisfaction could be obtained from the Jouvaud family, the authorities of the town should take the matter in hand. This led to criticism of the Mayor and the Town Clerk. The Mayor didn't even live in the commune, and didn't care what happened to it. Back in the days when "poor Monsieur Prullière" was Mayor, things were different. He wouldn't have tolerated a scandalous situation like the present one with Paul Jouvaud loose in the village. The Jouvaud affair nourished the conversations of the gossip groups for several days, but on the morning in question the conversation came to an end when the town clock struck twelve. The women gathered up their sewing and knitting, exclaiming that they had forgotten about the time. Madame Favre hurried home, and Madame Pleindoux followed her slowly holding Dédou by the hand.[30]

Wylie's description is precise and intuitive and evokes in the reader not only a plastic picture of the working and gossiping women at the corner of the town hall square but also spontaneous recollections of similar experienced situations. But Wylie is obviously not interested in the phenomenon of gossip for its own sake. The gossip group and their conversations for him are only a vehicle for creating a glimpse of the microcosm of village life for us. Thereby his descriptions draw their force from the fact that he does not infuse them with analytical and theoretical constructions. Wylie proceeds as if he has in mind Walter Benjamin's maxim, which states that, "it is half the art of narration to keep repetition free of explanations."[31] Wylie's presentation relies on our everyday understanding of gossip. In favor of a narrative presentation of forms of village life it rejects the analysis of gossip as a vehicle of this narrative presentation.

In the same way as Wylie, other ethnographers have also rejected the analysis of gossip in their texts in favor a of its reproduction. Gossip was used by Evans-Pritchard expressly as a means of better understanding a foreign culture. During his study of the Azande in the Sudan he discovered "that the writing down of imaginary conversation episodes was a great help in understanding the thinking and behavior of the Zande." Among "Zande Conversation Pieces" (the title of Evans-Pritchard's work) we find a long bit, "Two Women Gossiping," from which the following excerpt is taken:

A: Oh sister, are you speaking the truth?
B: Do I go about my dear! I sit in my place and hear all the news. Have you not heard that Baiwo's wife has revolted against him?
A: Speak it out sister! Has she seen another one again? Oh that girl, she has always been fond of going from one man to another!
B: My dear, do I go about! They say Baimeyo "has come out for her" and is vastly enjoying himself with her.[32]

In contrast to Wylie, Evans-Pritchard does not tell a story about a gossip group but allows the gossipers—although in an imagined dialogue—to speak for themselves. But like Wylie, Evans-Pritchard does not make any effort to elevate gossip to the level of a subject of analysis. For both, the depiction of gossip is a means to an end. And both assume readers who make use of their everyday understanding of gossip.

This documentary-style, pictorial treatment of gossip was pushed to the extreme by the anthropologist Elsie C. Parsons. Her ethnographic work on the Zapoteco-speaking Pueblos of Oaxaca (Mexico) of 1936 contains an almost 100-page chapter on "Town Gossip" in which she does nothing else but divulge the numerous stories she heard, as well as their background, in narrative form. It is interesting to hear the reason Parsons gives for this method. "In any systematic town survey," she writes at the beginning of the chapter on gossip,

> much detail is necessarily omitted and the life appears more standardized than it really is; there is no place for contradictions or exceptions or minor variations; the classifications more or less preclude pictures of people living and functioning together. In my last visit to Mitla I spent a good deal of time visiting and gossiping, and I would recall these scenes, as well as a few from earlier years, in order to convey personal aspects of the townspeople and some of the variability in their lives.[33]

Gossip is unconditionally bound—and this is Parsons's point—to concrete events, apparently insignificant particularities, and personal affairs. It is essentially *idiographic*. And this structural characteristic predestines it in large part for use in ethnographies as a literary means of compensating for the undesired consequences of scientific systematization, namely, to set against the desiccation of an ethnographic comprehension of life.

A second principle of gossip of the ethnographic literature is to bracket the presentation, that is, to presuppose as familiar, much of the gossip process itself, and to describe *individual factors that characterize the circumstances of the realization of gossip*. This process is found in an ethnography about life on Truk, an island belonging to Micronesia in the west Pacific. The authors of this ethnography, Thomas Gladwin and Seymour Sarason, also deal with gossip in a chapter entitled "Non-violent Aggression":

> A more common and less explosive means of expressing aggression, both within and without the lineage, is gossip which the Trukese refer to as "lots of talk" and recognize as a menace and also a very effective sanction. The patterns of gossip would be familiar to any American. There are the inveterate gossips, particularly women, who spend a good part of their working hours in scandalized expostulation over someone's real or imagined peccadilloes, and keep a sharp eye out for everyone's movements in hopes of smoking out a trysting couple. These are at the extreme, but all Trukese, men and women alike, gossip, particularly when something especially shocking and circumstantial comes to light. It was for example almost to be taken for granted that every week or so when the boat came over to Moen a new story would be reported to be making the rounds of Romonum concerning the three or four young men and women who lived in our house and helped with the homework. It is usually possible to get a fairly complete account of a man beating his wife from anyone on the island within an hour of its happening. It appears that most Trukese are

prepared to believe without further examination the worst about their fellow man. At the same time the victims of gossip do not appear to be able to shrug it off; however preposterous a story may be they worry about it, and worry everyone will believe it.[34]

This description of gossip structurally characterizes a majority of ethnographies. The gossip process as linguistic activity is—often, as in the above example, with express reference to the reader's understanding—more or less by-passed. The presentation concentrates entirely on the distant and proximate circumstances of the emergence and effect of gossip. In no case does this occur—at least not obviously—in accordance with a pregiven descriptive schema. And yet it is always only a short list of factors that are comprehended by the ethnographer. The factors named the most are the following:

- In principle all members of a society count as *participants* in gossip. Yet there are fixed circles of conversation in which gossip is cultivated without restriction.[35] Women and old men almost always count as particularly gossipy. Yet in the Pacific culture of Tchambuli, for example, the men are viewed as more liable to gossip.[36]
- *Places and occasions* for gossip are found everywhere acquaintances—accidentally or intentionally—meet, pass the time undisturbed, or better still are able to combine the passing of time with other activities. Examples from the ethnographic literature include the above-mentioned knitting of French village women,[37] the sewing circles of English ladies,[38] communal bread baking of Spanish country women,[39] as well as the communal cleaning of vegetables in a Chinese village.[40] In Africa[41] or Melanesia[42] the watering hole functions as the center of gossip, just as do the water queue at a well in Nepal[43] or Greece,[44] the Maniok-hut for the Mundurucú indians of the Brazilian Amazon,[45] the Tofu business in a Japanese village,[46] bars and barber shops in Spain,[47] or small shops in Newfoundland.[48]
- The *victim* of gossip can in principle be anyone. But often we can detect specific groups of persons who are readily gossiped about, as are, for example, single women and widows,[49] daughters-in-law,[50] teachers,[51] or doctors in the hospital.[52]
- The *subject* of gossip always consists of observed, conveyed, or suspected stories about personal qualities and idiosyncrasies, behavioral surprises and inconsistencies, character flaws, discrepancies between actual behavior and moral claims, bad manners, socially unaccepted modes of behavior, shortcomings, improprieties, omissions, presumptions, blamable mistakes, misfortunes,

failures—preferably from the area of the relations between the sexes.[53]

- The *effect* of gossip is twofold: for the participants themselves gossip is entertaining and, to the extent that it slakes their curiosity, satisfying. On the victim, however, it exercises a sinister effect. He fears the talk of other people. Of men in particular it is said that they are afraid of the gossip of women because they fear that their status in society will be upset.[54] A particular motive underlies the fear of gossip in preindustrial societies: gossip is a conspicuous medium for casting the suspicion of witchcraft or charging others with it.[55]

Many ethnographers who turn their attention to gossip restrict themselves to contributing to the factors mentioned above that concern the circumstances of the realization of gossip. If we consider this list, which has been distilled from a long series of ethnographic works, from some distance we will not be able to help wondering whether ethnographers, in dealing with gossip, had ever heard of Lasswell's famous formula, "Who said what to whom with what effect?"[56] But between the ethnographic factorization of gossip and communication science's analytic formula there exists a conclusive parallelism in two respects.

On one hand, in both cases a variable grid is placed over a formally closed social subject—a film, a radio broadcast, a newspaper article, a political speech, or even gossip—and with the help of it the imprint of individual characteristics can be grasped and compared. Such factorization gives social researchers the possibility of taking stock of the opaque material they investigate in all its ramifications. They analyze their subject in order to create a representative picture of it out of its parts—à la dot-matrix newspaper photographs. But just as a picture emerges out of the thousands of individual points that compose the newspaper photo only through the understanding of the observer, so the gossip factors named in the ethnographies, and more or less described in detail there, compose a picture of gossip only with the help of the understanding of the reader.

The second parallel between the ethnographic determination of factors and Lasswell's formula resides in the fact that both share a basic methodological shortcoming. In Lasswell's analytic formula, "Who says what to whom with what effect?" this shortcoming is clearly revealed: the only part of the sentence that is not transformed into a question, the predicate ("to say") is what designates the real process of communication. Although the formula investigates the sender and receiver, the content and the effect of communication, the act of communicating itself remains an unquestioned presumption that social researchers use as a resource to formulate their scheme of analysis. And the situation is not any different in the case of an ethnographic inventory of the individual factors of gossip. As much as we learn from the ethnographies of *gossip*, the activity of *gossiping* and the capacities required for this remain unclear. But this is a more than merely tolerable omission. To the social scientist who accepts gossip as a given social fact, access to the preliminary question of what makes gossip gossip is in principle closed. The specific performances of actors that allow interaction to be perceived as gossip by them or an observing third party cannot even be formulated by the social scientist as a problem.

The above passages reveal that the ethnographic literature concerned with gossip still manifests further affinities: it is replete with explicit or implicit explanations of gossip. Many times these explanations are developed in an ad hoc manner and remain without further clarification, as in Gladwin and Sarason's case for whom gossip is a means of the nonviolent articulation of aggression. More frequently, however, the ethnographic literature mentions only a few authors, beginning with Max Gluckman's 1963 essay entitled "Gossip and Scandal," who have made a serious theoretical commitment to the phenomenon of gossip. These approaches to the explanation of gossip will be presented and discussed in Chapter 5. Therefore, they do not need to interest us here because, in the social scientific research process that is built on the intersubjectively preconstituted quality of the social reality, explanation can always be the second step. It is preceded—explicitly or not—by a phase that provides an interpretively reconstructive appropriation in which the selected social fact is observed, described, and interpreted in detail. This chapter is concerned with the difficulties of such work.

The methodological functionalization of gossip within the context of field research remained inextricably stuck in the "naive" understanding that determines our daily practice of gossip. This merely practical appropriation of gossip was already surpassed in the ethnographic studies. Narrative or dramatic documentation provides a differentiated picture of individual gossip conversations and situations; the descriptive presentation of individual factors of the realization of gossip reveals not only its ubiquitous dissemination but also some of the components that characterize its internal structure. In face of the question, how does a conversation in the communicative behavior of people preserve the meaning structure of gossip?, ethnographic descriptions stand as if before an invisible barrier. Clearly, this question interests an ethnographer as little as precise chemical processes that occur in baking or fermentation interest a cook. The following will be concerned with developing a framework of investigation in which it will be possible to question what so far has remained unquestioned in works on gossip.

Chapter 2

Gossip as a Reconstructive Genre of Everyday Communication

ON THE DISCREPANCY BETWEEN TALKING ABOUT GOSSIP AND ITS PRACTICE

Gossip is a concept from daily life. We encounter it in conversations and letters, in novels, films, and in the daily newspaper:

"Only Coffee Klatsch Is Better"

(Reykjavik) While cozily drinking coffee in an airport lounge steward-esses of "Icelandair" this Tuesday simply forgot about their job: the plane took off without them. The absence of the cabin crew was only noticed ten minutes after take-off when a passenger asked for service. The plane thereupon turned around and returned to the Reykjavik airport where the captain found the women lost in conversation. The passengers' amuse-ment about the event was not shared by the airport administration. They explained the failure as "a serious break in security" and announced steps to avoid similar happenings in the future. (Deutsche Presse-Agentur, Jan. 23, 1968)

In this newspaper report the concept of the "coffee-klatsch" serves to typify the conversation of a small group of women. This typification also conveys connotations—as it were with a wink—that create the report's newsworthiness and that the newspaper editors obviously thought would attract the attention of readers through the use of the concept of coffee-klatsch in the headline. What kind of connotations these are is not said. In order to figure them out we, as readers, depend on the use of our everyday understanding of gossip. As readers we can, for example, develop an interest in the cited newspaper report because we "under-stand" that gossip is a thoroughly mundane activity practiced everyday by everyone and because this "understanding" of the banality of gossip contradicts the fact that a coffee-klatsch in Reykjavik was found worthy of mention in a newspaper report. This contradiction leaves in us, the readers, the expectation that something else—a remarkable or in any event, newsworthy event—lurks behind the coffee-klatsch. The head-line makes us anxious. But if the ensuing story only told us that some of the "stewardesses" in the airport in Reykjavik were sitting around gos-siping, we would be disappointed because this would not amount to news for us. Actually, the newspaper report begins with the information that the stewardesses missed their flight by sitting around "cozily drink-ing coffee." Just like the headline, this information "lives" off our every-day understanding of gossip. We know that interest in gossip has to be absolutely subordinate to one's professional obligations. But we also know how time flies when we are lost in gossip.

The present remarks were not intended as an analysis of the above newspaper headline. (For this, we would have to know that the headline clearly presents a playfully ironic variation on the well-known slogan: "Only Flying is Better.")[1] Their goal, instead, was to show that an every-day understanding was connected with the concept of gossip that goes far beyond the lexical meaning and essentially determines its application and perception. However, a sociology of gossip cannot limit itself to this aspect. The fact that we *designate* something as gossip in our everyday experience is one thing; that we *practice* it is another.

It makes sense to separate the concept and practice of gossip for no other reason than that the designation gossip does not appear at all in the vast majority of cases in which we gossip with others. Of course, it may happen in many situations that one of the participants expressly speaks of gossip in order to announce, for example, his interest in this type of diversion. Doris Lessing opens her novel *The Golden Notebook* in this way:

> The two women were alone in the London flat.
> "The point is," said Anna, as her friend came back from the telephone on the landing, "the point is, that as far as I can see, everything's cracking up."
> Molly was a woman much on the telephone. When it rang she had just enquired: "Well, what's the gossip?" Now she said, "That's Richard, and he's coming over. It seems today's his only free moment for the next month. Or so he insists."[2]

In order to initiate and conduct gossip, however, metacommunicative "formulations"[3] of the type of Molly's "Well, what's the gossip?" are neither required nor usual. As with other communicative actions it is also true of gossip that we perform it without having "to call it by its proper name." This refers to the fact that we possess a practical knowledge by means of which we can reliably recognize gossip in our everyday experience and competently participate in it. If we start from the plausible assumption that not every conversation is gossip, then we must assume that our partners have the capacity to evoke gossip as an autonomous, intersubjectively shared form of communication, which implies the capacity to decide from individual indicators when a conversation is gossip or turns into it. This capacity to gossip competently can also be considered as a form of everyday understanding. It corresponds to what Gilbert Ryle calls "knowing how"—in contrast to "knowing that"—and what Schütz and Luckmann, analyzing this rigid contrast into a spectrum of knowledge types, call "habitual knowledge" ("Gewohnheitswissen.")[4]

The "substantial" everyday understanding that reveals itself in our talk about gossip and the "procedural" everyday understanding that constitutes our capacity to gossip do not comprise, of course, two completely separate types of knowledge. Although there are overlaps and fluid transitions, their distinction itself remains meaningful and necessary. This is strikingly shown in the case of gossip by something that has been recorded in the literature but whose significance so far has not even begun to be clarified. This concerns an obvious but still noteworthy discrepancy that exists between talking about gossip and its practice— the *discrepancy between the collective public denunciation and the collective private practicing of gossip.*

The fact that gossip is practiced throughout the world has already been clearly demonstrated by numerous ethnographic studies. But what about its "public denunciation?" How is this to be understood? And is this more than a merely historical, possibly even accidental, trait of gossip? In order to be able to answer these questions it is necessary to find access to statements and texts in which a public discourse about gossip is conducted. A remark by Karl Vossler, the philosopher of language, puts us on the trail of one of those types of texts. In an essay published in the year 1923, in a book dedicated to the memory of Max Weber, Vossler recommended "viewing the treatises on persuasion, viz., the old rhetorics, as the first attempt to investigate language sociologically."[5] If we follow this recommendation, we see immediately that, already at the time when the first theories of human commerce and rules of conversation were written, gossip was also a subject of discourse and resolutely discredited as an offense against good manners, as discourtesy and tactlessness.[6]

Thus Theophrastus, Aristotle's student—to cite only one of numerous examples—in his famous "Characters" describes the "backbiter" with the remark: "He is prone to malign one of the company who has gone out; and give him but the opportunity, he will not forbear to revile his own kin, nay he will often speak ill of his friends and kinsfolk, and of the dead."[7] In the "Book of Jesus Sirach," in which the ethical ideas of the Old Testament were summarized into an ethical treatise, and which later was called "Ecclesiasticus," we find the words, "Whoever rejoices in an evil will be admonished and whoever repeats gossip is lacking in understanding."[8] In his mid-sixteenth-century influential work "Galeatus," a treatise on the "forms that one must observe or avoid in dealing with others," the Italian bishop Giovanni della Casa dedicates a separate chapter to the question: "How one should curb his tongue when he speaks about others."[9] It is hardly surprising that the founder of the pietist sect of the Moravian Brotherhood, Nikolaus Ludwig Count Zinzendorf, in his "Thoughts on Speaking and the Use of Words" (1723)—a radical regimentation of conversation and of social intercourse in general—rails vehemently against the immorality of gossip.[10] The moral weeklies of the Enlightenment period are full of sketches and character studies in which court gossip, empty compliments, and court intrigues are criticized, as much as is the gossiping of the lower classes, with the moral realism that characterizes this literary genre. Any proper bourgeois family would study Fontenelle during their labors, for example, while canning fruit.[11]

From antiquity to the nineteenth century the denunciation and condemnation of gossip have appeared in all the books devoted to conversation as well as in the behavioral theories that formulated the compulsory code of duties and rules of correct social intercourse for an epoch or social group. In the nineteenth century this line was split. Normative aspects were separated from descriptive-analytical ones. This line found its normative continuation in the genre of books on manners and treatises on decorum, which in Germany relied mostly—in a normatively abbreviated version[12]—on Adolph von Knigge's treatise *Über den Umgang mit Menschen* (1788), and which, then as today, experienced numerous printings. Even today books about decorum still unanimously condemn gossip. For example, it occurs in one that, not immodestly, calls itself "the Knigge of the 20th Century": "Thou shalt not speak ill of thy neighbor and spread idle gossip. This not only shows your bad character but also isn't smart, for the next victim might be yourself!"[13]

Information about the actual practice of gossip, in contrast to its official denunciation, cannot easily be gotten from the theories of conversation. From the fact that the condemnation of gossip was so persistently repeated we might draw the opposite conclusion, namely, that its denunciation remained relatively inconsequential for its actual practice and therefore had to be formulated and propagated anew time and again. But this would be a weak proof. Historical ethnographies and social novels, however, contain adequate references to the fact that gossip has been diligently cultivated at all times and places.[14] And yet cryptic remarks are found in many treatises on conversation that demonstrate the discrepancy between a behavioral proscription and behavioral practice of gossip. Thus the Enlightenment figure Christian Thomasius writes in a 1710 work, "Kurze Entwurf der politischen Klugheit, sich selbst und anderen in allen menschlichen Gesellschaften wohl zu raten und zu einer gescheiten Conduite zu gelangen" ("A Brief Outline of the Prudence of Advising Oneself and Others Well in All Human Associations") about "showing discretion in daily conversation," and in this context postulated that, "(the prudent man) speaks only good of those who are not present," in order then to continue resignedly: "although this rule is very seldom taken in the intended way."[15]

The demonstrable gap between the behavioral proscription and behavioral practice of gossip is not systematically thematized in the different ancient, court, and bourgeois theories of conversation. All these remarks and instructions for a binding culture of conversation remain basically normative—normative at first still in regard to a correct life but then later only in regard to conventional forms of civility. These texts contained the specific behavioral standards held as binding in the respective epoch or social group for the different conversational types— for example, sociable conversation, salon conversation, court ceremonial or recreational conversation. As a separate type of conversation gossip experienced the same fate in all these texts: it fell through the normative grid. It was treated like a poor relative of true conversation; one with whom it was wise to have no dealings, against whom one warned others, and on whom one otherwise did not waste any words.

The possibility of conducting a nonnormative discourse about gossip begins to present itself clearly—as already remarked—only in the nineteenth century. To be sure, some of the bourgeois theories of conversation had already abandoned the purely normative standpoint and begun to describe the phenomenon of "gossip."[16] But the descriptive-analytic parts of these theories had not yet taken on a form of their own. The fact that such a development occurred in the nineteenth century is due to multilevel reasons that can only be touched on here. In part, a role was played by the fact that in nineteenth-century Germany a bona fide philosophy of conversation emerged with Romanticism, one that opted, in opposition to the moralism of the Enlightenment, for humor, irony, and enjoyable fellowship.[17] Furthermore, it is significant that, at the beginning of the nineteenth century, Wilhelm von Humboldt's writings on language and his argument that conversational fellowship itself causes new formations in language, initiated an entirely new theoretical interest in language and conversation.[18] And finally it is significant that the ethnic psychology that developed around the middle of the nineteenth century in connection with the ideas of Herder and Humboldt established the idea that "the psychical" lives only in its social and cultural objectifications and that therefore it should be determined by exact methods.[19]

Against this cultural background there emerged the first program for the scientific investigation of everyday conversations. Its author is the ethnic and cultural psychologist Moritz Lazarus, a student of Simmel's, and it appeared in 1878 under the title "Über Gespräche" ("On Conversations").[20] Lazarus is aware that he is treading new ground. But nowhere in the literature, as he writes, has he been able "to discover anything that contains a scientific treatment of conversations." Because he also assumes that readers might misunderstand the theme of his treatise in a normative or aesthetic sense he is anxious clearly to tout the everyday ordinariness of his subject: "This is only a matter of conversations in the simplest, narrowest sense of the word, not of any dialogues at all—ones that might be created in a literary style as an artistic form for the sake of poetry or science—of real, daily conversations carried on by everyone all the time."[21]

With Lazarus, we can safely say, the idea of conversation finally shifts from normative thinking to the domain of scientific research—of course, only to be captured there like an illegal border jumper and either put into quarantine or "sent back" once again. In his great work on the history of literature entitled "Der Dialog" ("Dialogue") Larazus's student, Rudolph Hirzel, shows no doubt that for him only dialogue, as a higher form of conversation that is "connected with a discussion," is worthy of investigation. "Or does anyone think," as his rhetorical question asks, "that any conversation or chain of conversations that gracefully circulates around a coffee or beer table can be called a dialogue? We require of a dialogue, if I may say so, something more." Thus Hirzel excludes from his investigation all those conversations in which "only an exchange of any kind of news of a higher or lower kind occurs." Conversations of this type miss the essence of the dialogue, "because the latter is fused into its subjects by discussion and therefore cannot flit from one subject to another like a butterfly."[22] Hirzel's sharp contrast of dialogue and conversation sounds remarkably modern but can still be found—differently conceived and in part monstrously exaggerated—to this very day. Today, it is absolute "discourse"— understood "counterfactually" as "undistorted" and "free of domination"—that decides rationally and consensually about good and evil, and pushes banal daily conversations over the threshhold of scientific noteworthiness. But the "communicative action" that enjoys the blessing of grand theory does not include diverting conversation, chatting, and gossip. If gossip finds a mention in this theoretical context at all, it happens—as perhaps in Agnes Heller's investigation on "Everyday Life"—as a "kind of alienated conversation."[23] The consequence of this evaluation was already formulated for Heller twenty years earlier by B.F. Skinner.[24] Gossip was banished from his utopian community *Walden Two.* ("It was hard to put it into practice, but I think we've really done it.")

The practice of playing gossip out against "good" conversation has a tradition. Even Larazus, who so emphatically declared the "real, daily conversations carried on by everyone at all times" as a subject of scientific investigation, unexpectedly undertakes normative deletions once again in the clarification of his program when he refuses to concern himself with idle talk and other "dark sides of conversation." So it is hardly more than a lucky accident that in his early essay he briefly discusses gossip. After he distinguishes the individual types of conversation from one another he continues, "We will leave it, then, to the writers of natural history to decide where that genre has gone, which, in the beginning, distinguished the German language with the two noble sounds K and L (noble when they signify the sound in all Indo-Germanic as well as Semitic languages) and in the end with a subtle symbolism, with a muted, hissing natural sound (gossip)."[25]

Lazarus's remark on gossip is hardly more than marginalia and yet it is instructive in many regards. He skillfully plays on the contradictory structure of gossip, already identified above as the discrepancy between its public denunciation in talking about gossip and the widespread private traffic in it. Although Lazarus himself neither proves nor clarifies the contradictory nature of gossip, numerous social researchers after him have shown that this discrepancy always and everywhere is part of the phenomenon of gossip. Such is the case, for example, in one of Edwin B. Almirol's ethnographic studies of a Filipino community in a small California town. Almirol writes: "Although gossip is viewed as 'shameless behavior' because it ignores the obligation of good neighborly relations it is widespread and occurs daily."[26] In his study of life in Portuguese villages José Cutileiro maintains that, "It is a main concern of villagers to find out as much as possible about the lives of other people. This interest, however, is frequently displaced by the open asseveration of the opposite intention "¿Que me importa a mim a vida dos outros?' " ("What do I care about the lives of others?").[27] And in his ethnography of the Mehinaku, a small indian tribe in the Brazilian Mato Grosso, Thomas Gregor reports that anyone who gossips is denounced as "miyeipyenukanati"—literally "Garbage Mouth"—and is threatened by the rest of the village with a series of sanctions. But the Mehinaku, nevertheless, "find gossip infinitely fascinating" and accordingly "it flourishes despite all the sanctions."[28]

This list could easily be extended to many other societies—including our own. Gossip also "flourishes" among us. And our public talking about gossip is characterized by the same deprecatory tone. Now and again we hear the adage: "Gossiping and lying go hand in hand." As the official definition we find that "gossip = nasty, deprecatory, ugly talk about one's neighbor."[29] Or when we want to dismiss some information we call it "mere gossip." But what about the case when we ourselves gossip? Do we find gossip's official denunciation anywhere in our own gossiping? Or does our forgetfulness in this case refer to the impropriety of our action?

To answer questions of this type we need a framework of investigation. This is the second reason why Lazarus's remark about gossip is instructive. His proposal to distinguish individual types of conversation on "analogy to the poetic genres" leads him to the question, "where that genre has gone, which, in the beginning, distinguished the German language with the two noble sounds K and L (. . .), and in the end with a subtle symbolism, with a muted, hissing natural sound (gossip)." Lazarus himself did not pursue this idea any further. For the present work the idea of designating gossip as a genre provides the decisive conceptual point of departure.

THE CONCEPT OF GENRES OF COMMUNICATION

In every human society there are communicative processes that demonstrate—although in different situations and performed by different persons—a high degree of uniformity. This uniformity can result from the fact that the actors themselves possess a routine knowledge of the communicative forms they use and that they realize through their activity while they guide themselves by these forms. In the following such communicative forms, which can be viewed as "fixed" because they predetermine the action of the participants over a certain period of time like a model, will in accordance with the usage[30] common in the "ethnography of communication" be called "communicative genres."

Not all communicative processes are characterized by the fact that the participants follow such fixed forms. We can see this in a distinction introduced by Gregory Bateson. Using the example of dance, Bateson shows that the decision of the dancers about the type, course, and coordination of the individual dance movements can be organized in two different ways. For the extemporaneous dancer the respective state of movement that he—and possibly also his partner—have arrived at is the continuously changing basis of the decision about the continuation of the movement that immediately follows. Bateson calls this "spontaneous" form of organizing the course of the dance "progressive integration." But if the dancer follows specific movements (perhaps complicated Balinese dance figures or the standard dances we know), then an entirely different organization underlies the dance. Decisions about the continuation of movement are then made by a choice from among a limited number of known alternatives (insofar as this freedom to decide is not restricted to a large extent by a high degree of ritualization). Bateson calls this "fixed" form of organization "selective organization."[31]

Communicative genres form—in Bateson's sense—a model of the selective integration of communicative processes. They steer the selection of relevant communicative units and in this way suggest courses of action. And they adjust the integration of these units into a communicative occurrence that is experienceable as unified. Just as an experienced person can tell from the music which dance he has to choose—only beginners have to agree that "This is now a fox-trot"—so communicative participants can tell from the communicative "musical accompaniment" (intonation, mimicry, initial elements, etc.) which forms, that is, genres, will guide their communicative behavior. And just as the "choice" of a dance type intersubjectively binds the dancers to a definite, learned pattern of movement—anyone who begins with a waltz and suddenly changes over to a tango can cause painful collisions—so the "choice" of a communicative genre binds the actors to forms and rules that are specific to the genre.

Accordingly, communicative genres are real cultural objects. We can view them as a kind of cultural species—comparable to the way in which biologists consider species of plants and animals.[32] The advantage that the concept of genres (within communication) offers to scientific description lies in the fact that individual communicative processes of a broad type can be interpreted as actual, interpretive realizations of more general types of communicative action. There might be doubts about the need to introduce such a level of typological description when we accept the general epistemological premise, central to hermeneutics, that an individual meaning can be understood only through its relation to a specific type of meaning. Accordingly, the meaning individual communicative processes have can be disclosed only through reference to transindividual types of communication. Depending on their general function, these types are to be understood as communicative forms or guidelines that can be used by the producers and recipients in the same

way. Because these types of communicative action on one hand are
internally differentiated and on the other enjoy a kind of family relationship to one another and can be grouped into individual "families," it
makes sense to call them "communicative genres." What is meant here
is not concrete instances but different types of abstract—although socially institutionalized—entities.

Communicative genres owe their existence to the fact that they are
used by the respective participants in communication as orientational
models, are constantly reproduced in this way in their action, and are
readily recognized by them. For this reason communicative genres may
not be understood simply as logical or functional classes for whose
construction a more or less arbitrary feature or an external, functional
determination is selected as a class characteristic. For the social world it
generally holds that it is already arranged and ordered before the social
scientist begins to introduce categories of order to describe it and to
undertake classifications. The concept of communicative genres is essentially directed toward the reconstruction of a group of ordering schemata that possess relevant meaning for the action of the participants in
communication themselves.

On the basis of its special ontological status it makes sense not to
replace immediately the concept of genres with that of an ideal type. The
ideal type, as Max Weber had conceived it, is a cognitive tool based on
abstraction, used by the social scientist to develop a general concept of
something and against whose background the particularities of an individual case can be comprehended and described. Thus for Weber the
goal of the conceptual formation of ideal types is not something like a
genre but, on the contrary, the disclosure of the individuality of cultural
phenomena.[33] To be sure, there exists a certain relatedness between the
concept of "ideal types" and that of "genres," as it is used here, to the
extent that the concern is not the idiographic description of concrete
individual phenomena but the comprehension through abstract typification of socially sanctioned forms of communication. In contrast to the
concept of the ideal type, however, the concept of genres in the sense
intended here remains more empirical because it does not designate
"merely" heuristically relevant conceptual constructions of the scientist's but empirically effective orientational and productive models of
everyday communication.

The concept of communicative genres refers to processes of typification in our everyday understanding that are the source of the conceptual
formation of ideal types in science.[34] Therefore, in contrast to the analogy introduced above, we cannot proceed as the biologist does in a typological disclosure of animal and plant genera in describing the typology
of communicative genres. We have to remember that in the description

of the forms of human communication we cannot fix autonomous typological categories because the actors themselves control (ethno-) categories and taxonomies of communicative genres—the category "gossip" from daily life is the best example of this. Therefore "first-order constructs" (Schütz) cannot be neglected in the analysis of the typology of "communicative genres"—second-order constructs—because they decisively codetermine the projection and performance of the actions of those who are interacting. Furthermore, we must begin with the fact that the actors themselves have certain (ethno-)theoretical ideas as to which genre suits which situation and which does not, as to which social "image" a genre has, which social and psychical consequences the realization of a genre can have, and so on. The discrepancy presented between public talk about gossip and its private practice already reveals parts of such an ethnography of gossip.

Like other social institutions, communicative genres can also be understood as fixed, that is, routine, solutions to social problems. Or expressed hermeneutically they are to be interpreted as formally rigidified answers to questions. This way of looking at things has a desirable methodological consequence. But it forces us to investigate, in addition to communicative genres, the specific kind of social problems that communicative genres solve. Formulated once again hermeneutically, this is the investigation of the question to which the communicative genres are the answer.[35] As far as the individual genres are concerned this question cannot be answered in advance. On a more general level, the problems directed toward communicative genres can be determined in the following way: in every society there is the elementary problem of the way in which events, issues, knowledge, and experiences can be thematized, arranged, managed, and handed down in an intersubjectively binding way and under different criteria of meaning.[36] For these problems—just as for the elementary problems of securing subsistence, preservation of the species, socialization, conflict regulation or the formation of structures of domination (*Herrschaftsbildung*), there must be organized, that is, nonaccidental, solutions. Once such models of solutions have become part of the stock of social knowledge, the elementary problems usually appear "unproblematic" for the members of the society.[37] So it can very well happen that, despite all our efforts, in a specific situation one of our "jokes" falls flat. Yet we know in principle what a joke is, when which kind of joke is appropriate, how one tells a joke "properly," or what reactions typically follow a joke.

Instead of calling communicative genres "fixed" forms of solutions to communicative problems, we can also say that they always manifest a certain level of institutionalizing. Not only do they contain models of communicative processes, that is, do they fix the repertoire and sequence of the constitutive elements of these processes, but they also show to the participants in communication relatively constant relational models. Communicative genres therefore distinguish themselves by a kind of "relative autonomy." Their realization at any time is always characterized only to a certain degree by individual features and contextual givens. Of course, this does not mean that communicative genres imply an automatism, that once set in motion they will run, like a mechanical toy, undisturbed by external circumstances. Genres are not themselves the actualization of genres. Communicative processes are only "indicated" by communicative genres. Their factual realization occurs in the performance of action and is thereby, like every communicative act, subject to the principles of linguistic utterance (syntax, semantics); the principles of interactive organization (mechanisms of the frequency of the give and take of talking, sequence formats, etc.); and the diverse principles of contextualization (perhaps the obligation to tailor one's utterance to the specific recipient).[38] This clearly shows that the concept of communicative genres resides on a middle level— midway between universal structures and singular events, between the purely normative and the purely factual. This determination prohibits the degrading of the context of action to a mere case for applying schemata of communicative genres. Contexts of action can themselves be modeled through the specific choice or execution of a communicative genre.

Individual communicative genres are distinguished from one another, among other things, by the extent to which they obligate the actors to follow a preindicated model of communication in a precise way. Such an obligation can be an extremely rigid and fixed one, leaving the actors little freedom for interpretation and formation. This can range from individual formulaic turns of phrase about proverbs all the way to long-winded and minutely detailed rituals of communication. (Of course, an actor's skill can be demonstrated by his ability cleverly to play with these rigidly fixed forms in his communicative behavior.) Other genres, however, are rather weak and nonbinding in their obligatory character. They thereby already border on the "spontaneous" form of organization described above and can be recognized as genres only with difficulty. Thus, for example, a family conversation at the table within one family may take a downright ritual form; within another, however, it may occur so freely or chaotically that one will hardly be able to recognize it as a communicative genre.

On the whole, however, it appears fruitful to establish a typology of genres according to degree of obligation. The obligatory character is only *one* structural component of communicative genres, perhaps just as the dimension of communicative modality, which concerns either the communicative medium (oral, written, pictorial, or in a slide show, mixed) or the communicative context (serious or light, formal or informal). Besides this, we can introduce still other structural components of communicative genres and use them equally as typology-generating features: the relational structure specific to the genre (cooperative or confrontational, egalitarian or nonegalitarian, etc.) or a genre's active function (narrative, argumentative, purely phatic, etc.). To establish typologies of communicative genres along the lines of these components is not dangerous because in this way groupings and family relations of genres, which only emerge with the analytic and comparative determination of the internal structure as well as the morphology of individual genres, are already implicitly written down and at least touched upon.

Thus we will start with a purely heuristic classification, such as the one Dell Hymes has proposed.[39] Hymes performed a really global bifurcation and subdivided communicative genres into elementary or minimal genres on one hand and complex ones on the other. The elementary genres include formal turns of phrase, proverbs, puzzles, curses, word games, small verse forms, prayers or number rhymes. The complex ones encompass verbal duels, ritual abuse and insults, courtship rituals, speeches and sermons, praises, demonstrations of merchandise, children's games, recitations of the genealogies of dynasties, or funeral rituals. The complex genres also contain reconstructive genres that extend from anecdotes about adventures, biographical stories, the reports of informants, tall tales, jokes, sagas, legends, all the way to national epics and can be singled out as a subgroup for no other reason than their internal differentiation and diversity.[40]

How this incomprehensibly broad spectrum of communicative genres can be brought into one context of order, one no longer based merely on the heuristic framework of the scientist but on the relational network and structure that the genres have among themselves, is a problem whose practical research as well as theoretical solution is hardly visible at present. A direction in which this solution might be found has been provided by Thomas Luckmann with his proposal to conceive the totality of communicative processes that influence the permanence and change of society as a "communicative budget."[41] As its own entry this communicative "budget" would also have to contain spontaneous communicative processes. But its core would be systematically organized and would consist of a "field of communicative genres." By means of analytically determining society's stock of communicative genres it would then be possible to estimate the total communicative budget—at first of one society. Of course, this concept of a communicative budget initially remains situated on a relatively abstract level. But it offers a conceptual bracket for investigations in comparative culture, social history, or conversation analysis of individual communicative processes and genres, all of which are subject to the danger of a love of detail and case blindness, even as it acquires ever more empirical content through these investigations.

RECONSTRUCTIONS OF EVENTS AS GENRES

Part of the essence of social events is their transitory nature, that is, the fact that they pass with their very occurrence and irrevocably become part of the past. The idea that events appear and disappear again seems, of course, trivial to us—trivial because in our everyday experience we always assume the past of a social occurrence and always have socially institutionalized solutions for this structural problem, which thereby becomes an "unproblematic problem" for us. Once it has occurred, an *occurring* event does not dissolve into nothing but becomes an *occurred* event. We know that events are transient. But we also know that past events can be retained in memory, named, typified, thematized, and presented in conversation. For human social intercourse these conversational techniques, which open up the possibility of the consciousness of history and the formation of tradition, possess elementary significance. Research on the consciousness of history of illiterate peoples proves that "for all the ethnic groups known to us the past is not accepted as something self-evident or even indifferent, but that in it events that have occurred are viewed as essential both to the present and the future of the affected group and are made the subject of reflection and tradition."[42] Although social events plunge with their occurrence into the stream of what has been, this does not mean that every occurrence liquidates itself, as it were, with its actualization. In this case, too, Odo Marquard's striking remark holds: "To a great degree men are in the position to do something else instead."[43] In the place of the forever and eternally past event steps—its reconstruction.

The assumption that, because of their transitory nature, we can control social events only in the form of reconstructions seems to contradict the fact that social processes frequently lead to material states or facts that outlast them and that form an ever-available document of the past event. Whether such material witnesses of past events are sought as criminal evidence, or for historiographic, archaeological, or (in the application of so-called non-reactive procedures[44]) sociological reasons, they provide the observer with something tangibly "secure" insofar as these objects escape the transience of the original flow of events. But this security is a false one when it means that the presence of a material trace immediately brings the past back into the present. Even tracks mean to be "read," that is, the observer must organize these data so that, as the historian Carlo Ginzburg writes: "An occasion for the narrative sequence arises whose simplest formulation could be: someone has passed by here. Perhaps the idea of narration itself (in contrast to magic spells, curses and conjurings) arose for the first time in a society of hunters and from the experience of tracking. (. . .) Thus the hunter would have been the first to tell a story because he was the only one capable of reading an interconnected series of events in the mute—if not invisible—tracks of his quarry."[45]

How plausible Ginzburg's speculation about the source of the idea of narration is remains to be seen. His remarks are interesting here for a different reason, namely, on one hand, they show that, even when social events leave a trace behind for the observer, that the original process has disappeared still remains a chronic problem. The remaining traces of an event, no less than immediate participation or direct eyewitness, require a subsequent reconstruction. On the other hand, Ginzburg's remarks on the origin of the idea of narration make clear that the structural problem of the communicative presentification of past events cannot be solved arbitrarily or ad hoc but that societally institutionalized models of solutions have to be developed for this, namely, communicative genres that specifically serve to reconstruct past events or, in short, reconstructive genres.

Why do I speak of reconstructive genres and not simply of stories, tales, or narrations?[46] There are essentially two reasons for this decision that are similar in that familiar—everyday (story, tale) or scientific (narration)—concepts possess too normative a significance, which does not allow them to do justice to the manifold possibilities of the forms of reconstructive reference to social events. First of all, these concepts are, at the very least, blind to all non-narrative forms of reconstruction. So, for example, we can observe that after a sporting event, the players—and sometimes even the fans—reconstructively presentify individual events or passages in a mixture of reactualizations of scenes, critical or euphoric evaluations, and imagined possibilities about alternative hypothetical courses of the game. In this situation, in which all those who are present participated as actors or eyewitnesses to the past occurrence, narrative elements hardly play a role. Yet this is a case of reconstruction—and of a communicative genre of its own kind, namely, that one must have command of the rules of this form of communication in order to be able to participate in it.

Concepts such as "story telling" or "narration" not only reduce the plurality of forms of reconstructive genres externally. They also dramatically narrow the spectrum of forms of internal reconstruction. Everyday narration occurs for the most part in forms that do not possess the fully developed format of a story. Through observing family conversations, for example, we can notice surprisingly that hour-long events and occurrences are thematized, that is, "told," but that "tales" remain a rare exception. Instead, brief depictions of new matters, rehearsals of old matters, suggestive anecdotes, individual observations of unusual things, and so on succeed one another, sometimes rapidly, sometimes with persevering sloth. These communicative forms have gone unrecognized for a long time by social and linguistic scientists. Supposedly they counted as pre- or post-levels of true narration and were ignored as subjects worthy of investigation because they did not manifest a formal quality of their own. This disdain can be explained by the fact that it was based on a normative conception of "narration" that was still powerfully characterized by the traditional literary ideals of the forms of narrative, even if these artistic ideals of form latently influence the analyses of everyday narration, as a kind of paradigm. In comparison to them the outlined "primitive forms" of narration must appear like an unimportant trifle.

Paradoxically, however, writers such as Jane Austen, Theodor Fontane, and Leo Tolstoy, who use dialogue as a main narrative device,[47] have recognized these "primitive forms" and their conversational significance and reproduced them in their works. As an example we can take a passage from *Anna Karenina* in which Tolstoy describes the conversations of the guests at an evening party in the house of Princess Betsy:

> The conversation began amiably, but just because it was too amiable it came to a stop again. They had to have recourse to the sure, never-failing topic—gossip [. . .]
>
> Round the samovar and the hostess the conversation had been meanwhile vacillating in just the same ways between three inevitable topics: the latest piece of public news, the theater, and scandal. It too came finally to rest on the last topic, that is, ill-natured gossip.
>
> "Have you heard the Maltischtchev woman—the mother, not the daughter—has ordered a costume in *diable rose* colour?"
>
> "Nonsense! No, that's too lovely!"
>
> "I wonder that with her sense—for she's not a fool, you know—that she doesn't see how funny she is."
>
> Everyone had something to say in censure or ridicule of the luckless Madame Maltischtchev, and the conversation crackled merrily, like a burning faggot-stack.[48]

Tolstoy has intuitively seen that a conversation can crackle "merrily, like a burning faggot-stack" through the introduction of trifling news, the continuation of and comments on "piquant" information, and that it is gossip, above all, that is nourished by these rudimentary narrative forms of reconstruction. To be sure, it is not unusual that such piquant information in gossip can develop into whole stories. But in order to comprehend the entire spectrum of the reconstructive forms and sub-forms that are found in everyday diversions we need another concept less radically prejudicial than "narration." This desideratum was the occasion for the introduction of the concept of "reconstructive genres."

THE ANALYSIS OF THE GENRE OF GOSSIP

With the determination of gossip as a reconstructive genre a program for the sociology of knowledge and communication is outlined that the following will clarify with respect to its methodological implications and the difficulties involved in its realization. As a point of departure we will compare gossip's objective reference with the reference of the sociological analysis of gossip. This reveals that a homology exists between them, namely, gossip thematizes social events that are past events for the participants and therefore must be reconstructed. But the communication of gossip is itself a social event that, with its occurrence, becomes a part of the past and thereby forces the social researcher who investigates gossip to reconstruct it.

In principle, the social researcher, as far as the transitory quality of social processes is concerned, enjoys no privileged position compared with actors in everyday life. He too can approach his subject only from an a posteriori position, which means that the data with which social research normally operates (official and processed data, interview data, data of observation) preserve the social matter that they depict in a reconstructed form. This situation, which for a long time has gone un-studied in social scientific methodology,[49] causes no small problem for a sociology that takes its departure from the process of gossip.

The problem contained in the fact that an interpretively reconstructive transformation of social occurrences normally already exists in the raw social scientific data—and not only in its subsequent processing—can be shown from the earlier example of the distinction between talking about gossip and its practice. Every gossip-conversation forms a primary context of meaning as a result of the goal-directed social actions of its participants. The meaning of the acts of gossip is constituted in situ; if "when the action is performed the goal has been attained—or one misses the goal completely—then the original meaning comes to a definitive conclusion too."[50] Gossip emerges as "gossip" through the performance of actions that are distinguished, perceived, and answered by the partici-pants specifically as acts of gossip in the concrete action situations. Nevertheless, the talk about gossip—whether in a book of etiquette, in an everyday conversation or in an interview—forms a secondary context of meaning that must be distinguished in principle from the primary, actual meaning of the actions in the course of gossiping. In subsequent thematization, which can itself fulfill a prescriptive function, a past occurrence is typified, interpreted, reinterpreted, explained as "gossip." And these ascriptions of meaning—in contrast to the object-bound, ephemeral meaning of the acts of gossip themselves—can be repeatedly clarified, revised, or fixed time and again. However, the primary context of meaning of the course of actions can be determined only in a highly speculative manner from these representations. The secondary context of meaning sits like a veil, having its own models of motives and coloration, over the interactively generated structure of meaning of the original course of actions. Social scientific data that transfer only the secondary context of meaning of reconstructive interpretations are thus not suitable, as a database, for an analysis of the primary context of meaning of a course of actions. If the sociological investigation of gossip relied only and exclusively on data that consisted of statements *about* gossip, then it would have to answer the question: how do the actors themselves turn a conversation into a gossip-conversation, that is, in what does the ability to conduct gossip-conversations consist?

In order to be able to investigate gossip as a form of communication that is realized through the actions of the participants in a conversation, data are required that do not themselves reconstructively preserve the reconstructive conversation but that preserve as much as possible of its detail in its actual course, that is, preserve the record.[51] This form of continual, disinterested, non-interpretive documentation of a social occurrence has been made possible by recent technical developments in the procedure of audio-visual recording. Of course, such recordings cannot directly reproduce the primary context of meaning of a real social process. But they create the possibility of determining this context indirectly from the observed behavior in which it manifests itself. For, as the observers of recordings of communicative processes, we benefit from the fact that the actors themselves continually "reveal to each other" through linguistic, prosodic, and nonverbal means how an utterance is meant, how a partner's utterance was heard, in what context the present utterance has to be viewed, and so on. Behavioral reports based on technical recordings allow the observer—without using the questionable method of empathic recreation—to gain access to the primary context of meaning that the interactors locally produce in and through their actions. At the same time, through the reproduction of sections of the report, the observer can also examine and clarify for the reader which of the primary processes he or she used to develop secondary interpretations and analyses.

Working with data that preserve the record of a social process confronts the researcher with new kinds of methodological problems that have for a long time been recognized and reflected only by a very few authors.[52] To this very day, many of the so-called "qualitative" social researchers use recordings and behavioral reports naively as direct reproductions of social processes without worrying about the particular textual quality of these data. This omission, however, leads with a certain necessity to the processing of textually represented recordings of interactions as the analysis of their content. In this way the recordings' decisive potential to provide information—that they preserve and provide access to the analysis of the process structuring interaction that temporalizes the factual structure of a social state of affairs as a "continuing" event—is lost too easily.

The deficiencies of this procedure, which ignores the process of the social construction of gossip in the actions of the participants, can be clearly shown in an ethnographic study of gossip that is among the very few works that include transcripts of gossip-conversations. In *Gossip, Reputation, and Knowledge in Zinacantan* (1977) John B. Haviland describes, from a primarily ethnographic perspective, the gossip-communication of a Tzotzil-speaking indian community in south eastern Mexico.[53] Because in his fieldwork he mentioned that the Zinacantecos avoid gossiping in his presence Haviland thought up a special procedure. He instituted so-called "Who's Who eliciting sessions" in which he incited the villagers attending the session to discuss and tell stories about the reputation of other Zinacantecos included in a "Who's Who" list he drew up. Beginning with the broad definition that all conversations about anyone absent is gossip, Haviland consolidated the elicited stories into a body of gossip and determined from them the main themes of gossip, the reputation of the victims of gossip, as well as evaluative "gossip-words." Because Haviland treated the stories he elicited as written texts he minimalized the significance of their pragmatic context of emergence, although he should have known better from the initial experience of being excluded from gossip by the Zinacantecos. Gossip, therefore, cannot be determined and understood by Haviland as an interactively produced social affair. If we, as Haviland did, analyze and classify gossip-conversations semantically in terms of their content in disregard of their interactive unfolding, we skip over the preliminary question of the production of conversations as gossip by the actors and its identification by the social researcher.

Now how can these technical recordings of a communicative occurrence be used to determine the principles of structuration that turn this occurrence into an ordered, identifiable social affair? Within sociology during the last ten to twenty years two research approaches—"conversation analysis" and "objective hermeneutics"—have been developed and separately used by people to answer this question. For essential reasons both approaches almost entirely reject statistical, social, and interview data and in their procedure rely mainly on visual and sound recordings and transcriptions of the detail of "natural" interactions. In order to solve the methodological problems they encountered in working with this kind of data both approaches independently developed procedural programs that are almost identical in their essential parts. This agreement is even more remarkable in that both approaches pursue different interests and are connected with quite different theoretical traditions.[54]

It is not necessary here to present and discuss the methodological programs and, as will be shown elsewhere, the complementary relationship of both research approaches once again.[55] We must mention, however, that both approaches, in contrast to other qualitative modes of procedure, are characterized by the fact that they are basically guided in their interpretive procedure by an ordering premise that states that no textual element appearing in a transcript of an interaction is to be viewed as a product of chance but is to be determined as a part of an order that reproduces itself through the action of the participants. For conversation analysis the independent principles and mechanisms of interaction form the ordering context in which a singular event can be determined as a methodologically produced object and thereby loses its accidental character. On the other hand, for objective hermeneutics the specific, "individual" selectivity of a system of interaction forms the ordering context in which an individual textual element can be described as "motivated" and thereby as a nonaccidental product.

Because the interest of the present work is in gossip as a communicative genre, that is, as a socially institutionalized, independent model of communication, the primary methodological orientation is that of conversation analysis. When we will be concerned, at different places, with going beyond the determination of genres and investigating the process of individuation that gives every real gossip-conversation its appearance, the procedure will approximate objective hermeneutics analysis of individual cases. This results in a methodological procedure whose main stages can be clarified in the following five points. The order of these five points parallels more or less the course of empirical research.

Preconception. A well known cliché of the philological theory of genres is the "problem of beginning" that forms part of the question:

how is it possible to ascribe a text to a genre when no standards for genres yet exist but when these standards have to be developed from the mass of individual historical works? Since we must already have an idea of the standard to be established in order to be able to assemble a corpus of relevant works, we seem caught in a vicious circle.[56] Of course, this argument constitutes a misadventure for the hermeneutics that works with the fiction of a "basic error" (Gadamer) and, as we can add, with the false hope of a final understanding. Understanding can never begin from nothing. Prejudice (in its hermeneutically rehabilitated sense) is an essential part of it.

The same holds for the analysis of the genre of gossip. After conversations are characterized in the rarest of cases by a self-referential formulation as "gossip," we cannot help but begin to localize relevant investigative material by means of a preconception of gossip. This already holds for the decision concerning which situations as such are to be considered for observation. Based on what we know, for example, we will not expect that doctor-patient conversations, oral examinations, or political discussions will possess a "mother-load" of gossip. Yet even family conversations or informal conversations between friends, acquaintances, and fellow-workers are not automatically gossip-conversations. In order to be able to identify these conversations as gossip the social researcher necessarily depends on a preconception of it.

Since the preconception of gossip with which investigation begins is replaced in the course of analysis by empirically proven determinations, a separate defining effort is not required. Everyday linguistic circumscriptions or simple lexical determinations are enough, perhaps like those found in Wahrig's *Deutsches Wörterbuch*, which says that gossip consists of "bits of news about the personal business of others."

Acquisition of Data. The observation and classification of gossip encounter problems that already betray something about it. First of all, there is the express resistance of the gossipers themselves: either they object to having their "officially censured" activity recorded, or they fear that cameras and microphones will turn the absent person who is the subject of gossip into someone present, that is, into an eyewitness of how and what is said about him or her—at the very least the feeling of being recorded gossiping is rejected as being an intrusion of privacy. (Through its rejection it becomes clear that gossip in everyday life can survive only in the special "culture" of privacy.) Even when people—perhaps seduced by an attractive fee—say they will allow their conversations to be recorded, this is no guarantee that they will gossip in these conversations.[57] (This too reveals something characteristic: gossip begins "spontaneously" and is hardly ever planned or produced under experimental conditions.) However, if we, as participants in a conversation, covertly try to direct our "second" attention toward the forms of gossip, we will see that we are so strongly drawn in by the power of gossip that we will only recognize afterward that what we have just done is gossip and that we have once again neglected to pay attention to the particulars of gossiping. (In this case we encounter the above-mentioned phenomenon of the gossiper's self-forgetfulness.)

A possible way out of this situation would be to use the gossip already contained in newspapers, journals, correspondences, diaries, auto-biographies, or novels as a database. Of course, "gossip" thereby would be radically restricted to a literary phenomenon that basically distin-guishes itself from oral communication solely through its "public" char-acter. This does not mean that journalistic and literary gossip, the subject of the literary historian Patricia M. Spacks' 1985 book,[58] would be completely irrelevant for the present work. But the social significance and function of utterances would be radically altered by being written down. The writing would also alter, as Georg Simmel's remarks on the sociology of correspondence show,[59] precisely the area that plays a cen-tral role for gossip, namely, the relationship of determinacy and ambi-guity, of the revealed and the concealed. To be able to determine the specificity of literary gossip an understanding of the primary, everyday oral forms of gossip is necessary. If this understanding is not scien-tifically developed, we must rely, as Patricia Spacks does, on our own intuition and on the everyday understanding of gossip.

Thus in order to acquire data on gossip we would have to resort to an everyday proven method that is intimately connected with gossip itself: to listen where propriety says not to listen. James Joyce tells of how, while staying in a London hotel that had thin walls, he listened all day to the conversations in the next room in order to ascertain, from its differ-ent linguistic colorings, ever-new nuances of the English language for his work.[60] Indiscretions of this kind, which are almost unavoidable in our daily experiences, can therefore be as easily justified in principle as condemned. It may be judged ethically dubious surreptitiously to listen in on conversations and record them. But different measures (for exam-ple, the subsequent explanation and request for approval, changing the names and circumstances in all transcripts) can reduce the problem this contains to an acceptable minimum.

The passages of gossip cited in the following chapters are taken from conversations that, in very different situations and personal contexts, were observed and in part written down in records, in part recorded on tape and then transcribed. Video recordings of gossip were not possible at any time. How people conspire when gossiping was impossible to investigate systematically, only illustrated with individual observational notes on nonverbal behavior.

Regularities. In order to determine gossip typologically, as well as to differentiate different generic strata of the genre, individual texts (transcriptions of conversations) have to be viewed as specimens of a genre, that is, recognized as variations of an unchanging form. The way to this determination passes through the observation of regularities. For if gossip is really an independent genre of communication, regularities must reveal themselves in the communicative action of the conversational participants, and they must be recognizable for the interactors themselves and then secondarily also for the external observer of this conversation. The genre of "gossip" is reproduced in these observed regularities. The communicative dimensions and processes in which these regularities manifest themselves cannot be decided in advance. The genres that communicative processes refer to may consist of legal participants and models of social relations, modes and styles of speaking and themes, situative embeddedness, communicative modality, and especially the model of interaction.[61]

A special problem results from the fact that the regularities to be observed are not obvious. An individual gossip-conversation is not the genre of gossip itself but only an individual, exemplary realization of a communicative model. Not only can this model be varied, ironically mediated, concealed or explained, interwoven with other models, differently modalized, contracted and expanded, the model of gossip itself is only one of many orientational variables that determine the communicative behavior of the participants in the conversation. Thus gossip-conversations are not "cloned" specimens of a pure ur-type of gossip. Different communicative lines always "intersect" within them.

To prevent the particular traits of gossip-conversations from becoming universalized as genre traits, the peculiarities not specific to the genre must be filtered out of the available individual textual manifestations. This cannot be done in one step. In a successive process, which in its logic is not unlike chemistry's principle of fractionation, the conversational material is subjected to a three-step separation process: analysis of individual cases, structural hypothesis, and broadening of the corpus, as long as contextually independent uniformities of gossip-communication can be delineated over a plurality of texts.

Organizational Principles. Describable regularities of gossip-communication are always a collective performance of all those participating in the gossip. Even the—apparently monological—narration of a gossip-story requires that the others contribute to the emergence of this story through their corresponding activity as listeners. Therefore, uniformities in gossip-conversations may not simply be reduced to the autonomy of an initiated behavioral program. They are interactively produced and have to be explained from the perspective of the history of their interactive production. Thus uniformities in gossip-conversations refer to an interactive organization of gossip that occurs in and through the action of its participants. Of course, "organization" in this case is not to be understood in the sense of the sociology of organization but— following the usage of this concept by Charles H. Cooley[62] or Erving Goffman,[63] for instance—as a process of forming and ordering in which a social state of affairs emerges as a quasi-organic whole, or better, is continually created. The fact that gossip is interactively organized means that—in reciprocal agreement and by using rules, principles, or (ethno-)methods—the interactors turn their conversation into a gossip-conversation through their action.

The interpretive disclosure of the organizational principles of gossip makes it possible to determine the dynamics and contextualization of gossip-conversations, their internal "logic-in-use" (Kaplan)[64] that connects utterance with utterance. Only the knowledge and mastery of these organizational principles, and not just the knowledge of models of gossip, constitute what we can call "gossip-competency." An example of another communicative genre may help to clarify this distinction. In their study "Proverbs and the Ethnography of Speaking Folklore," E.O. Arewa and A. Dundes cite the comment of an African student in an American university: "I know the proverbs but I don't know how to apply them." Because of his western-oriented education in Nigeria, the student had no access to the everyday use of proverbs among the Ibo. So he could remember the Ibo's text of numerous proverbs but was unsure exactly how and when they were to be applied in specific situations.[65] To be able to describe a communicative genre, it is in no way sufficient to understand only the isolated model of the genre. Its determination also essentially entails the principles and rules by which a communicative model is realized under specific circumstances and thereby becomes an individual communicative event. These individual specifications are for themselves not accidents or "contingencies" but—in this the ethnography of communication, ethnomethodology, conversation analysis, and objective hermeneutics agree—the result of a process of specification that itself obeys universal principles of structuration.

Presentation.　　Conversation analysis and hermeneutic investigations of communicative occurrences by means of recordings and behavioral records encounter unexpected problems if they, following science's requirement of public availability, are to be published for the "scientific community." The basic problem resides in the fact that result-oriented conventions of presentation and text structures of the standard literature form an inadequate framework of presentation for the process-oriented logic of research of the interpretive procedure.[66] Interpretive hypotheses do not acquire their validity via statistical operations but via a careful demonstration that the interpretation comprehends a context of meaning toward which the interactors themselves are directed and that is reproduced by them in the continuation of the interaction. The mode of presentation of this demonstration is the *form* of an analysis of individual cases in which an interaction passage is interpreted utterance by utterance with regard to the principles of organization and the content of the structure of meaning reproduced in it. It would contradict the logic of the interpretive procedure to argue from the perspective of a ready result of investigation and thereby degrade the cited sections of transcription to a mere illusion. This can be avoided if we replay the process of the acquisition and of the securing of knowledge, which is modeled in this case explicitly on the interpretive procedure of the interactors, and thus present it to the reader.

In conversation analysis,[67] as well as objective hermeneutics,[68] there are works that use the form of the analysis of individual cases to synchronize the course of the presented interpretation with that of the real course of the social interaction. In these works knowledge is not postulated and then justified, instead the reader is taken by the hand as it were, and led step by step to knowledge—even over detours. Thereby the intersubjective reproducibility and validity of the scientific interpretation is primarily sustained by the process of presentation, which, therefore, is no longer a mere vehicle of the transport of ready-packed knowledge but becomes a part of the method itself.

The analysis of individual cases—as an investigative method as well as a form of presentation—reaches its limits when it tries to view the empirical material as a morphological problem, that is, to use it to determine distinct modes of modeling and types of variation of a communicative form. This can only occur through a comparative analysis of different cases—a procedure that has long since become an important part of the methodology of conversation analysis. But because it would be hopeless—and also rather pointless—to want to present all case interpretations in the same minutely detailed way in the form of an analysis of individual cases, the only remaining possibility is to choose other, rather subsumption-oriented modes of presentation. The explicative style of presentation in which the progression of interpretation clings closely to the progression of interaction cannot be maintained uninterruptedly. To be sure, the brief encounters with this mode of presentation have to appear more emphatic in the case of the investigation of gossip than in that of the investigation of other interaction phenomena. Whereas, for example, in the case of shorter interactive sequences, comparative analysis can proceed explicatively to a large extent,[69] in the case of the relatively large-format phenomenon of gossip the point at which the favored diachronous mode of presentation has to be surrendered in favor of an abbreviating—and often also encroaching—synchronous mode of presentation is reached much sooner. Thus the style of presentation in the following chapters is not unified. Phases in which individual segments of gossip are analyzed almost pedantically and applied indiscriminately alternate with sections in which relatively "generous," that is, detailed, larger interpretive brush strokes are made.

Chapter 3

The Gossip Triad

THE RELATIONAL STRUCTURE OF GOSSIP

The German term *Klatsch* unifies two semantic components so intimately that they can hardly be distinguished. Yet it is only their separation that makes it possible to recognize the wisdom contained in their consolidation within one concept.

On one hand, gossip designates the *content* of a communication and is also lexically defined in this sense, that is, as "news about the personal affairs of another." "Gossip" also serves to designate a specific communicative content in phrases such as: "carrying around gossip," "spreading gossip," and "dishing out gossip." On the other hand, gossip designates a communicative *process* and is paraphrased in this sense most often as "babble" or "talk." These semantic components are even more dramatically evident in expressions such as "chatter," "titter-tattle," or "prattle." The designation "gossip" therefore unifies the fact that news of a special type is communicated with the way in which it is communicated. In everyday experience this difference is hardly ever noticed. The fact that there are always specific forms of communication for specific types of news is obvious to us. The fact that it is desirable, for the sake of analysis, to begin at this point is made clear by another example in which the transmission of specific news is important.

At least in the case of western societies it is true that a person's death triggers a differentiated communicative process. We would now like to ask, what is the connection in this case between the communicative content (the death announcement) and communicative process (the transmission of the death announcement)? David Sudnow, to whom we are indebted for his interesting remarks on this subject,[1] shows in his investigation of two clinics for the terminally ill that a death is generally viewed as a "unit event," that is, as an event-for-a-social-unit because it

45

is only for the members of such a unit or group that the death is relevant at all. The reason for this is to be found in the fact that with membership in such a unit the right to be informed as well as the duty to inform other members are connected. In the case of a death the most important social unit is the family. The bearers of the duties and rights that are to be activated in case of a death are most importantly the family members of the deceased.

Sudnow goes on to show that the members as well as the doctors in the hospital observe rather strict rules in the transmission of death notifications that follow a "correct sequence." In accordance with this "rank order of notification" all the persons who have to be informed in the case of a death can be viewed as an arrangement of concentric circles. Members of the inner circle are distinguished from those of the outer circles not only by the measure of urgency of the transmission of the notification (—should one create a special contact or does one simple wait for the next occasion to communicate?) but also by the procedures of transmission "at their disposal," which may be personal or impersonal, dramatic-affective or neutral-informative. The fact that the participants follow such a hierarchy of notification is expressed in the fact that that those persons who view themselves as members of the social group and are notified either "too late" or not in the proper manner (e.g., only through a newspaper obituary) or are not notified at all, feel overlooked, forgotten, or excluded.

If we relate this observation to the semantic difference of communicative content and communicative process contained in the term "gossip" that was presented at the beginning of this chapter, we can see that a *network of social relations* holds between both components as the decisive mediative authority. How the death notification is communicated depends essentially on the kind of relation that exists between the transmitter and the receiver. In fact, we can even say that a death becomes a "notification of death" as such only through the activation of the deceased's social network.

The degree of care with which social networks are observed in everyday communicative commerce may be particularly high in the case of the transmission of a death notification. But it is never restricted to this specific communicative content. The fact that participants follow their relational network with painful exactness is made clear by the following interview with a pregnant woman:[2]

> Interviewer: After you had discovered you were pregnant, you
>   told John [husband]—and who else did you tell?
> Subject: Well, everybody.
> Interviewer: Everybody?

Subject: Well, no. We went away to Toronto. We camped on our way and saw relatives in Winnipeg, and we told them, and told everyone in Toronto. And then we came back and told my parents. The only reason I can think of for not telling is that—well, most people wait until they're about four months pregnant—is that either they've had a miscarriage before and they're afraid of losing it. I see no other reason for waiting.

Interviewer: Did you tell your mother before you left?

Subject: No. She was away. She left a couple of days before I found out. She was away and I didn't think I should tell my dad, you know, because then my mom would come home and my dad would tell, and she'd be all disappointed because I didn't wait until I told her.

Interviewer: So your father didn't know until you came back from Toronto?

Subject: Right, uh huh.

Interviewer: And your sisters?

Subject: No, no. No one here knew. We left about five days after I'd found out. Well, we thought we should tell mom and dad before we told my sisters.

Interviewer: They're in town too?

Subject: Yea.

Interviewer: Did you tell any of your friends here before you left?

Subject: Oh, Yes there's one person I told. I told one friend. I couldn't keep it to myself.

Interviewer: Why would you feel that you shouldn't tell your sisters before you told your mother?

Subject: Because my mother would be hurt if she didn't find out. <?> And because she was getting back before we were, and she would be talking with my sisters and she would be bound to hear it. She's the type who would like to tell everybody.

The woman's descriptions clearly show the extent to which she is concerned with situating the "news" of her pregnancy within the relevant relational social network and carefully observing a determinate sequence in disseminating it. Individual persons—in this case her mother—were ascribed the right of receiving the information first hand. Other persons—a friend, but not her father—could be informed "out of sequence"—perhaps because her circle of friends formed a branch of her relational network separate from her family. To be sure, the woman does not say whether she transmitted the news of her pregnancy to different people in different ways. With some certainty, however, we can assume that the way that this news was disseminated within her circle of friends and the way that the woman herself announced this news, for example, to her doctor, are distinguished by some characteristic features.

Just as in the case of the transmission of a death notification or the announcement of a pregnancy, *in the case of gossip the news to be communicated is always a "news-for-a-social-unit."* In all these cases it makes little sense to determine the communicative content and the communicative process in isolation from each other and then to investigate the social relations between the communicative participants separately. For, whether an event is considered as worthy of communication and thereby becomes "information," when, to whom, and in what sequence this information is to be imparted as a message, and how this message is actually to be transmitted, all these questions are decided in the participants' action through recourse to relevant relational networks. As far as gossip is concerned, this means that the dissemination of a bit of gossip-information is steered by mechanisms of social selection and relational processes in a way similar—although not identical—to the transmission of a death notification or the announcement of a pregnancy and that this actualization of the specific network forms a constituent element of gossip.

At the beginning of this chapter it was determined that in its everyday meaning gossip designates a communicative content and at the same time a communicative process. In contrast to the position that holds that the structure of social relations is a constitutive element of the gossip participants, both these determinations contain no direct reference to a special relational quality of the participants. To be sure, both determinations implicitly presuppose that a specific social relation exists between all persons who are engaged in gossip; a social relation that obviously consists of the fact that the further dissemination of the very same bit of information may at one time be gossip and at another not, depending on who gives it to whom and whom it concerns. To take a classic gossip-theme, if a woman has an extramarital affair then we would surely call her friends' and neighbors' discussions about this event gossip, but not the injured husband's discussion about it with his divorce lawyer. That is to say, whether *news about another person is news about his private affairs (and thereby could be the content of a gossip-conversation) depends not only on the content of this news but equally on the relational configuration of those who disseminate it, perceive it, and are affected by it.* As we can now see, gossip content and gossip process are united in the specific relational structure of the gossip. And viewed from this perspective, this is what justifies the fact that both determinations are unified in the designation "gossip" and gives it its deeper meaning.

In order now to be able to determine the specific relational structure that is actualized in gossip the figures that typically participate in gossip have to be identified. It is not difficult to see that the basic model of gossip to which its different, conceivable constellations can be reduced always encompass at least three figures of action: "A gossips to B about C," which is the concise formula to which Leopold von Wiese reduces the triadic structure of gossip[3] in his *Beziehungslehre*, and which—again within a normative context—was mentioned in much earlier works. "Why is gossip like a three-pronged tongue?" asks a proverb of the Babylonian Talmud and answers by saying: "Because it destroys three persons: him who disseminates it, him who hears it and him who is its subject."[4] In the following these three figures who compose gossip will be designated as the gossip subject, the gossip recipient and the gossip producer, and discussed in succession together with their respective relations.

THE SUBJECT OF GOSSIP

The reason for beginning with the figure of the gossip subject, that is, with the person about whom one gossips, is that he is in principle distinguished from the other two figures of the gossip triad by his status. He is excluded from the communication of the gossip an active participant, that is, he is present only as someone *about* whom one gossips. This negative determination of the subject of gossip is a constitutive feature of gossip as such: it is essential that anyone who is the subject of gossip be absent.

The fact that the *absence* of the subject of gossip is a structural condition of the emergence of gossip about *this* person can always be clearly shown when this condition is not or no longer fulfilled. Thus, for example, we frequently encounter and observe situations in the university, the hospital and in other professional contexts where someone, for example, a colleague, is the subject of gossip and he suddenly appears. Most of the time this constellation of people puts a rather abrupt end to their conversation, an embarrassing silence follows before the conversation—now with a new theme—slowly begins again or the subject knowingly leaves with a "I'll see you later." Another example is provided by the anthropologist Don Handelmann who has described situations in which someone present is the subject of gossip but who, through various measures taken by the gossip producer and recipient (having their bodies turned away from him, lowering their voices, distancing themselves from him, avoidance of eye contact), for the time being turns into a nonperson, that is, someone who is physically present but interactively absent.[5]

Both these examples show that the rule that the person who is the subject of the gossip must be absent is not merely a statistically comprehensible behavioral uniformity or a relation imputed by an observer but a structural feature of gossip that is used as a norm to guide the actors in the gossip. Of course, this rule should not be interpreted to mean that situations in which news and stories about those present are told do not exist. In Bavarian and Swabian carnival celebrations, for example, news and stories with an unmistakable gossip value—often in rhymed form—are disseminated even in the presence of those concerned. Only in this case it is not gossip but another, although gossip-related, form of communication (called *derblecken* in Bavaria).

The absence of the subject of gossip is surely a necessary but not sufficient condition of the emergence of gossip. Not all conversations about absent third parties are at the same time gossip-conversations. If someone tells stories about a family's strange eating habits that he observed during his last camping vacation, then, to be sure, the conversation revolves around "the personal affairs of other people." But we do not view this as a gossip-conversation because a further condition of this is that the absent party, who is the subject of the gossip, is known to the gossip producer as well as the gossip recipient. Besides absence, the *acquaintance* of the subject of gossip is viewed as a structural condition of the emergence of gossip.

Of course, the argument that a person has to be known in order for a conversation about him to be called gossip requires differentiation because a person can be "known" in more than one way. The most important mode of acquaintance for gossip resides in the fact that the relation, which one calls "acquaintanceship," actually exists between the subject of gossip and the gossipers. Acquaintanceship means reciprocal acquaintanceship: each knows the other, that is, one can identify each other through previous knowledge, information, and earlier encounters. And one knows that the other is aware of this reciprocal acquaintanceship.[6] The degree of this reciprocal knowledge can vary a great deal from one acquaintanceship to another. What two persons who are acquaintances know about each other can be limited, as Georg Simmel has remarked, to a minimum of what one reveals about oneself to the other. "The fact that persons reciprocally 'know' each other in this sense does not mean that persons reciprocally know each other, that is, directly intuit the true individuality of their personality but only that each, so to say, has taken note of the other's existence. Characteristically, the concept of acquaintanceship is satisfied by naming or 'presentation': the knowledge of the 'that,' not the 'what,' of the personality is what conditions acquaintanceship."[7] This kind of fleeting acquaintanceship can gradually intensify through frequent contacts into a relationship of being "well acquainted with someone" and even become a relationship of friendship. An essential part of this is the argument *that this reciprocal relationship of acquaintance forms the primary relational structure of the gossip triad*. Given this determination, two cases in which acquaintanceship with the subject of gossip is justified in a different way need to be distinguished.

1. On one hand, there must be the possibility that the subject of gossip is known without a relationship of acquaintance existing between him or her and the gossipers. In what kind of activity are two conversational participants involved who exchange news possessing gossip value about an absent third party they know but to whom they are convinced that they are unknown? They practice what we could call *gossip about well-known persons*. For this one-sided acquaintanceship relation is precisely the defining characteristic of prominence and fame. "Fame" means that the circle of those who know of a person because of his or her deeds, successes, and status and know something about him or her can be very large and—viewed relatively—is always greater than the circle of those with whom this person enjoys a relationship of reciprocal acquaintance.[8] Thereby two types of famous persons can be demarcated: on one hand, nationally and internationally famous persons whose status is almost exclusively provided through mass media; on the other, locally famous persons who are more familiar than others only within a limited, observable context of action. In the one case gossip—often even in the interest of the subject of gossip himself—is driven commercially into forms of presentation that are developed specifically for this purpose. We can mention the "personality columns" of serious newspapers, investigative reporters of the tabloid journals, or diverse video-magazines and talk shows on TV. These mass media forms of the dissemination of gossip-information make up, simply because of their special modality, a genre-family of their own that can be philologically and communicatively investigated with respect to their own specific features.[9] In the other case, however, in which locally famous persons, such as the mayor of a small town, a CEO or a university president, serve as a subject of gossip, gossip is a form of conversation that is embedded in everyday face-to-face communication. Even though no reciprocal relationship exists between the subject of gossip and the gossipers, they are still in most cases bound together in the form of a relatively brief, to be sure latent, but

activatable chain of acquaintanceship. Accordingly, this type of gossip about prominent figures is already more closely related, from the perspective of its communicative conditions, to the primary type of gossip for which the subject and actors stand in a relationship of reciprocal acquaintance. It is still too early, however, to speculate about the effects of different relationships of acquaintance on the factual course of gossip. But the fact that the kind of acquaintanceship between the subject of gossip and the gossipers can exercise an influence on the emergence and course of gossip-conversations is shown by the following case.

2. A special constellation of gossip occurs when the person who is the subject of gossip is not only known but, in addition, enjoys an intimate, familial relationship with one of the gossipers. We can imagine the situation in which A and B gossip about C who is known to both. And into this conversation suddenly comes—not C himself but his wife. This situation as well introduces an abrupt change in the theme of the conversation. For in all societies there is, with respect to gossip, an additional restriction of the kind, *that a person counts as virtually present and thereby cannot be the subject of gossip when one of the gossipers forms an intimate social unit with him or her.* That is to say, that, as a rule, the intimately related life partners of a gossiper—in the above example A's, B's, and C's spouses, parents, and so on—are not allowed to be subjects of gossip, although they enjoy a reciprocal relationship of acquaintance with the other gossipers. This is the reason why persons without family relations are the favorite subjects of gossip in all communities. They have no one whose presence would exercise an inhibitory effect of the emergence of gossip. In her ethnography on a Greek mountain village Juliet du Boulay reports that "The young widow of the village, about whom at one time there was a flood of gossip, said several times to me that when her brother came back from the Merchant navy the community 'shut up.' This brother has the reputation for being quickly roused to anger, and his very presence in the village curbed, though it did not end, the talk."[10] Therefore, the fact that one of the participants in the conversation is related to a potential subject of gossip can obstruct the emergence of gossip about this person. This is manifested indirectly in the fact that the reciprocal relationship of acquaintance forms the central relational structure of the gossip triad.

Besides "absence" and "presence" we can still describe a third structural condition that must be fulfilled for a person to become a subject of gossip. The point of departure for the determination of this condition is the observation that there are types of people who—even though countless stories have been told about them—are obviously unsuitable as subjects of gossip. In any case, we feel that the conversations about them are not gossip. For example, little children. Parents constantly like to talk about what their kids have done to anyone who wants—and doesn't want—to listen. And, although even the "most intimate" of details are revealed, we do not feel that these conversations are gossip. It is impossible to gossip about little children—but why?

When we gossip about other persons who are known to us we are playing with a structural feature of social relations whose sociological discovery and description are due mainly to Georg Simmel.[11] In his remarks on a sociology of secrets Simmel shows that one cannot do justice to the individuality and dynamics of social relations if one only follows the, in itself, correct observation that social relations arise only where the participants know something about one another. All social relations, from professional agreement about goals to intimate marital relationships, presuppose, says Simmel, a certain measure of ignorance, a variable measure of reciprocal secrecy. When we form our utterances from a perspective of reason, value, the consideration of the understanding of others, we conceal from the other our internal actuality. Even the most personal details that we reveal to others are always a "teleologically directed" selective transformation of what is occurring within us. "As such," says Simmel, "no other commerce and no other society is possible than the one that rests on this teleologically determined ignorance of one person about another."[12] That this ignorance is an obvious condition of social life is demonstrated by the fact that what we intentionally or unintentionally conceal is respected by the other in an equally intentional or unintentional way. Even in an intimate relationship an absolute knowledge about the other would not be desirable: it would harm the liveliness of the relationship and, since there would be nothing new to learn about the partner, make its continuation appear as genuinely pointless. Thus, according to Simmel, it is a constitutive element of social relationships not only that the participants know something about each other but also that they keep secrets too.[13] In fact, for Simmel, the secret is "one of the greatest achievements of humanity. In light of the puerile state in which every thought is immediately expressed and every undertaking is publicly revealed, an enormous advance is achieved through the secret because many of life's contents cannot be made fully public as such. The secret, so to say, offers a second world in addition to the revealed one."[14] And so, in connection with Simmel's distinction, we can say that *the central theme of gossip lies precisely in this tense relationship between a revealed "first" and a concealed "second" world*.

Gossip draws an essential part of its energy from the tension between what a person does publicly and what he or she seeks to keep secret as his or her private affair. If we follow this observation, then it becomes immediately clear why it is impossible to gossip about little children. At the stage of development in which they find themselves and in which, as Simmel remarks, "every thought is immediately spoken and every undertaking is publicly revealed," the world has not yet split into a public and a private one. It lacks that social feature that, besides "absence" and "acquaintance," has to be fulfilled as a third structural condition for a person to become a subject of gossip: *privacy*. In the prohibited transgression of the boundary into the sphere that the subject of gossip would claim as "private"—if he or she only knew of this conversation— lies a constitutive element and at the same time essential stimulus to gossip.[15] Therefore, even conversations about little children and other individuals to whom we deny the capacity to claim privacy for themselves or to respect it for others are not felt to be gossip.[16] Even when something "intimate" is revealed the feeling does not arise in and through this conversation that a boundary has been crossed into a domain that the subject of gossip could claim as private living space.

Absence, acquaintanceship, and privacy, we can safely say, are three constitutive features of the figure of the subject of gossip. The persons who are talked about in gossip-conversations are excluded from the conversation as its active participants. They stand in a reciprocal relationship of acquaintance with the gossipers (or are at least one-sidedly known to them—at least as locally famous persons), and they have, like all competent adults, their private domain of action and decision that is a source of information. Of course, it is not always the case that when the private affairs of someone who is known but not present are talked about, this is automatically gossip. That is to say, the three features of the subject of gossip mentioned above name (only) the necessary but not sufficient conditions of the emergence of gossip. Other observations about the subject of gossip cannot, of course, be given cardinal importance in this way. Although we can observe, for example, that in most cases people gossip about the living, about individual persons, and about social equals or superiors, these are not constitutive features of the subject of gossip. Gossip also occurs about the dead (for example, about a married doctor who together with his lover committed suicide) about collectives (for example, about how a "simple," working-class family can afford such an expensive vacation), and about an inferior (for example, about one's unemployed neighbor who drinks too much). Whether, however, a certain "logic" lies hidden behind these observable frequency distributions of the features of the subject of gossip can only be clarified in the course of the investigation. Even the justification of the figure of the subject of gossip itself, which was introduced as "constitutive," had to remain in large part hypothetical because the argument could proceed only in anticipation of other, still-to-be-determined, structural features of gossip communication.

THE GOSSIP PRODUCER

The second figure in the gossip triad, the gossip producer, is the central one throughout the process because he or she manages all the gossip information. On one hand, he knows the personal affairs of the absent third party, and, on the other, he transmits this information to his conversational partners who are present. The gossip carousel, as it were, revolves around the producer and, therefore, it is not surprising if we find that there are a number of names for him in many languages—in fact, not surprising if we find that the name of the gossip producer is sometimes identical with that of gossip itself. Thus, for example, "gossip" in English means not only "gossip" but also designates the person who is gossiping—or more properly, she who gossips. For the second meaning of "gossip" is uniquely female and in German most precisely translated as "tattletale" (*Klatschbase*). As names for the producer of gossip, "gossip" and "*Klatschbase*" provide a fitting occasion to pursue more closely the position of this figure within the gossip triad.

The Well-Informed Klatschbase

First of all, it is worth noting that both designations name a person who is an outsider to the familial or friendly relationship of an immediate family circle. In the case of the *Klatschbase* this is easy to see: in the narrow sense *Klatschbase* designates the daughter of an aunt or an uncle; "in the broader sense all distant female relations are called *Klatschbasen*."[17] In order to demonstrate this relational element in the case of gossip we must consider etymology. "Gossip" is derived from the old-English expression "god sib," which designated a specific relationship between a family and a relative or a friend of the family. This relationship had to be so strong that relatives or friends were chosen as godparents for the family's children. In the course of time, "god sib" became "gossip" and in this sense originally designated relatives or family friends who, to be sure, did not belong to the immediate family circle but who as godparents—perhaps through participation in family celebrations, births, funerals, and so on—enjoyed a close contact with the family.[18]

Accordingly, the terms *Klatschbase* as well as "gossip"/"god sib," in their root, etymological meaning, indicate in a significant way the special interactive position of the gossip producer within the relational network of the gossip triad. He has access to the closed circle of a social unit and in this way gains insider information about the private, outwardly inaccessible life of the circle of persons to which he belongs as a fixed member. If he reveals his information outside this circle, then those about whom he gossips are neither strangers, nor does he enjoy an intimate connection with them. The French word for idle talk and chatter *commérage* also signifies similarly distant familial relations and is connected with *commère* (godmother, *Klatschbase*) as well as the Spanish *comadreria* (gossip, talk) that derives from *comadre* (midwife, godmother, neighbor). All these designations incorporate the intermediary position of the gossip producer in the gossip triad that already appeared in the presentation of the subject of gossip. Neither complete estrangement nor close family bond, but distant relationship and, generally, reciprocal acquaintanceship are characteristic of the relationship of the gossip producer and subject. Against this background we can understand why in patrilocally organized societies so much mistrust is brought against the woman who has married into the society and why she is viewed as the woman with the "evil eye," namely, because she now has access to her husband's family secrets and at the same time retains strong feelings and obligations to her ancestral family.[19]

The special intermediary position of the gossip producer provides an occasion to indicate that the communicative genre of gossip is rooted in a problem from the sociology of knowledge that Alfred Schütz developed in his essay "The Well-Informed Citizen," namely, the problem of the social distribution of knowledge.[20] He constructed three ideal types for the purpose of his investigation: on one hand, the "expert," whose knowledge is limited to a rigorously circumscribed area but that within this area is clear and well founded. He contrasts the expert with the "man in the street" who has a recipe-type of knowledge that tells him how, in typical situations, he can reach typical results through the use of typical means. Schütz then constructs the "well-informed citizen" as a type that "stands between the ideal type of the expert and that of the man in the street. On the one hand, he neither is nor aims at being, possessed of expert knowledge; on the other, he does not acquiesce in the fundamental vagueness of a mere recipe knowledge or in the irrationality of his unclarified passions and sentiments."[21] Of course, these types are not mere constructions because in everyday life each one of us is at any moment "expert," "well-informed citizen" and "man in the street" with respect to different regions of knowledge. Schütz himself views this construction of three ideal types, in which the social distribution of knowledge is crystallized, as a means to reach a well-founded sociological theory of vocations or authority or a better understanding of the relationships between artists, the public, and critics. We can now go further and apply Schütz's idea of a social distribution of knowledge to a special region that Schütz himself did not consider: "knowledge about private affairs."

Knowledge about private affairs is, we can say, *per definitionem unequally distributed in society*. Something is private precisely because it is withdrawn from the view of others, or expressed more generally, is withheld from the knowledge of others. Even more, when someone views something as his private affair he contests the right of another to acquire knowledge of it. "This is none of your business," "this is my business," "do not mix in the affairs of others"—everyday such utterances are used to claim and defend a private domain of action and decision against the intrusions of others. Now if knowledge about private affairs is unequally distributed in society, can equivalents for Schütz's ideal types be found in this context? In fact, such equivalents promptly emerge. In relation to "knowledge about private affairs," the equivalent of Schütz's expert can be found in him who—for himself alone or together with intimate partners (who can very well be unacquainted with each other)—possesses a knowledge of his own private affairs. We all, so to say, know best about our own personal affairs. The opposite of this is someone who does not know anything specific about the private affairs of another but only something "typical," for example, that people in our society typically dress and behave more carelessly "behind the scenes" than "on stage;"[22] that they are more childish in private than in public; and that they secretly have greater or lesser vices and sinister aspects in their life from which they quickly distance themselves in the presence of others. Anyone who possesses only "typical" knowledge of the private affairs of others in this sense forms, within the context of "knowledge about private affairs," the equivalent of Schütz's "man in the street." And *so, just as in Schütz's case, the "well-informed citizen" occupies a position between the "expert" and the "man in the street," so the gossip producer occupies the position between both contrast types of the person who knows everything about his own affairs and the person who knows nothing or only what is typical about the private affairs of others as far as knowledge of private affairs goes*. Thus the *Klatschbase* who is "well informed" about the personal affairs of another is a direct appendage of the Schützian ideal type of the "well-informed-citizen."

But she is only an appendage. For in contrast to the "tidy," innocuous knowledge about the technical and practical domains of the lifeworld that constitute the theme of social distribution for Schütz, the "knowledge about private affairs," whose social distribution is important here, is entirely different. Knowledge about private affairs can have a downright malicious character in the hands of those who turn it into gossip information.

- Knowledge about private affairs is not merely distributed in a neutral sense but is *socially segregated*. The gossip producer benefits from this circumstance insofar as his knowledge about the private life of another possesses a certain exclusivity and he can disperse his *knowledge about the scarce resource "intimacy"* like a dealer in information, as it were. Of course, he must be careful to put his information into circulation quickly because all news has a short shelf life, that is, it possesses value only as long as it is topical. But the faster and more freely the gossip producer transmits his privileged information about the private affairs of others, the faster it also loses value.[23]
- The knowledge about private affairs that the gossip producer has is essentially *morally contaminated*. That is to say, because this information intrudes on the truly respectable private sphere of another, it can destroy the reputation of its transmitter, in fact, harm its possessor permanently. We would therefore expect the gossip producer not to distribute his knowledge carelessly but to take specific precautions to guarantee that his invasion of the privacy of another does not come back on him. As we shall subsequently show (see Chapter 4, Section 3), the presentation of the genesis of gossip information plays an important role here. For as far as our everyday understanding is concerned, it makes an important difference whether someone who disseminates gossip information has acquired his indiscreet information accidentally or has made special efforts to get it.
- Knowledge of private affairs has value in the hands of a person who would like to trade in it only if the content of this knowledge *actually makes a difference in the real and the virtual social identity of the subject of gossip*.[24] Thus the gossip information must concern something that does not agree with the subject of gossip's self-presentation and whose "public disclosure" for the subject of gossip would probably evoke a feeling of embarrassment or shame. The spectrum of such gossip information extends from trifling "piquant" news to supposedly great blunders of the type that typically are the subject of blackmail.

Beginning from these sociological observations on the character and the social distribution of "knowledge about private affairs" we can discuss, without falling into a politically correct language, a feature of the

figure of the gossip producer that was already addressed at the beginning of this section: the figure's sexual status.

"Gossiping like a Washerwoman"

The fact that "gossip," as mentioned, designates not only gossip but
also the *Klatschbase*, that is, the gossip producer (female gender), expresses in a compromising way the universally widespread opinion that
gossip is *typically a female form of communication*. Gossip—this is almost
always and exclusively a matter of women: female gossip. The association of gossip with women has become a part of so many figures of
speech, anecdotes, proverbs, caricatures, and other presentations that it
even determines our picture of gossip where it is not explicitly formulated. The view that it is primarily women who indulge in gossip clearly
possesses a great deal of evidence in the scientific context too. In any
event, there are not a few authors who, in their works, view this connection as simply given and are only interested in its explanation. In his
essay *Ressentiment*, for example, Max Scheler develops the idea that
woman is "the weaker, therefore more vindictive sex. Besides, she is
forced to compete for man's favor, and this competition centers precisely
on her personal and unchangeable qualities." Therefore she always
finds herself in a situation that is charged with a large dose of "resent-
ment." Scheler then goes on to say that, "The strong feminine tendency
to indulge in detractive gossip is further evidence; it is a kind of self-
cure."[25] A more recent example of a "scientific" explanation of female
gossip is provided by those psychoanalysts for whom, "the greater capacity of women to divulge their most intimate secrets is directly connected with the effects of the castration complex."[26] And a similar tactic
is followed by those authors who, à la human ethology, see a parallel in
the gossip of women and the incessant attempts of female primates to
care for the newborn and young of other animals and explain this as a
typically female form of "caretaking."[27] All these works, therefore, try to
localize the causes of female gossiping in the special psychical constitution of the woman.

Now to deflect the precipitous acceptance of the opinion that gossip is
primarily a domain of women, a series of empirical studies can be produced that prove that men hardly take a backseat to women when it
comes to gossip. Here too we have to be satisfied with a reference to a
few works: the ethnologist Donald Breinneis describes in detail a genre
of gossip ("talanoa") used by the Hindi-speaking Indian community on
the Fiji Islands in which almost exclusively men participate. In the eve-

ning after their work the men of the village gather in small groups, drink a lightly alcoholic drink ("grog") and talk about "the less-than-worthy doings of absent others." To be sure, women also gossip, but their gossip takes place in other contexts and is not called "talanoa."[28] For the Creole-speaking inhabitants of the Antilles island St. Vincent, male friendship relations form, as Roger Abrahams shows, a constant threat to family loyalties because in large part the conversions between friends consist of gossip and in gossip—particularly when it is malicious (melée)—internal family matters are discussed.[29] In an exploratory study that is based on observations obtained without the knowledge of the partici-pants in a student dorm of an American university, J. Levin and A. Arluke come to the statistically supported result that females gossip marginally more than males (71% vs. 64%) and show a much greater readiness to gossip about close friends and family members. As far as injurious tone and the themes addressed were concerned, however, there was no significant difference between males and females.[30]

From the present investigations that contain findings on the factual participation of the sexes in gossip, we can draw the conclusion that gossip is by no means the sole province of women. To be sure, there may be gradual and stylistic differences in the gossip behavior of men and women, and between different societies these differences may in part vary to a great degree. But *on the whole, the argument that gossip is a typically female form of communication can be viewed as refuted* and thereby—as it seems—be put to rest. However, such an argument would mean committing a decisive mistake. It would overlook the fact that the be-lief that women are the gossiping sex is not a scientific—empirically falsifiable—investigative thesis but an "everyday theorem" about gossip that as such needs to be taken seriously and made a theme of investiga-tion. For, to follow William Thomas, who himself had investigated gos-sip, a sociologically relevant fact is already provided by the fact that women's gossiping in their everyday life is "defined as real."[31] The question whether women actually are the gossiping sex can be com-pletely omitted in this context.

There are also countless examples of our typically attributing commu-nicative processes, for which we possess ordinary designations, to spe-cific groups of persons. This attribution often becomes part of generally used phrases; perhaps when we say that someone "cries like a little kid," "gives orders like a sergeant," "swears like a stable boy," or "gos-sips like a washerwoman." Attributions of this kind refer to an organiza-tional principle of everyday knowledge that serves us in our everyday action as an important perceptual and interpretive resource: we know, in fact expect, that specific categories of persons typically carry out activ-ities; this connection is so strong that we can use it to draw inferences not only from a category of persons to their typical activities but also conversely from an activity to the coordinate personal category of its actor. This interconnection, which is designated and investigated in conversation analysis with the concept of "category-bound activities" introduced by Harvey Sacks,[32] clearly occurs where a person identifiable in a specific category does not carry out the activity expected of him. A "child," for example, who gives self-possessed judgments about himself and advice to adults, that is, who carries out activities that are not viewed as typical of the category "child," becomes an occasion of interpretation for adults and is viewed by them as "precocious" or "premature." Against the background of the concept of category-bound activities the following observation regarding gossip by the anthropologist F.G. Bailey receives a special significance:

> Valloire is a village in the French Alps. It has a population of around 400 and you can walk from one side of the village to the other in a few minutes. Housewives in Valloire avoid being seen talking to one another. In the winter, when the snow lies deep and one can walk only along narrow cleared pathways, these women stay indoors. If they need something from the shops, they try to find a child who will run the errand for them. There is no reason why the husbands should not go to do the shopping, and if they happen to be around, they do so: being men, they combine the shopping with a visit to a café, and in fact one is said to *aller boire le shopping*. For men to sit around in public and gossip is quite acceptable since, it is generally assumed, this exchange is *bavarder*: a friendly, sociable, light-hearted, good-natured, altruistic exchange of news, information and opinion. But if women are seen talking together, then something quite different is happening: very likely they are indulging in *mauvaise langue*—gossip, malice, "character assassination."[33]

Bailey's remarks make clear that in the French community the *publicly condemned communicative form of gossip is attributed to women as a category-bound activity. The same finding is also reported about countless other societies and ethnic groups*[34] *and not least of all for the German-speaking region too.* In German dictionaries and etymological lexica one rarely finds a designation for a male gossip producer (exceptions are *Klatschvatter*, *Klatschfink*, and *Klätscher*). Yet there are many expressions for gossipy women: from *Klatsche*, *Klatschweib* and *Klätscherin* to *Klatschhanne*, *Klatschtlotte*, *Klatschlise*, *Klatschfriede* and *Klatschtrine* to *Klatschtasch*, *Klatschbüchse*, *Klatschfutter*, *Klatschkasten*, *Klatschdose*, and *Klatschloch*.[35] The fact that gossip is categorically bound is expressed even more strongly than by this collection of names for gossipy women in the fact that a man who gossips too much can be ridiculed with the title of an "old *Klatschbase*." The names for male gossip producers obviously do not suffice here for this—this is quite clear from Gotthold Ephraim Lessing's following characterization of a man: "He is an old gossip; if such a stupid as well as malicious gossiper (gossip-monger would be much too good) is so shameless."[36] Men, it seems, do not gossip; they chat, discuss, have a talk, but they do not gossip—and if one should indulge in gossip he would make himself appear ridiculous and bring upon himself the scorn of the people because he then would be assuming a typically female mode of behavior. "If a man is found to be a gossip," remarks a anthropologist about a Filipino community in America, "insinuations are made that he has effeminate qualities."[37]

If we pursue the etymology of the word "gossip,"[38] we come upon something that makes a connection between gossip and women, once again, interpretable within the context of the sociology of knowledge. Gossip and its original form, "klatz" (Middle High German), were as onomatopoietic interjections originally imitations of a resounding slap, such as happens with a box on the ears or the crack of a whip. In particular, the onomatopoietic sense of the word designated "the effect of something wet" (a splashing downpour, a drenching, a wet towel slap). But, in addition, the etymology of gossip also included the sense of a "wet spot" or "stain" left behind, perhaps, by a "dollop" (*Klack*) of butter or marmalade. (Grimm: "no doubt should remain here that in earlier times a stain got its name from the sound that occurred when it was made. both concepts are often found together in the same derivation.") The meaning of gossip as "prattle" or "malicious talk" appeared for the first time in the seventeenth century and with it at the same time—the expression "an old gossip" is authenticated for the same period—its attribution as a typically female form of expression. How did this attribution arise? What connection is there between the meanings of gossip as (1) an onomatopoietic paraphrase of a resounding slap, (2) its designation of a stain, and (3) its pejorative designation as the prattle that is typical of women?

Generally, whenever one constructs etymological connections and derivations one has to go rather far out on a limb. With this in mind, it may seem pure speculation to say that a specific social context of action, namely, the communal laundry (washing place) of women, in which the different meanings of gossip fit together like a jigsaw puzzle and form a whole, is—at least symbolically—the birth place of the communicative semantics of "gossip." In working together "washerwomen" produced "resounding slaps" when they beat and worked on their wash with mallets in order to get rid of every stain. At the same time, however, the women were together and, therefore, we may assume, also quite willing to pass the time of their monotonous work exchanging news and opinions. This could hardly have been different at other places. Yet the washing place assumed special significance because while doing their wash, which contained the bodily dirt of its user, "revealing" stains and worn out places and holes, the women constantly came across traces of the private and intimate affairs of others.[39] Washerwomen thereby structurally assumed the position of gossip producers who acquired morally contaminated information about the private affairs of others or at least could figure this out from traces (visible evidence). If the resounding slaps of the mallets and the voices and laughter of the women could be heard in the village then in time these sounds assumed for the villagers—especially for the men—a significantly threatening character, and "gossip" thereby became accepted as the designation for the socially condemned, feared, and specifically. female form of conversation about the private affairs of others.

We could provide many references to prove the argument that *the washing place is the symbolic birth place of (female) gossip* is not mere speculation. However, we will will only mention a few of these. For example, in his *Wörterbuch der deutschen Sprache* (1808) Campe defines the verb "klatschen" ("to gossip") in the following way: "To talk duplicitously and disdainfully, too much and uselessly; in particular, to reveal negative things about others or things that should remain unsaid; which one loosely calls washing and chatting." This meaning of "washing," which is no longer in use, is also found in Goethe's negative judgment: "this is wash and gossip," as well as in the synonymy of "gossip mouth" (*Klatschmaul*) and "wash mouth" (*Waschmaul*) (found in Grimm). And in Jean Paul's story "Das heimliche Klaglied der jetzigen Männer" (1801), the wife of the protagonist is described as a woman who never allows into her apartment the large mechanical washing machines (tea or coffee is poured in as a detergent) in which whole families are soaked, processed, and thrashed all at the same time.[40] All these references, as well as the current designation "chatter," prove that the etymology of "gossip" is intimately connected with the social occurrence that plays itself out at washing places and laundries—an occurrence that reveal traces of the private affairs of absent acquaintances and provides those present with the occasion for interpretations, memories, and comments. To this extent the etymology of gossip ultimately leads to the problem of the socially unequal distribution of knowledge about the private affairs of others as a structural condition of the emergence of gossip.

This interpretation should not mislead one to think that the "shameful" activity of gossiping was (and is) uniquely attributed to women as a malevolence specific to their sex. On the contrary, it should once again open up a perspective in which this fact becomes analytically accessible after it no longer seemed possible to speak about it otherwise than in an empty, analytically obtuse rhetoric of emancipation. In recent years countless contributions and essays about gossip have appeared in the so-called "feminist" literature,[41] all of which seem to follow the same explanatory model: gossip is viewed in these texts as a specifically female, conspiratorial form of solidarity that presents a potential offsetting power to the domination of men, and therefore is feared by men, discredited as the shameful, malicious pursuit of women, and ridiculed as well as suppressed by appropriate measures.[42] Even if we liberate this explanatory model from its heroic and conspiratorial ingredients the argument of male supremacy, for which in fact a whole battery of ethnological and prehistorical findings speak,[43] proves rather useless in the analysis of gossip or any other concrete social phenomenon. Although in accepting this argument it is hardly possible to learn anything from this interpretive attitude toward gossip that one did not already "know" beforehand. That is to say, research is limited to subsuming gossip under a theoretical postulate whose validity claim is so global that it becomes unfalsifiable. Gossip's discreditation and its essential attribution to females are then—just as, for example, the minimalization of chances for promotion, the more or less gentle coercion to perform unremunerated housework or the limited access to public places—only perceptible as renewed examples in which men manifest their domination. And so we obtain an "explanation" of gossip without needing to know much about this form of communication.

The proof that an essential connection exists between "gossip" and "wash" is revealed by the possibility *that the everyday knowledge about the socially unequal distribution of knowledge about the private affairs of others forms the basis of the process of the sexually specific attribution of gossip.* Based on this idea we can say that, through their work, not only "washerwomen" had an insight into the private sphere of others and thereby assumed the position of a potential gossip producer for their neighborhood. The phrase "to pick a person apart," which is another way the activity of gossip also can be paraphrased, refers to an entirely different "gossip-endangered" profession. Le Roy Ladurie wrote of the maids of rustic thirteenth-century society: "Such servants, who might sleep in their mistress's bedroom, would be her confidantes in love-affairs. They were half duennas and half bawds, and often knew things of which their husbands were ignorant. To anyone they liked they were apt to reveal the secrets of the household which employed them, and thus were one of the main elements in the village's cultural and information system."[44] In the nineteenth century it was the servants in the cities who, because of their proverbial garrulousness about the powerful families for whom they worked and about whose internal matters they could gossip, were notorious and feared.[45] In a novel that contains a naturalistic depiction of the circumstances of servants in Berlin at the turn of the century we find the following passage, which because of its plastic presentation of the gossip situation and fashion should be presented in detail:

[A favorite meeting place was the porter's apartment or the grocer's cellar where the servants came in the evening]. They gathered there talking on buckets and barrels; dipped their finger in here and there, tasted this and that, inspected each others clothes and hair styles, blustered and blew their own horns. Here they picked their bosses apart like the flax drawn through the sharp teeth of a flax-comb. One boss was too rigorous, another too indulgent; this one too slovenly, that one too greedy; that one too fond of sweets—for those inside at the table nothing good enough, for the servants outside everything too expensive. One mistress was a lush and her husband an ass; another too fastidious, a third sanctimonious, a fourth foolish, a fifth licentious, the sixth had a lover and her husband molested the maid. And so it continued. It could hardly find an end. [. . .]

All the maids screamed in indignation when one of them told an especially frightful story particularly well. How could one put up with such a thing! Because of burned soup! A deafening noise arose, a clamor and a cackle, a wild tumult of clamoring, derisive and threatening expressions, of scornful laughter and angry invective. All the while, the great cylinder whirled in the background, rattling and creaking indistinctly as if it would go against its grain to roll the boss's linen and damask smoothly.[46]

Because of the specific work that they performed washerwomen, maids, and servant girls found themselves in a situation where they constantly acquired information and news about the private affairs of others and thereby naturally became potential gossip producers for their neighborhoods. We have to view this as the decisive reason why these women were especially gossipy. The question whether they actually participated more than other groups in the collective gossip effort seems to be of secondary importance. This argument is confirmed by the observation that, in spite of specific sexual attribution, vocational groups in which it was not women but men who acquired information about the private affairs of others could also be viewed as gossipy. Even today it is still true, for example, that barbershops in many societies are centers of gossip or places where it is exchanged[47]—an assessment that goes far back, as we can tell from the following malicious remark by Georg Christoph Lichtenberg: "Barbers and hairdressers introduce the frivolous news of the city into great houses, just like birds carry seeds from the trees into church towers. Both germinate there often for the worse. The only difference is the mode of planting—the former through speaking and the latter through. . . . Wives too."[48] A prototypical gossip position is also occupied by a landlord who over time can acquire a detailed knowledge of the personal circumstances of tenants through direct observations of their apartments, in removing their trash, and through hearing their complaints and stories about the neighbors. And significantly, one of the greatest problems with which the landlord has to deal is the—anticipated—poor reputation of that profession.[49] Finally, we would like to remark that mailmen,[50] newspaper deliverers,[51] and small shopkeepers[52] can be viewed as groups who distinguish themselves through their gossipy nature, which in this case may basically be reduced to the fact that, because of their daily contacts at work and encounters with other members of their social network, they are very apt to be transmitters of information.

The argument that *it is above all the groups that acquire a glimpse of the private sphere of others through their daily work that have the reputation of being the biggest gossips,* is not a law of nature. It describes a context that arises out of the interplay of social and interaction structures and thereby can be modified or even eliminated through appropriate social regulations. Nowhere is this clearer than in the case of modern societies where there is a large number of people who, because of their profession, have intimate information about the private lives of others and who do not gossip about it. Doctors, psychotherapists, lawyers, bank employees, tax advisors, personnel administrators, and so on learn things about their clients in carrying out their work that are so personal and intimate that they would hardly have been revealed if there was not legal protection to prohibit their dissemination as gossip. Like a priest's obligations regarding confession, the members of these professions are subject to strict rules concerning the repetition of the private secrets of their clients. The German penal code (§203. Transgression of Private Secrets) threatens with imprisonment anyone who "reveals another's secret, namely, a secret belonging to the sphere of his personal life, without authority," with which he was entrusted as a member of a professional group. Above and beyond any legal obligation, the guarding of private secrets of a professional nature is also a postulate of professional ethics. Thereby prevented through internal and external social controls from transmitting professionally acquired information about the private affairs of others to those not authorized, the members of this professional group do not fall into the position of potential gossip producers and also do not acquire the reputation of being gossipers.[53] If this argument is valid, then we could venture the thesis that, for example, secretaries would lose their reputation for being gossipers if their profession could be professionalized as "skilled labor for office communication."[54]

In summarizing we can say that the gossip producer is a "transgressor" in two senses: he penetrates—by crossing the border between the back stage and proscenium—the inner space of another's social existence and then—disdaining the social system of inclusion and exclusion for the time being—pushes outward with his information as the booty of his raid. Expressed paradoxically, *the gossip producer externalizes what is internal*. His reputation and position within the gossip triad is essentially determined by the potential and factual access he has to the unequally distributed information about another's private life and the extent to which the dissemination of this information is subject to socially enforced restrictions. The fact that women as a rule are attributed a category-bound gossipy nature essentially has its basis in the fact that women structurally fall into the position of gossip producers to a greater extent than men do because of the organization of the division of labor specific to their sex. Much points to the fact that men and women do not significantly differ in their actual productivity of gossip.

THE GOSSIP RECIPIENT

The last figure of the gossip triad, the gossip recipient, is by no means merely a passive participant whose presence—or more exactly willingness to listen—is necessary for communication but who otherwise has no special significance for the specific communicative process of gossip. On the contrary, it is only through his having a specific relation to the gossip producer and the subject of gossip that a conversation finally becomes gossip.

The kind of relation that has to exist between the gossip recipient and the subject of gossip was already discussed: on one hand, the subject of gossip must be an acquaintance of the gossip recipient or at least be known to him indirectly through intermediaries or local "fame," because the news he hears is personally relevant for him only if it is not about a complete stranger. On the other hand, the gossipers follow the rule that persons who enjoy an intimate familial or friendship relationship with them are taboo as subjects of gossip.[55] Conversational participants can, in fact have to, express their disapproval or even register their "veto" if their friend or family member is made the subject of gossip in the conversation.

Not all communication partners are suitable, as gossip recipients, to be a conversational participant who is ready to disseminate information possessing gossip value. And so we can observe, for example, how an ongoing gossip conversation is abruptly ended or turned to a different theme as soon as a stranger enters the conversation.[56] A typical condition of gossip conversations is that the gossip producer and gossip recipient are both known to each other. And so, as Moritz Lazarus and Georg Simmel have shown,[57] conversations between two complete strangers—

as happens during travel—develop an openness and intimacy for which there is really no internal basis. Still, gossip usually does not occur in situations, or at best only rarely, in which strangers in their conversation discover someone known to both of them. Nevertheless, to take the other extreme, we can ask whether we should call gossip the conversations between spouses in which they exchange news about the personal affairs of third parties between themselves alone. This surely is a borderline case for which there is no single answer. I think that in this case it would be incorrect to speak of gossip because these conversations lack the *element of openness* that is so characteristic of gossip among friends, acquaintances and relatives. It is common that men as well as women bring home gossip that they heard during the day.[58] Yet the conversations they have about this resemble more of a mutual exchange of information about the gossip than its continuation within a domestic context. This can be seen in, among other things, the fact that in this domestic reportage about the latest gossip the participants' "thrill" and commitment does not nearly reach the normal dimensions of gossip conversations. However, these domestic gossip "briefings" are not insignificant— if for no other reason than because with their information the spouses can actively participate the following day in nondomestic gossip conversations.

The relationship between the gossip producer and the gossip recipient that is based on mutual acquaintanceship is specifically characterized by the special kind of information that is transferred in their interaction. Information about another's private affairs is morally contaminated information and thereby places those who exchange it in a relationship of co-informers. The gossip recipient finds himself, as it were, in the situation of one who accepts a gift that he as well as the giver knows is stolen.[59] This co-informership binds the gossipers together in brotherhood and affects the ability of their relation to last. In the transfer of gossip the tone of exchange is one of equality; distinctions of rank are hardly tolerated.[60] Because of its *equalizing effect* gossip between superiors and subordinates, namely, between persons of unequal rank, is generally rare. Of course, it is not impossible, although the gossipers in this case have to proceed with special care that their rank-effacing behavior is not interpreted and answered as strategically motivated "cozying up" (L. von Wiese),[61] that is, as ass-kissing.

The relation between gossip producer and gossip recipient is not least of all determined by the expectation that the gossip recipient at the moment he acquires morally contaminated information can then appear as a gossip producer himself within other contexts. To be sure, the ethnographic literature time and again reports about the astounding rapidity with which gossip information is disseminated through a village and even over longer distances.[62] Phrases such as "something is making the rounds," "a little bird just told me," "something is spreading like wild fire," "someone is a hot topic," "someone is on everyone's lips," or "something is hot off the presses" reveal that *gossip's rapid rate of diffusion* is a part of its everyday understanding. Yet this everyday understanding in the sense of a "self-destroying prophecy" can be the reason why the dissemination of gossip, at least in its initial stage, is tied up or delayed for a short period. After all, to anyone who wants to report interesting gossip, the first person brought into his confidence as a gossip recipient becomes a possible competitor who could "steal his thunder" by transmitting the just acquired news to others before him. Against this background, we can understand the observation made by the anthropologist James Faris.[63] In his study of a small fishing village in Newfoundland, Faris remarked that men who returned to the village with interesting news initially revealed nothing of it in individual encounters with other men nor gave evidence of anything unusual even later on. In this way they guaranteed themselves a public as well as the attention that they would have had to share if they disseminated the information too quickly to other individuals. This strategy was continued in evening conversations in that the men did not give out their information by itself and en bloc but made their listeners "drag it out of them" by questions and answers and thereby put themselves "in demand."

Of course, the gossip producer can try to obligate the gossip recipients to silence by means of metacommunicative instructions. Yet it is a common experience that *restrictive admonishments* of the type: "this is only between us," "this must remain between us," "only for you," "no word of this to X," are not very effective. To be sure, they excuse the gossip producer, if he is ever reproached with being a gossip, insofar as he can always refer to having obligated the gossip recipient to silence. Yet everyone knows that the gossip producer actually has very little influence over what the gossip recipient does with the information entrusted to him. The gossip producer also knows that gossip recipients as a rule, "at first place their hand over their mouths and afterwards let a little slip through their fingers" (G.C. Lichtenberg).[64] This situation of absent control over the subsequent course of gossip points the gossip producer directly again to his network of social relations. For even if he cannot prevent the fact *that* gossip is retold, he can still make sure, through his appropriate selection of gossip recipients, that gossip is transmitted only *to the right people*. Examples of such measures are, for example, adults excluding children from their gossip, even when these are only passive recipients.[65] The danger is too great that, out of ignorance, children will tell other people things that are not meant for their ears.

In its selective actualization of social relations gossip distinguishes itself, moreover, from another communicative phenomenon that erroneously is often thrown together with gossip—*rumor*. The expression "rumor" suggests that the dissemination of information occurs in a rather unspecific way. If not etymologically, then at least connotatively in German, "rumor" (*Gerücht*) contains the meaning "smell" (*Geruch*). The composites "kitchen rumor" and—more drastically still—"lavatory rumor" also depend on this olfactory component of its meaning. We may attribute the reason for this semantic association to two features that are as characteristic of smells as they are of rumors: they are easily disseminated in all directions, and no one knows who started them and where they originated. To be sure, rumors distinguish themselves from gossip mostly because they do not refer to individual persons ("classical" cases of rumors are, for example, the imminent end of the world, the horror stories of conscientious objectors, or the cooking of rats in "fast food" restaurants).[66] Yet the decisive difference between rumor and gossip is that rumors do not require the construction of a specific network so characteristic of gossip. Rumors contain unauthorized messages that are always of universal interest and accordingly are disseminated diffusely. Gossip possesses relevance only for a specific group and is disseminated in a highly selective manner within a fixed social network.

The determination of the gossip recipient brings the presentation and discussion of the individual figures of the gossip triad to a close not only in a formal sense. The determination of its position and its relations to the two other figures reveal that a circle is completed: *gossip occurs—lege artis—only through friends and acquaintances and only with friends and acquaintances*. Therefore, in its concrete social situation, the gossip triad reflects a specific model of intimacy within the relational network of its three participants. The law of gossiping only about particular people, that is, of hearing and repeating—morally contaminated—information about their personal affairs, is a privilege that is extended only to those persons who mutually recognize themselves as members of this relational network. Gossip is therefore to a great degree a "clique phenomenon."[67] If two persons in the presence of an oblivious third party begin to gossip, then it necessarily produces one of those situations in which a stranger discovers with painful clarity (or later comes to discover) that he does not belong.[68] When one gossips with an acquaintance about someone they both know, both show that all participants belong to a circle, a "gossip cell,"[69] and thereby have the right and duty to respect the virtues and vices of the other members. The fact that one gossips *with* others is thereby—sociologically considered—almost as important as the fact that one gossips *about* them. Elizabeth Bott[70] has provided an impressive formula for this connection: "no gossip, no companionship."

Chapter 4

The Gossip Sequence

THE SITUATIONAL EMBEDDEDNESS OF GOSSIP

Anyone who investigates the social, spatial, and temporal circumstances of gossiping is confronted with such a multiplicity of possible situations that it may appear at first glance hopeless to go beyond individual descriptions and the establishment of lists. For whenever the gossip triad finds itself in a social situation it is possible for the interactors to set the "gossip machine" in motion. Of course, on closer inspection we can see that the actual—and conceivable—gossip situations, in addition to the relational structure of their participants, manifest similarities that allow them to be consolidated into individual groups—groups that do not crystallize in isolation from one another around individual situative particles but that can be arranged, with fluid transitions, along a continuum. Such a continuum breaks down into sections when one localizes the situations in which gossip occurs along a line drawn between the contrasting contexts of sociability and work. Along this line, which extends from the domain of activity to that of inactivity, two groups of gossip situations can be identified as ideal types.

1. At one end of this line, namely, the domain of purely sociable interaction, we encounter a situation that is—at least in the judgment of the social environment—so completely gossipy in nature that it even owes it's name to it: the coffee-klatsch. Gossip seems to manifest itself in its purest form in the coffee-klatsch. From everyday experience a coffee-klatsch is typically a circle of acquaintances who—either in a café or at home in a living room—gather for coffee and cake and unburdened by pressing obligations, turn their attention to one thing: the discussion of the flaws and actions of their absent acquaintances and endless talk about things that do not concern them. The coffee-klatsch forms, so to

speak, the institutionalized form of gossip-communication. It is the social form of sociability reduced to gossip.

The disdain that always accompanies our everyday use of the term "coffee-klatsch" has a historical basis. The first coffee houses appeared in Europe in the sixteenth century.[1] They functioned primarily as places of business and they played—at a time when the press did not yet exist in the modern sense—an important role as centers of communication in early bourgeois economic and cultural history. The worldwide insurance company Lloyds of London, for example, began as "Lloyds Coffeehouse." It was opened at the end of the seventeenth century in the center of London and quickly developed into a meeting place for people that had maritime business. In the eighteenth century the coffee houses served the editors of the London moral weeklies as editorial locations and were even cited in the pages as business addresses. Women were largely excluded—in England by law—from the conversational culture that developed in the coffee houses and that also exercised no small influence on literature. It is known that the coffee houses, probably because they were refuges for men from domestic life, awakened the mistrust and resistance of women.[2] But to the extent that coffee moved from the public sphere of the coffee houses into the private sphere of bourgeois households women—by following the model of the coffee house culture of the men—could establish their own talk circle around the drinking of coffee: and so the "coffee circle" was born. Whether it was because bourgeois men were not entirely at ease with this striving for independence by their wives or because the private affairs of third parties were actually talked about in these coffee circles—since the end of the eighteenth century, in any event, women's "coffee-klatsches" have been the butt of men's jokes. They could view their domestic-female copy only as a caricature of the exclusively male coffee-house culture.[3]

Although the coffee-klatsch in the meantime has long since left the private domain and has superseded the coffee houses—that became cafés—this historical background may contribute to its derogatory and ironic evaluation. To be sure, a second factor that structures interaction played a role in this. The real "scandal" of the coffee-klatsch is not *that* gossip occurs there—gossip also occurs in other places—but that gossip occurs there *unrestrained*. The participants in the coffee-klatsch hardly take the trouble to conceal that the intention and goal of their being together is to gossip about other people. That is to say, they engage in an activity that is officially condemned without showing that this offense makes any moral difference to them. The coffee-klatsch not only brushes aside like any other gossip the prohibition of gossip; instead it ignores this prohibition when it refrains from neutralizing its unseemly character through appropriate measures and, thereby implicitly, from respecting the prohibition on gossip. This is precisely the reason, as we shall soon see more clearly, for the particularly bad reputation of the coffee-klatsch. One is not a gossiper simply because one tells stories. Instead, one is a gossiper only if one does this without specific measures of care and neutralization. Therefore we can also say that the genre of gossip is performed in the coffee-klatsch in its purest form. For in the coffee-klatsch, which like all gossip breaks rules, not one rule goes unbroken that ought to be observed by a competent gossiper.

The domain of sociable interaction also provides examples of the situational embeddedness of gossip that are more or less structurally—and therefore in their social reputation—identical with the coffee-klatsch. Thus the following description can be used to describe more than one society:[4] in villages or small towns it usually happens in the summer that small, closed groups composed mainly of the older inhabitants congregate during the day on a veranda or some other shady location and sit around for hours with nothing to do but drink, smoke, talk, and pass the time concerned with someone who has provided them with an occasion to gossip. These groups hardly care to conceal the fact that they are gossiping and, therefore, they are viewed as particularly persistent and malicious nests of gossip. (Moreover, this is also the reason why old

Figure 1. Nineteenth-century caricature of the "Coffee Circle." From W. Schivelbusch 1980. Reproduced by permission of the publisher.

people who no longer are part of the work force easily acquire the reputation for being gossipers.)

It is characteristic of these idle groups that—directing their attention to what is happening in their village and with their neighbors—they find themselves as it were in a *state of constant readiness to gossip*. Their conversations—like conversations in general—contain a *large measure of local sensitivity*, that is, anything that transpires before them, in their perceptual range, can be addressed, thematized, and processed in their conversations as extended commentaries and disputes. "Stroll by a bunch of wives *Kaffeeklatsching* on a lawn and you will feel very forcefully their inquiry." With this remark a sociologist indicates the uncomfortable experiences he had in a study of American suburbia.[5] These groups constantly feed themselves the smallest bits of information in order to satisfy their unquenchable hunger for gossip, at least for a short time.

Gossip, of course, can also occur in entirely different sociable contexts. Whenever acquaintances meet at a bar,[6] at a party,[7] in a sauna,[8] or playing cards,[9] there is occasion to exchange news about absent—or at least out of earshot—third parties. In contrast to the coffee-klatsch the situational embeddedness of gossip already distinguishes itself in these cases in an essential point. Gossip occurs here within the context of—we could also say under the cover of—socially accepted sociability. Gossip is not the telos of these social gatherings but—as perhaps also in the case of family celebrations (marriages, funerals)—a by-product that emerges of itself and without planning as a result of the personal constellation. Gossip thereby appears as a more or less accidental event. And this situation alone is enough to protect the actors to a certain degree from the reproach of gossiping. Of course, it can happen that actors who find themselves in these sociable contexts show a great deal of energy for gossip because they fancy that they enjoy a kind of carte blanche. But this is not the rule. Instead, we observe that in these sociable contexts a clear tendency emerges to put off gossip, that is, to conclude the "official" part first, for example, the card playing, and afterward to change over to the "unofficial" part, namely, gossip. This *postponing of gossip* is also a technique that provides the interactors with the possibility of gossiping without running the risk of appearing to gossip.

2. If we quit the context of sociability for the context of work we encounter a second group of gossip situations in the no-man's land between these two regions. The fact that these situations assume an intermediary position in more than a metaphorical sense can be shown with the following examples. Anyone who uses public transportation to go to work often finds himself in the situation of sitting together, willy nilly, with someone from work and gossiping with him during the trip

about colleagues or locally well-known people. Or in a doctor's waiting room we quite accidentally encounter an acquaintance and before we know it we start to gossip. Or before the theater lights are dimmed and the curtain goes up theater goers look about in the audience for people they know and gossip with their companion about someone they see— possibly only on the way home. Or at the end of the short breakfast break a person leaves the cafeteria not only to have coffee and a roll but often to take (or give) a piece of gossip too.

It is not difficult to see what these examples have in common. They form that amorphous, intermediary web that fills in the gaps and holes that continually and unavoidably materialize in everyday life as a result of the sequentialization and segmentation of larger blocks of social action. Waiting times, pauses, trips to and from work, and the like are transitory, social aggregate states of forced "inactivity" that appear on the periphery of contexts of action and are socially accepted insofar as the conditions of the management of what we could call (with Erving Goffman) "dominant involvements"[10] are created within them, or the consequences of such involvements can be eliminated.

These peripheral activities[11] now form a specific situational context for those gossip conversations that we can, using a part for the whole, call *diversion gossip* (gossip for the sake of diversion) (*Pausenklatsch*). The special potential for gossip of these peripheral episodes is based on the fact that the actors are temporarily released from the performance of urgent occupational obligations as well as from the duty to participate in specific sociable forms and thereby find themselves in a relatively unstructured situation that does not make complex demands on them. Among other things, this means that in these situations the diverse activities of self-engagement, that is, the forms of egocentric, self-forgetting action (such as leafing through magazines, picking one's teeth, cleaning one's nails, dozing, etc.)[12] regularly arise despite the presence of other persons. If in such situations, whose lack of structure is likely to give the participants the feeling that they are condemned to inactivity, two acquaintances should meet, the temptation to "beat" the empty time "to death" with gossip is generally very great.

Remarkably, diversion gossip occurs with relative openness even in the presence of other persons, that is, without the actors having to partition themselves off from their interactive environment through whispers or similar maneuvers. Therefore, it can be observed frequently and easily in cafeterias, on buses, or in waiting situations by an observer who secretly directs his attention in this direction. To be sure, these conversations are usually incomprehensible to the secret listener. The actors who converse as mutual acquaintances about another familiar acquaintance speak an extremely presuppositional language that to a large extent excludes an eavesdropping third party who does not share what the actors presuppose. It almost seems as if the actors had an intuitive knowledge of this protective mechanism and therefore gossip openly. Under certain circumstances diversion gossip can become coffee-klatsch (and vice-versa), in which case the situational embeddedness of gossip clearly becomes evident. Thus a sociologist[13] has reported, for example, that many of the women who showered and dressed in a locker room after playing tennis gossiped about common acquaintances during this activity. It occurred to two women (obviously housewives) to make this more than just an occasion for gossip and after their game, which was always in the morning, they regularly opened a bottle of sherry and transformed the normally short dressing period in the locker room into an extended gossip hour. The gossip that initially was bound to the peripheral activity of bodily hygiene, dressing and cleaning up, and so on had now become the main activity. What was indicated in this case as planned and intended in advance through the routine of drinking sherry can in other cases occur as a spontaneous, situationally generated, and relocalizable continuation of gossiping. And so, perhaps, when two acquaintances who meet on the bus to the university make a beeline for the cafeteria to continue their conversation.

3. At the end of the line that began with the context of sociability and then lead to the domain of peripheral social activities we come to the context of work. The presentation of the essential etymological connection between "gossiping" and "washing" (*Wäschewaschen*) already clearly indicated that—carefully formulated—gossip and work are by no means radically separate activities. On the contrary, there is much to support the argument that the domain of work is even a preferred context for gossiping. Such a connection is evident not only in current designations such as "office gossip" or "employee gossip;"[14] anyone who—attuned to gossip—follows the employees of a hospital or a university in their activities will encounter pairs or groups who gossip during their working hours. And if people are asked where they meet others to gossip, frequently the first answer is not the afternoon coffee or another sociable context but a work locale.[15]

In order to be able to determine the embeddedness of *gossip within the context of work* we first have to clarify the relationship of these two forms of activity. As the ethnographic literature always notes, gossip and work are two forms of activity that to a great degree are mutually exclusive. To be sure, there are two professional activities in which the actors can also concern themselves with gossip: one is the case of firemen who wait in the firehouse, village women who wash their vegetables together in the brook, or truck drivers who can converse undisturbed with their riders about common acquaintances during their trips. But in many other cases gossip cannot be combined in this way with the performance of one's work. The consequences that result when gossip accompanies the performance of one's work—not as an aside but as the main focus—are shown by Jeremy Boissevain's following observation, which could be supported by similar findings of other ethnographers: "In Gozo (a farming village on Malta) it happened that a group of women were seen conversing on the street. When, however, such groups are observed the people say that these women are bad and are not doing what they ought to be doing."[16] The rule that anyone who gossips during work time is neglecting his or her work also belongs to the core of our everyday understanding of gossip. Gossip is viewed as sociable inactivity and thereby is incompatible with work. Anyone who gossips to the detriment of working runs the twofold risk not only of being discredited but also of acquiring a bad reputation.

Why then is work time always transformed into gossip time? Because one's colleagues are preferred as gossip partners (and subjects)? Possibly, but the problem, then, is only displaced to the question of the reasons for preferring this gossip network. Because, as a kind of "banana time,"[17] gossip provides the workers with the possibility of interrupting their dissatisfying work routine with informal interaction? This cannot be excluded, but it also holds for a series of other activities (teasing, flirting, smoking, etc.) and does not say anything specific about gossip.

In contrast to justifications that resort to external factors, we can now show that gossip itself contains a structural feature that demonstrates that, paradoxically, the context of work has to appear as a convenient environment for gossip. Gossipers are in principle confronted with the problem of participating in a socially disreputable form of interaction. They can simply ignore this fact in their gossiping, or reflect it with the help of appropriate behavioral accentuation. The fact that these are not interchangeable but have very different consequences can be shown by the following example. Anyone who arrives at work in the morning drunk can expect understanding and tolerance only if he succeeds in isolating his unacceptable behavior through appropriate explanations (winning the lottery, the birth of a son, etc.) as a situationally conditioned exception. On the other hand, anyone who does not make it clear that his faux pas is attributable to special circumstances and that he is not flouting the rule of sobriety in this case will very quickly acquire the reputation of being a drunk. As far as gossip is concerned, this means that *anyone who wishes to avoid the reputation of being a notorious gossip must try to contextualize his affinity for gossip so that it appears as the unintended, accidental, and thereby excusable activity of an occasional gossiper. This contextualization can be achieved, however, if the gossipers situate their behavior within the context of work.* Such a contextualization technique requires for example, that the actors not retire to a corner to gossip after they have met but carry their work around with them (depending on the circumstances: books, briefcases, shopping bags, etc.) while conversing.

In this way the gossipers visibly document that their conversation still occurs within the context of their work, that they have only momentarily interrupted their work for the sake of conversation (standing is more acceptable than sitting!), and that, because of their heightened sensitivity to the situation, they are prepared at any moment and without much ado to stop talking and return to their work. In other words, their work is put aside during their gossiping, but the significance of their work as a framework of social encounter—for reasons of self-protection—is constantly indicated by the gossipers.

Through its accentuated localization within a work context gossip acquires and preserves the character of being accidental, occasional, and transitory. The gossipers demonstrate to each other and to others that, even if they momentarily indulge in gossip, this does not form the telos of their being together. The fact that this mechanism is not unknown to the gossipers themselves manifests itself perhaps most strikingly in the frequently described phenomenon of housewives who, instead of visiting each other obviously for the purpose of gossip, often prefer to contact their neighbor—a contact which then can lead to gossip—for some other important reason—to borrow eggs, to return a key, and so on. (Even work gossip can evolve into diversion gossip and coffee-klatsch). The fact that gossipers clearly accentuate the context of work only so that they can freely indulge in gossip under the appearance of an accidental, transitory encounter, is, of course, seen through by those around them. The illustrator of the "Satirical Handbill on the Vices of Servant Girls" had given this idea an ironic twist in the figure of the youth who brings the two girls at the "gossip market" a chair. But we should not fault those we encounter gossiping in the halls of the university as well as standing at the market. By standing they symbolically express their respect for the prohibition on gossip that they are actually breaking.

The presentation of the situational embeddedness of gossip within three different contexts of action—the domain of sociability, the domain of peripheral activities, and the domain of work—has repeatedly encountered a single theme, namely, the problems that emerge for the gossipers as a result of the fact that the activity in which they indulge is socially discredited and that they thereby run the risk of damaging their reputation. We encounter the same theme once again if we pursue the

345. Nürnberger satirisches Flugblatt auf die Untugenden der Dienstmägde. 1652

Figure 2. "New Council of the Servant Girls." Satirical handbill on the vices of servant girls. Nuremberg, 1652. Taken from E. Fuchs 1906.

embeddedness of gossip to the question of how gossip occurs in interaction, that is, in conversations.

THE INTERACTIVE SECURING OF GOSSIP

The fact that gossip occurs *in* conversation as a genre of oral communication can be initially disguised by the trivial fact that utterances, which in themselves have nothing to do with gossip, precede and succeed the gossip-communication itself. For example, we would not call gossip the greeting with which a conversation begins, nor the farewell with which it normally ends. Thus in the one case gossip is embedded in a sequence of interaction, and this embeddedness provides the analysis of gossip-communication with a point of departure. To be sure, the flow of the interaction within which the gossip occurs cannot be deprived of its temporal structure, and thereby have its temporal succession overlooked, because it is analyzed by pregiven categories of observation into individual, fixed, conversational activities. Instead, the fact that a sequence of interaction occurs in a clear and ordered way should be understood as a performance of the interactors that produces, as an articulated structure of interaction in situ, what is presented in and through their utterances in succession. Therefore, the assumption that gossip is embedded in a sequence of interaction should not disguise the fact that it is the interactors themselves who mutually accomplish this embedding.

The participants in an interaction are in principle obligated to possess, and as a rule do possess, the corresponding competency to coordinate and harmonize their utterances and behavioral decisions in many different ways. Anyone who, "out of the blue," that is, without any forewarning, tells a joke will, if he succeeds, evoke irritation if not anger in his partners regardless of his remarkable behavior. Conversations will be successful only if the participants repeatedly indicate, communicate, confirm, and ratify to each other what-they-are-at-present-concerned-with-and-what-they-intend-to-do-next. This agglutinative way of writing should indicate that these harmonizations and coordinations are not verbalized in most cases but are to be conveyed to one's partner indirectly and in "bodily" form through the communicative acts themselves. Of course, this intersubjective securing of agreement is urgently required when the ongoing conversation is to be turned to a different theme or when one model of communication is to be superseded by another.

Such a situation occurs when the interactors try to transpose a conversation that has not yet become gossip or to end a gossip-conversation that is already in progress. Thus we can assume that the external boundaries of a conversation as well as the internal boundaries of a gossip-communication—their opening and their concluding phase—are organized in specific ways by the interactors for the purpose of the intersubjective securing of agreement and concretized for the scientific observer.[18] Roughly speaking, this produces a tri-partite sequential structure for the internal organization of gossip-conversations

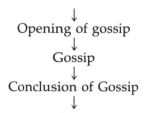

$$\downarrow$$
$$\text{Opening of gossip}$$
$$\downarrow$$
$$\text{Gossip}$$
$$\downarrow$$
$$\text{Conclusion of Gossip}$$
$$\downarrow$$

that formally not only characterizes gossip but also characterizes the performance of other communicative models of conversation. The present and following sections will try to determine the specific organizational sequence of gossip, that is, to use observational records and transcripts to determine how gossip is distilled as a genuine form of communication out of the flowing stream of activity of a conversation, how it is performed in linguistic interaction and how it is finally brought to an end.[19]

The preceding presentation has shown that in initiating gossip within an ongoing conversation the interactors have to manage two specific complexes of tasks. (The general problem of thematic organization will be omitted for the time being.) On one hand, there is the *relational problem* of clarifying whether and how the absent person, who is to play the role of the protagonist in the conversation, is mutually known to the conversational participants, and thereby can be thematized as a subject of gossip. On the other, there is the *interactive-moral problem* of making sure that the socially condemned practice of gossiping is shared by all the participants because this is the only way in which the gossip producer can avoid the unpleasant and fatal situation of appearing as the only one who is gossiping. Since both complexes of tasks concern the conditions of the communication of gossip they are typically solved by the interactors before or at the very beginning of the real gossip. We should then expect that the central interactive sequence in which the gossip is transmitted and processed is preceded by a presequence in which the interactors test whether the conditions for entering on gossip exist.

Presequences have already been a subject of investigation of conversation-analysis for a long time.[20] Many works have shown that such phases of communicative clarification can precede the most diverse interactive sequences. They refer principally to the fact that the interactors imagine the prospective course of their conversation and anticipate possible undesired developments. Accordingly, these presequences are constituted by the actors' efforts to detect an immanent "nonpreferred" course of conversation as early as possible and, through appropriate measures, to prevent the conversation from actually developing in this direction. For example, if someone wants to avoid having his invitation to the movies ("Would you like to go to the movies with me tonight?") turned down, he can use a presequence ("Are you busy tonight?") to determine whether his invitation will have any chance of success. If he can determine from the presequence that his conversational partner is unlikely to accept his invitation ("I have my Italian class tonight"), he will then know not to ask. Generally, presequences serve to coordinate the actions of the interactors in advance and to harmonize them. With their help intentions are indirectly revealed, interests discreetly articulated, goals covertly indicated, rejections implicitly expressed, and conflicts avoided before erupting. In this way abrupt rejection, open refusal, and thereby rebuff and loss of face can be avoided.

Establishing the Subject of Gossip

When we use transcripts to determine how the interactors manage the first complex of tasks, namely, the introduction of the future subject of gossip into the ongoing conversation, we always encounter the same observation:

> [1]   [*High-Life*: GR: 22][21]
> [Mrs. Hein and Mrs. Ring, residents in a development for the homeless, are sitting with students Paul and Gunther, who previously worked with both women in a coalition for the homeless. All are having a coffee-klatsch in Paul's apartment.]
>
> P: (You want) coffee, or⌐beer instead?
> G: ⌊hm
>   (3 sec.)
> H: I prefer a beer, as long as you're asking.
> G: Hehe
> H: Hehehe
> P: No (I'm asking) just so I can turn off the coffee.
> G: Hm
> →   The . . . the Theissens moved out, huh?

R: Yes⌜she did all⌝right for herself
H: ⌞(   )⌟
R: ⌜Ten thousand Marks.
P: ⌞(   )
G: That's what she got? As a one-time subsidy, huh?

The way in which G in this passage introduces "the Theissens," who were not yet mentioned in the conversation, into it reveals that he implicitly assumes that the identification of the persons named would not be a problem for the participants in the conversation. Except for a few references that he achieves through the definite article and the "recognitional form" of a family name,[22] he declines to supply further proposals and clues to localize and identify his focus group. And it is precisely this restriction to a minimal, definite form of reference that expresses the speaker's assumption that the persons named by him possess the status of "acquaintances" for the participants in the conversation. This economic form of referring to the person who becomes the subject of gossip in the conversation by means of his first or family name (many times even by means of a nickname) is a typical element of the presequence that precedes gossip.

As a rule, the participants have no trouble in immediately identifying the persons (and future subjects of gossip) introduced with this form of reference. Most of the time the recipients immediately recognize them in their successive utterances through pronouns, and thereby confirm not only that someone is an "acquaintance" but also that the sequence initiator has correctly presupposed this acquaintanceship in his form of reference.

[2]   [*Careers*: AK: EM 21][23]
K: Yes that Schleifinger woman is now making a "career" of it in Mainz—
→ S: How's that? *Her*? How did she get to do that??

When S unhesitatingly uses the anaphoristic, astonishment-eliciting "*Her*!" as well as the dialect pronoun "she" to refer to "that Schleifinger woman" whom K introduced into the conversation in a familiar way using the definite article + the family name, she establishes between herself, "K," and "that Schleifinger woman" the triadic relation of acquaintanceship that forms the basis of gossip. (Of course, this does not mean that the gossipers are also known to "that Schleifinger woman" or to "the Theissens".) In summary, we can say that the task of introducing an absent third person into the conversation as a subject of gossip who is known to the participants, and thereby as a potential subject of gossip, is performed by the interactors quickly, easily, and without problems. This shows that the participants in the conversation clearly know *something about the sample of their respective circle of acquaintances.* This knowledge spares the interactors from initially having to clarify the troublesome question "whether my acquaintance is also your acquaintance." Even more, in this expeditious process of identification the interactors mutually demonstrate and guarantee a suitable measure of familiarity with each other's personal life. And this familiarity is one of the conditions of the interactors' being able to enter into a relation of gossip.

Of course, it can happen that the person named by a participant cannot be immediately identified by a recipient. The following segment of conversation illustrates such a case:

[3]   [*High-Life*: GR: 28]
G: Are the Große-Schürups still living in the development in— on
     Oswald Street?
     Mrs. Großs-S⌐chürup
R: ⌊Große-Schürups?
P: Kröll.
R: Don't know her.
H: Frieda Kröll.
R: Ahhhh ah⌐hhh
H: ⌊heheh⌐ehe
R: ⌊ahhhhh Große-⌐Schürups
H: ⌊yeah, sure—that Frieda
     is living again in (⌐   )
R: ⌊exactly!
H: yes
R: That clod!

In this case Mrs. R can make as little sense of G's personal reference ("Mrs. Große-Schürups") as with P's help in identifying someone ("Kröll"). And it seems as if G has introduced someone into the conversation who—contrary to his assumption—is unknown to Mrs. R ("Don't know her"). Only when Mrs. H provides the first name of the person in question ("Frieda Kröll") does Mrs. R signal ("Ahhhhh ahhhh") that she knows her. What is more interesting in this case than the process of the creation of the reference[24]—embedded in a separate sequence—is the difference of knowledge reflected in the fact that the same person who was called "Mrs. Große-Schürup" by G is known to Mrs. R and Mrs. H as "Frieda." Someone who refers to an adult person by a first name in the German language indicates, as a rule, a relatively equal and familiar relation, which also includes a knowledge of personal and private things. He thereby finds himself in the position of a potential gossip producer for any interaction partner who refers to the same person by his or her family name and thus indicates a rather formal, distant relation of acquaintanceship. What is revealed here in the case of personal reference can be generalized as a more encompassing structural component: *the gossip presequence not only secures the acquaintance of the future subject of gossip but it also clarifies the kind of knowledge the actors have of this mutually known acquaintance.* This process of clarification further reveals which participant can and should act as the—next—producer of gossip. Thus a segment of the conversation cited above shows:

[1]   [*Detail/Simplified*]
G: The—the Theissens moved out, huh?
R: Yeah, she did all right for herself?
R: Ten thousand marks.
G: That's what she got? As a one-time subsidy, huh?

that the person asking the question, and who introduced "the Theissens" into the conversation, is not completely ignorant of the mutual acquaintance, but, on the contrary, can understand the somewhat puzzlingly communicated information, itself possibly gossip ("Ten thousand marks"), and interpretively apprehend it through her knowledge ("As a one-time subsidy").

The information that Mrs. R repeats here does not yet qualify her as a gossip producer because her information is not newsworthy. Formulated more generally, *the positions of the gossip producer and recipient are worked out locally* through the clarification of the acquaintanceship relations, the knowledge of private affairs implied therein, and the newsworthiness of the information. The latter process is also of decisive importance in the management of the second complex of tasks with which the interactors are confronted in initiating gossip and that concerns the problematic moral aspect of their activity.

In principle, the initiative to gossip can begin with the producer as well as the recipient of subsequent stories. But, because they have to deal with morally contaminated material, both have to get about their work with great care in order to prevent a situation in which each alone appears interested in gossip. Structurally this situation is comparable to one in which a bribe takes place. A bribe can only be managed successfully if a consensus has been developed between A and B in regard to it, that is, if A's offer of a bribe corresponds to B's susceptibility to bribes. But A cannot offer a bribe with impunity, nor can B reveal his willingness to accept bribes. Each would thereby run the risk of morally discrediting himself in case he received a negative reaction from the other. In fact, he would put himself in a position of legal culpability because "the attempt is punishable" (as the *Strafgesetzbuch* (Penal Code) says in regard to the offering or soliciting of bribes). Thus, before the conduct of the real transaction can occur, the corruptibility of the other has to be secured and gradually transformed into an unambiguous consensus through guarded proposals and vague demands that permit one to back out without losing face. Starting from this comparison we can then ask which techniques the gossip producer and recipient use to create a consensus about the mutually shared willingness to gossip before the real gossip transaction between them occurs.

Invitations to Gossip

It might at first appear as if the moral problems of initiating gossip could easily be solved by having one of the participants openly assume the role of the recipient and ask his partner directly about the latest news. Through his open expression of interest in gossip the recipient would then assume as much of the responsibility for the situation as the producer who disseminates his morally contaminated information. Yet this simple solution of the problem of "complicity" contains a series of problems. The ethnologist E.B. Almirol has described the main problem in his study of a Filipino community in California with the following observation: "A woman who is reputed, perhaps unjustly, as a *tsismosa* explained that the 'art' of gossiping begins with a show of lack of interest in it, if not a vague contempt for it. 'If you show an active interest in knowing things about other people, you are immediately branded as *tsismosa* and as a consequence you do not get any information.' It is wise never to appear too inquisitive, or too interested in gossip, 'because gossip is like a butterfly, namely, the more you chase it, the more it will fly away from you, if you sit still it will land on your shoulders.' "[25] The fact that anyone who appears interested in gossip will have it withheld from him precisely for this reason may—as Almirol himself thinks—be based on the information-provider's fear that the person interested in gossip will foolishly repeat everything he hears and thereby do harm. Yet this is an interpretation that assumes for the interactors—especially for their informal domain of action—an overconcern with expediency. The boycott of an information-hungry gossip recipient can be reduced perhaps to the paradoxically sounding attempt of the gossipers *to gossip together, while at the same time not to appearing to gossip*. And because the reputation of being a gossiper is contagious, those who, as producers or recipients, acquire this reputation are isolated and excluded from the

broader network of gossip. (These can meet together as their own notorious network of gossipers—perhaps as the above described groups of
idlers.)

Thus there are good reasons for gossip-recipients not to appear interested in gossip. Yet how can interactors bring their partners to repeat
information without appearing to be curious? If we examine this question using recorded conversations, we can observe that the participants possess different techniques discreetly to encourage—or better
invite[26]—their partners to transmit information about the private affairs
of an absent third party. The way in which such invitations function
consists, in general, in placing one's partner in a position where he
willingly appears to produce more information than the initiating utterance actually requested of him. These invitations thereby are closely
related to those types of "fishing"[27] expressions that are frequently used
in informal as well as institutional contexts of interaction as a means of
pressuring someone to talk.[28] Two of these techniques will be described
in the following.

One technique consists of "innocently" signaling, through *repeated
thematization of apparently innocuous details or data*, an interest in the fate of
a common acquaintance—an interest that goes beyond the requested
details and aims at "more" than a simple confirmation or brief remark.[29]
The following two conversational segments, which are continuations of
segments [1] and [3], contain examples of this technique of the repeated
thematization of details and also show how these sequence-initiating
utterances are answered.

[4/1][30]   [*High-Life*: GR: 22]

- G: The—the Theissens moved out, huh?

                    .
                    .
                    .

- G: How long ago did they move
      fro⌐m Oswald Stre⌐et?
  R: ⌊(   )⌋
  R: Gunther! The moving van came.
      What gloves the workmen had . . .
      Yes, and afterwards they grabbed them, just like that, and
      tossed them into the trash can.
  H: So come on, you can see that Paul isn't as poor as you thought.
      <amused>
  R: And so I said—I did—⌐there are
  H: ⌊hihihi

R: They were next door, at the neighbors, washing their hands.
    That's how foul their stuff smelled.

[5/3]   [*High-Life*: GR: 28]

G: Are the Große-Schürups still living in the development in–on
    Oswald Street?

                                        .

                                        .

                                        .

R: That clod!
                              (2 secs.)
R: Bahhhh! <disapproving>
                              (2 secs.)
P: They lived on Wentruper Street┌before
H: └hum
R: (palaver   )
H: (   )
R: She'd stick out (wanted   ) her head through those stair
    rails, but that didn't work. They'd 've kicked her in the arse,
    eh.

In segment [4], after the conversation had already taken a different
direction, the question of the Theissens' move is taken up once again by
G with the question of the time at which it took place. Although till that
time it was not known that this theme was in any way gossipy, a gossip
story by R follows immediately upon this "innocent" rethematization of
events that were supposed to have occurred when the Theissens moved
and that concern the Theissens' lack of sobriety ("That's how foul their
stuff smelled"). To be sure, in segment [5] the first question of "the
Große-Schürups" home leads to R's malicious typification ("that clod").
Yet it is only the harmless rethematization of the question of residence
that produces the story about the—as it later turns out—tipsy Mrs.
Große-Schürup ("They'd 've kicked her in the arse, eh."). In both cases
the initiating utterances have a neutral, almost detached, character and
remain focused on details that appear as really unimportant. But it is
precisely through his persevering interest in irrelevant matters that the
speaker reveals his wish to learn more about the persons introduced by
him into the conversation, namely, to make them the subject of gossip.
The gossip initiators indirectly reveal that they have too little information to be able to ask for gossip intentionally (if for strategic reasons they
do not reveal themselves as less informed than they really are). The
combination of a lack of information and an interest is a concealed invitation to potential gossip producers to become active. Even if gossip

does not immediately commence, all participants can easily withdraw from the situation because of the "harmlessness" of the sequence-initiating utterances.

Another technique for inviting gossip consists of *evaluating already known information about the behavior of a potential subject of gossip to one's interlocutor, with the hope that the other party will supply more detail and comment*. Examples of this technique are found in the following two segments of conversation:

[6]   [*Sicilian*: AK: EM 14B]

J: And Aunt Bertha really liked it;
M: Oh, ┌and how!
A: └*Her*! My God=er=my God. Sunday morning I thought, "ha—I can't call her yet". . .

[7]   [*memorandum*]

R: And the Dischingers actually got themselves a dog.
G: Really, they're putting everyone on. A poodle! A real tiger . . .

First of all it is striking that in both cases the sequence initiators do not thematize a fact or an event that concerns a mutual acquaintance in the form of a question, but as a statement. This assertive structure also belongs in principle to other *"fishing"* expressions (for example, "your phone was constantly busy"). The speaker who uses these forms of expression tells his partner that he already has information about the issue he has raised, and that he is interested in learning more about its background. In spite of their assertive structure, because both utterances also contain indications of uncertainty ("really," "actually") the recipients—who should have the appropriate information—are invited to confirm or correct them. In addition, both utterances are restricted to formulating a result ("liked it," "got") that indicates a prior history (in the one case a trip, in the other a process of decision and the circumstances of the dog's purchase). All these features of the utterances are functionally directed toward enticing background information, prior histories, unofficial versions, and so on from the interlocutors—in a word, to lure them into gossip.

From the vigorous reactions ("Really, they're putting everyone on"), it is clear that the "fishing" character of these sequence-initiating utterances still refers to an entirely different dimension. Quite clearly this refers beyond the thematized issue to an evaluative characterization of the mutual acquaintances or relatives introduced in the conversation. Of course, in both utterances this evaluative orientation is expressed only latently and in reference to a mutually shared foreknowledge. In segment [6], through the anticipatory particle "really," as well as through the slightly evaluative—and as will later become clear, understated—descriptor "liked," the speaker J indicates that she views her Aunt Bertha as someone who knows how to take things in a positive way. (In the further course of the conversation M even says, ("Aunt Bertha has a really happy nature'.) In segment [7] R indicates his amazement over the purchase of the Dischinger's dog with a skeptical "actually." This amazement can be read in two ways: it can refer to the fact that the dog's purchase occurred against R's expectations or against what R thought was reasonable. It would be pointless here to try to try to decide which of these readings is correct. It is precisely the *ambiguity of this utterance that is such a specific and clever technique for initiating gossip*, because its "harmless" version forms the cover for the "critical" version, which is for the partner, if he is able to decipher it, a signal to come out with his presumably negative judgment.

In summary, we can say that gossip initiators have many techniques of inviting—not to say, deceiving—their partners into repeating gossip information in an indirect and guarded way. For these techniques are a very effective means of "sounding out" a partner about an absent person. Subsequent recipients avoid openly expressing their interests and intentions and in this way protect themselves against the danger of appearing as indiscreet and gossipy. A partner who operates in such a restrained way recommends himself, as it were, as a reliable gossip partner. But at the same time it is always possible that the potential gossip producer, by means of the way he initiates the gossip, can discreetly pass up the invitation to gossip. In the following segment,

[8]   [*High-Life*: GR: 37]
G: What's new with the Pelster?
       (2 secs.)
R: Oh, nothing
G: <faint laughter>

G openly and indiscreetly asks for news about the "Pelster" grocery store that is well-known to the residents of the homeless settlement as a gossip exchange. Such undisguised *invitations to gossip* generally appear (as in the present case) within already established gossip meetings or between persons who have established a fixed relationship for gossiping among themselves over a long period of time.[31] In segment [8] G's unconcealed desire for gossip is rejected in the same direct way. In an ongoing gossip-conversation, where all the participants "have already gotten their hands dirty," this may be an unproblematic, unforeseen event. But in a phase that is concerned with the interactive securing and framing of gossip-communication, the gossip initiator would disavow such a brusk rejection. However, a partner who is carefully and discreetly lured into repeating his gossip can—and must—express his rejection in a similarly diplomatic form (through hesitation, a change of theme, reference to his involvement etc.). As implicit and unexpressed as is the invitation to gossip in this case, its rejection remains just as implicit and unexpressed.

GOSSIP PROPOSALS

It has become clear that the gossip producer's morally contaminated information can also, à la radioactive substances, morally "pollute" anyone who reaches out for it unprotected. Of course, it is initially the gossip producer who is in possession of this explosive material. Therefore, in handling and processing this information he must be as careful as the recipient that something unforeseen does not occur, which might damage his reputation. That is to say, if a participant is interested in repeating his information he must first make sure that his partner is prepared to participate in the gossip-communication—otherwise he would be disavowed as a gossiper because he is forcing his indiscreet information on someone who is not interested in it. It is therefore not surprising that in initiating gossip the gossip producer takes precautions in the same way as the recipient, namely, in a presequence, which is directed primarily at checking the willingness of his partner to gossip.

In this case the presequence consists of the gossip producer's making a proposal of gossip to his interlocutors and withholding his information until they give a positive reply to it. Just like the recipient's invitation, the producer's proposal must be presented in such a way that a negative reaction without rebuff and a retreat without loss of face are possible. The basic principle of such proposals generally consists of *the potential gossip producer's causing his interlocutors to ask for information on their own, through his indication and announcement of it.*

This finding already shows that the invitation to gossip and gossip proposals essentially differ in regard to their sequential structure in one particular. In the case of the recipient-generated invitation to gossip the sequence, if it leads to gossip, is composed essentially of two components:

Model A: *Invitation to Gossip*

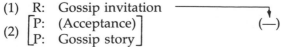

    (1) R: Gossip invitation
    (2) ⎡P: (Acceptance)⎤   (—)
        ⎣P: Gossip story⎦

As examples [6] and [7] show quite well, the acceptance itself is no longer expressed by the gossip producer if he accepts the invitation to gossip. It is omitted and the gossip-story begins immediately. Thus the presequence is reduced to a preliminary move by the potential recipient. Nevertheless, the sequence that begins with a producer-generated proposal of gossip always contains three components:

Model B: *Gossip proposal*
   (1) P: Gossip proposal ⎯⎯⎯⎯⎯⎯⎯⎯⎯⎯⎯⎯⎯⎯⟶
   (2) R: Inquiry   (—)
   (3) P: Gossip story

We might get the impression from this that the components (1) in model A are identical with the components (2) in model B. Both times the recipient addresses the potential producer with the intention of persuading him to provide gossip information. But on the basis of this schematic presentation we can already anticipate that the recipient's inquiry in model B will typically be much more open, direct, and undisguised than the recipient's invitation in model A. For the recipient's inquiry in model B is always preceded—although covertly—by the gossip producer's proposal, so that the recipient does not have to show as much caution.

This expectation is confirmed by going through the conversational transcripts. In most of the cases in which the participants indicate and announce gossip information (how this happens will be shown presently), the recipient inquires in a relatively direct and "curious" way, as perhaps in the following segment:

        [9]   [*Nichts Tolles*: AK: EM 13B]
        M: And Metzger, he has a professor in the town of X;
        E: *Yeah*.
        M: I still don't remember when he left

                              .

                              .

                              .

        M: ⌈he was a nice guy
        E: │ *Metzger?*
(1)   │   (1 sec.)
        E: │ °I don't think so°
        M: │ Hnhh?
        E: ⌊*Maybe* he was *sort of* nice!

(2) ┌ M: Yes, well I don't know him too well, only by sight, and from
     │   his manner, I always found him ˌ°only so-so°
     │ E: ⌊well, yeah:::,⌋
     └ M: But you knew him better, ˌor what?
(3) ┌ E: ⌊As far as I'm concerned,
     └   he was a real phony . . .

In this segment "Metzger" is a mutual acquaintance of the interactors, who M(onica) thinks is a "nice guy." E(rich) thereupon clearly indicates[32] that he does not share the opinion that "Metzger" is a nice guy. On one hand, E's utterances are characterized by that fact that they do not provide a reason for his negative opinion or allow us to figure it out. But on the other, E indicates with the utterance "Maybe he was *sort of* nice," which differentiates his judgment, that he knows something about Metzger that makes it possible for him to make an evaluation that goes beyond the global typification "nice/not nice." But it is precisely this *simultaneous indication and withholding of information about another person* that forms the central functional principle of gossip proposals.[33] M, too, interprets E's utterances in this way. At first she tries to play down her information about Metzger as superficial in order then to ask for E's indicated information directly. It is only in connection with this explicit inquiry that E begins to divulge his "insider information" about Metzger.

Segment [9] is an example of how, despite differences of opinion about an absent person, gossip proposals can initiate gossip. Thereby the appearance of gossip proposals within such argumentative contexts of interaction is systematically promoted by the specific conversational organization of disagreement that obligates the interactors to caution, withholding, waiting, and indications ("predisagreements"). Because disagreements generally possess a sequence-expanding effect, the course of the conversation, from the initial proposal to the final narration, in such discordant interactive constellations takes many moves, as segment [9] shows. Nevertheless, gossip proposals can also occur quite directly, trigger an immediate inquiry, and, as segment [2] already shows,

[2]

(1)   K: Yeah, and that Schleifinger woman is now making a career of it in Mainz—
(2)   S: How's that? *Her*? How did she get to do that?
(3)   K: Ha, the same way she did it here, too; . . .

after two preliminary moves lead to gossip. In this case the presequence is reduced to its basic format, which once again points to the fact that the

gossipers possess a mutually recognized, implicit foreknowledge about
the subject of gossip and/or an established gossip relation exists between them. The following segment refers to such a situation. In it, both
of the main gossipers, Mrs. R and Mrs. H, are asked at the end of G's
story where such conversations take place:

[10]   [*High-Life*: GR: 46]
H: Yeah, and Jochen=he ⌈went along ⌉=
R: ⌊walked over⌋
H: went over
H: ⌈hihihihihihihi
G: ⌊°hahahahahaha°
R: What a (mess   ) huh
G: Where are people talking about it? An⌈d=
R: ⌊Everywhere,
     all the time. When—
R: Suppose you're   H: (   ) when you're
     shopping when a—   just walking around and
     When I go shopping I   you meet someone you
     notice two women   know (   ) a
     standing by the door. So   conversation starts.
     I say "Hello."   "Have you heard what's
                                       going on?" and so on.
R: And then it starts "Did you hear?"
     Bzz, bzz, bzz—then you (   ).
     Yeah, and when I hear that, then I start to get interested
     in everything.
     Then I ask "when," "how," and so on.
                    (—)
R: ⌈(   ) did you hear about Zeunert?
(1) ⌊You heard it too?
     ⌊No, (but truthfully) now. The accident?
P: No
R: He had—Ferdi's brother . . .

Embedded between the two stories in this segment, the two women
describe, sometimes identically, how the women in their apartment
building gossip during shopping. Both women agree that the initiative
always begins with the one who has the information. It seems to characterize this situation that the women can assume their partner's enthusi-
astic willingness to gossip. This is expressed by the fact that in their
gossip proposals they do not even bother to check the willingness of
their recipients to gossip, but—"Did you hear?"—merely see whether

the information for *this* recipient possesses the status of news. Formulated more generally, *in personal relationships, where an established relation of gossip already exists between the participants, the complex of moral tasks involved in initiating gossip no longer needs to be worked through separately.* In such situations, the place of concealed, cautious gossip proposals can be taken by the simple format of an open "announcement of news."[34] As segment [10] shows, in this case as well the sequence initiator can begin to report his news only when the recipient allows him "free passage" through questioning ("what?," "what happened?" etc.) or through rejecting his information ("no," etc.). Thus there is no difference between the "proposal of gossip" and the "announcement of news" with respect to sequential organization. This once again points to the fact that if the moral problem of initiating gossip is worked out within a presequence it happens in a concealed and implicit way. Thereby, the sequence form of the preannouncement of news within the conversation forms the basis of the sequence form of the gossip proposal that can be viewed as a moral version of this type of presequence.[35]

Besides working out and ignoring the moral problem of the initiation of gossip we would like to present and analyze a third variant at the conclusion of this section, with the help of a conversational segment. In this variant the interactors try to deal with the morally doubtful character of their activity by viewing it as a problem that is, in fact, not serious and, instead of simply overlooking it as irrelevant to the situation, by *playing* with it. How this occurs can be shown quite clearly with the following segment:

[11]   [*High-Life*: GR: 29]

[The transcript begins at the end of a gossiping session between Mrs. R. and Mrs. H. about Mrs. S.]

H: She's a little touched!
R: She's ⌜nuts
H: ⌊She's totally, completely
     crazy! <vehemently>
G: <faint laughter>
R: ⌜They imagine—
H: ⌊<grinning> Well . . . the dilemma was more or less
     (—) my fault. I brought it on, even though I didn't want to.
R: Yeah, yeah (⌜)=
H: ⌊yeah
G: =what then? What⌜ happened then?
R: ⌊The word got round,=
     got round—

> H: [I can't possibly repeat what part
>   I played.
> G: <laughing faintly>
> R: The rumor went around that she—
> G: [This is getting exciting=
> G: =hehehe
> R: That she's always got some guy in the sack.
>   ?   hah ahaha
> H: [No, pay attention!
> R: So she's screaming—
> H: [I have my bathroom—Dieter's below
>   and she's at it with Dieter "You want me to spray you?"
>   And then she sprays him . . .

This segment reveals an interesting *expansion* of the sequence triggered by the gossip proposal that can be reconstructed in the following way: after R's and H's story about the "impossible" behavior of the—drunken—Mrs. S that concludes with some forceful characterizations ("nuts," "crazy"), H indicates that there is a story behind this story in which she herself was involved. This indication, which is made even more interesting and secretive by H's accompanying grin,[36] causes the potential recipient G to inquire with curiosity ("What then? What happened then?"). Here where H—following the model of gossip proposal—could present her story she shows restraint. Instead of the story that she had taken such pains to indicate, she stops the expected continuation of the sequence of action and says that because of her own—problematic—participation she cannot repeat this event ("I can't possibly repeat what part *I played*."). Of course, with her suppressed laughter she makes clear that the withdrawal of her proposal is not serious, only *that she is behaving affectedly*, in fact that she is *being coy* in telling a story in which she herself was guilty of participating ("the dilemma was more or less my fault"). With his statement, "This is getting exciting, hehehe," G skillfully enters upon the particulars of both significant features in H's hesitant behavior. He appeals to H to tell the indicated story despite the latter's objections and at the same time reveals through his laughter that he has perceived that the withdrawal of the proposal was not serious. Only then does H begin to depict the event. (This *re*construction omitted the fact that during this interaction, R—who is in competition with H who actually "heard" this story—makes several attempts to report at least its juicy part, to which H protests—"No, pay attention!").

We can summarize this reconstructed sequential expansion[37] in the following way as the continuation of the sequence model of the gossip proposal:

Model C: Gossip proposal (expanded sequence)

(1-a) P: Gossip proposal
(2-a) R: Inquiry
(1-b) P: Feigned rejection
(2-b) R: Renewed inquiry
  (3) P: Story

The significance of the hesitation (1-b) is twofold. It documents that the sequence initiator is aware of the moral dubiousness of his activity and objects to compromising himself through the indicated story. Although this (feigned) rejection causes the recipient to become clearly more interested in the proposed story, the moral "guilt" in initiating the gossip, which the subsequent gossip producer *qua* sequence initiator had to bear all by himself, is largely transferred to the "curious" recipient. This guarantees that the "reprehensible" practice of gossiping—according to the motto "go along, get caught"—is begun and concluded as a cooperative act of all the participants. But such mutual moral complicity of the gossipers is only one significant feature of this dilatory maneuver. The other is dramaturgical in nature. A kind of seductive game is played with the recipient in such a situation. He is at first enticed to express his interest in the indicated transaction, and then the initiator of the situation allows him to be "snubbed" with his feigned rejection. In this way the exciting suspense in which the recipient awaits, even feverishly, the furtively proposed story is intentionally increased.[38] But even for the initiator the thrill of the following gossip-communication is heightened by the fact that he "tortures" his partner for a little while. This shows *that the fact that gossip is a morally objectionable practice is not merely a subject of concern for the interactors but also a source of their enjoyment at the same time*. In compromised form this paradoxical relationship can be found to constitute a part of the very sense of the teasing that plays precariously with the validity of the norm.

THE GOSSIP INSTRUMENTARIUM

Gossip-producers are confronted with having to find a solution to a very general problem. They have to translate the information they possess into a linguistic presentation. (The fact that mimic-gestural and prosodic-paralinguistic means of expression play an important role in this will become clear as the analysis progresses.) If we now examine more closely how gossip producers transform their specific knowledge about events into a communicative presentation, we will observe that their presenting activity is not restricted in principle to the use of the often described model of storytelling—now under the heading of gossip—in order to reconstruct an event.[39] That is to say, the gossip quality of the reconstruction of an event is not simply reduced to the fact that it occurs after a gossip presequence is successfully managed. Instead, the gossip producers' activity always—and often preeminently—consists of *creating a context of interpretation for their information that is specific to gossip*. This observation follows the rule, used quite productively by ethnomethodologists, of directing attention in the analysis of texts to the question of how the performance of utterances and actions is interpreted and, for all practical purposes, explained (made "accountable") by the actors themselves.[40] From this perspective "context" does not signify an external, normative variable that the actors have to follow but a context *within* the conversation that they produce at the same time *through* their actions as a framework of interpretation *for* their actions. This reflexive structural coherence of utterance and utterance context, of the performance of action and its meaning clearly reveals itself in gossip by the systematic efforts of gossip producers to describe—often only indirectly—specific qualities, modalities, and implications of their information through and alongside its reconstructive presentation and thereby to reveal their activity as "gossip."

Thus the activity of gossiping is not restricted to repeating information about the private life of an absent acquaintance. At the same time, gossip always includes the willingness and the capacity of the gossip producer to supply in metanarrative a context of interpretation for this information. This happens—as we can say in anticipation of research findings—insofar as the gossip producer refers implicitly or explicitly in his presentation to the following qualities of his information:

- Gossip information is always characterized as *worthy of communication* by the way it is presented or through specific accentuations of the gossip producer. This is the reason underlying the generally dominant tendency in gossip-communication to emphasize the unexpected, the unconventional, the juicy, the strange, the improper, the immoral, the eccentric in the behavior of the subject of gossip when reconstructing an event. *This accentuation of the extraordinary that is specific to gossip* has two important implications. On one hand, it heightens the entertainment value of the information. And on the other, this tendency towards dramatization—especially when it is about the breaking of rules—indirectly legitimates the gossip producer's intervention into the private sphere of the subject of gossip. Scandal turns a private event into a subject of public interest.

- Gossip producers are in principle concerned with presenting the information they transmit to others as *believable*. Because gossip contains a built-in tendency to exaggeration, and because "gossip means confessing the sins of others" (Wilhelm Busch), gossip producers are always in danger of being called slanderers. The reproach of slander presupposes that someone circulates false statements about someone else for which he raises a claim—against his better knowledge—to truth. If and when a gossip producer's presentations contain false statements against the subject of gossip cannot, of course, be decided through the analysis of gossip-conversations.[41] We can observe, however, that gossip producers employ numerous *authentication strategies* within the framework of their reconstructive activity to try to prove that the narrative version they present is valid and that thereby their information is believable.

- Despite the different types of measures for interactively securing gossip communication, the gossip producers repeatedly reveal through their utterances that they have not lost sight of the *morally contaminated character* of their information. This is documented in their efforts to characterize their *information as passively acquired*, that is, as information that was given to them by others or that they had gotten in some other way, without making an active effort. Instead of referring to the genealogy of their information, gossip producers can also use the technique of *preventive denial* to try to protect themselves against the harmful consequences that can result from the spreading of morally contaminated information.[42] Gossip-producers sometimes begin their gossip contribution with utterances such as "I don't want to say anything bad about someone else, but. . ." or "I really don't want to tell anyone what to do, but. . ." Introductory elements of this kind (see also "This may sound chauvinistic, but . . ." and "I don't want to offend you, but. . .") serve in this case, as in other communicative situations, to anticipate the possible negative reaction of an interaction partner, to pre-empt the reproach of bad intentions, and in this way to make the formulation of a truly "impossible" utterance, the performance of a truly forbidden action, possible.

- Gossip producers do not present their information in the detached, neutral sense of a news broadcaster, because what is important for the gossiper is not so much the informative content of his gossip but his *commentary* and *evaluation* of it. Two of the most striking features of gossip-communication bear witness to this. On one hand, we can observe that what is stimulating about gossip for the gossiper is above all the *joy of speculating* about the background of the story and about the motives of the subject of the gossip. On the other, we can also see that the *morally indignant, to the point of malicious,* inflection running throughout the gossip is one of its characteristics. Gossip producers indicate early on, through evaluative accentuation and the choice of appropriate descriptive terms, how they want their story interpreted. Should the recipient agree with this evaluative commentary, such a mass of speculative and foolish remarks arises that an outside observer could easily get the impression that the information served the gossipers only— as a pretext for idle speculation, mischief, and mutual moral indignation.

• No less than in the reconstruction of the individual event itself, the gossip producers are interested in the *generalization* of their knowledge. No matter how shockingly entertaining it may be in itself, the story is always interpreted by the gossipers as typical of the subject of gossip. In fact, in most cases that begin with a story or a series of stories, the *subject of gossip is identified as a social type.*

We have to interpret correctly the significance of the five components of the interpretation of gossip-information that have been presented here in summary fashion. *Taken together they form nothing less than the indispensable instrumentarium of the production of gossip.* That is to say, whenever a participant presents his gossip-information, he must also be basically concerned in this interpretive process with its worthiness for communication and belief, its moral contamination, as well as with his commentary and the generalization of his knowledge. It is only in this way—and not through the dull narration of a story about an event from the private sphere of an acquaintance—that his presentation acquires the genuine character of gossip.

In the following sections we will try, with the help of conversational recordings, to show in what way this instrumentarium of the production of gossip can determine the sequence and realization of gossip-conversations. We can start with two observations. First, these instruments of production can unfold their effect in regard to *conversational subjects of very different sizes,* affect the smallest parts of an utterance as well as model entire conversational passages. Second, it is entirely possible that the *individual instruments of the production of gossip can conflict* with one another. For example, in his effort to emphasize the worthiness of his information for communication, a gossip producer can choose forms of presentation that cast doubt on its credibility. The following section will address this very contradiction.

THE RECONSTRUCTIVE PRESENTATION OF GOSSIP-INFORMATION

After the interactors have mutually assured themselves of their willingness to gossip, established familiarity with the prospective subject of gossip, agreed about the newsworthiness of the expected information, and worked out the roles of gossip producer and recipient—after all these, in most cases, extremely rapid and economically performed preliminary activities, the time has come for the gossip producer to act. In this initial phase, the organization of the speaking order was also implicitly modified in conversations so that the gossip producer is in a position to disseminate his information about the private affairs of a third party without thereby having to anticipate or fear that his interlocutor will thwart his efforts with his own contributions at the first occasion.[43] Since the presequence has indicated that he can assume the recipient's willingness "to participate" in the reprehensible practice of gossiping, there now seems the possibility of criticizing the subject of gossip, unencumbered by moral objections or restrictions of a temporal or interactive nature. How, then, does the gossip producer act within this mutually secured free range? Which structural principles determine this central part of gossip-communication, which reconstructively presents the gossip-information?

Using conversational recordings we can show that gossip producers in their linguistic behavior frequently brush aside recognized rules of civility and respected conventions of custom, and in this way seem to move about in a kind of free range. Gossip producers often use a coarse language. They are not afraid to use obscene expressions in their descriptions instead of vague, euphemistic paraphrases, as is expected and preferred in everyday conversation.

[11]
R: The rumor went round that she—
G: ⌊this is getting exciting=
G: =hehehe
→ R: that she's always <u>got some guy in the sack</u>.

And even the labels that the subject of gossip is given

[3]
H: Yeah, sure, that Frieda
    is living again in (   )
R: ⌈exactly!
H: Yeah
→   H: That clod!

are often anything but considerate and cautious. Yet, we undeniably come to a distorted estimation of the gossip process if we analytically isolate such conspicuously *vulgar language of gossip* as a stylistic feature and neglect to pay attention to the specific handling of this vulgar language by the gossipers. However blatant the gossip producers' malediction[44] may be—especially when this is presented in written form—it always shows on closer inspection that it is an intentionally used and carefully controlled element of the presentation of the complexly organized reconstruction of events in gossip. That is to say, even if the interactors in gossiping—in comparison to other conversational forms—take greater liberties regarding their means of expression, the gossipers, however, do not find themselves in a chaotic situation. As vulgar as it may be, their language is not uncontrolled.

The Authentication of Information and the Endangering of Reputation in the Production of Gossip

Gossip is concerned with the factual—no matter how far the gossipers ultimately stray from the facts. Anyone who tells a gossip-story is faced with the task of proving that his—as a rule rather negative—statements about the subject of gossip are not an outright invention. Gossip producers who have a firsthand knowledge about the event that they reconstruct seem to have a systematic advantage in this situation. They can refer to their own observations to prove the accuracy of their statements. If we start with the assumption that gossip producers have an obligation to prove their statements, this explains a phenomenon that regularly appears within gossip-stories and that may appear unusual at first glance. That is, in the reconstruction of an event gossip producers often mention different situational details, which on closer inspection do not reveal a connection with the continuation of the story or seem necessary for the recipient's understanding:

[12]   [*High-Life*: GR: 30]
H: So we were sitting around at night, and suddenly—thump
P: <faint laughter>

H: So I said <grinning> "I'll bet
    she toppled over."
    (   )
R: Yeah
→ H: That was at 8:15. A⎡crime show was on=
                        =⎣
→ R: "San Francisco"
G: <faint laughter>
H: Suddenly, on the bal(cony). . . .

[13]   [*High-Life*: GR: 31]
H: And then she started screaming upstairs.
    Then she, uh . . . uh, gulped down some pills
    and made it only worse.
P: Hm
→ H: And Sunday morning when I'm sitting on the toilet.
    Suddenly, I hear her again upstairs yelling
    "Ha- help, help". . . .

[14]   [*High-Life*: GR: 32]
R: You know what? She—
    she used to live on the *same* block as I, right,
    and she gave that kid
    sleeping pills.
→   The kid would sleep from 7 A.M. till (—) four in the
    afternoon.
    While she was away in town. Every day. Until the kid got
    some kind of a heart condition.
    Yeah, heart failure

In these segments the gossip producers weave painfully precise statements about the time of an event, where they were at the time and what they were doing, into the reconstructive presentation. The *mention of such seemingly marginal details* can be regularly observed in gossip-communication. Their main effect is to situate the event to be reconstructed clearly within the speaker's everyday perceptual context. And they function in this sense to indicate that the gossip producer's information is firsthand information.

If we take a closer look at segments [12] and [13] they also show that details help the gossip producer in this case to emphasize the fact that she was minding her own business and acquired knowledge of the event from the outside only as a passive recipient. Thus the significance of her implicit reference to the fact that she was not an eyewitness, but only heard of the event to be reconstructed. This reference acquires a special significance if we compare it with another segment from the same conversation. In this segment—which forms the continuation of segment [4]—the veracity of Mrs. R's statement concerning "the Theissens'" lack of sobriety comes into doubt from the other participants:

```
     [15/4]              [High-Life: GR: 23/Simplified]
     R:   . . . so they went next door to their neighbors
          to wash their hands.
          That's how foul their stuff smelled.
     H:   (                        )
     G:                  [(         ) at the Theissens? <in disbelief>
     R:   At the Theissens! <emphasizing>
     G:   I can hardly imag ine
 →   R:                   [I saw it
 →        as they were moving stuff out.
     G:   Yes, more coffee!
     R:   And all the stuff they left behind.
          Ba:::h, the people who moved in—
 →        the woman!
          She had to move in really fast.
          She had to (            ) remove bags and bags of rags and
          junk.
          Bags and bags!
 →        It's true. I saw it (             )
     H:                      [She always acts
          this way—
 →   R:   I was standing right there
     H:                       [as nice as you please. She always
          had everything (           )
     R:                  [The cellar was fu:ll of
          dirty laundry ba:::h
     G:                [But I know something about— about the
          Theissens from the time when they lived in the—
          small housing development. The place was always
          extremely well kept.
```

Confronted with the disbelief and disagreements of her partners, Mrs. R repeatedly refers to the fact that her statements are supported by her own observations and that she can produce a witness. But this does not eliminate the doubts of the others who themselves refer to firsthand knowledge about the "Theissens'" circumstances ("But I know something about the Theissens . . ."). In this situation Mrs. R changes her strategy and tries to argue that the others' opinion is based on a superficial impression and that her information is based on a deeper insight. But this only produces an unpleasant surprise for her:

[16/15]

G: . . . It was always rather well kept

R: Yeah, when you walked in and looked around I would

G: ⌊(   )

R: say it was always well kept.

G: ⌊Hm

R: But you have to look in the corners too.

P: <laughing>

?: (   )

H: ⌈You can't really go there

and look in the corners.

P: ⌊Hehehehehehe

G: (   )

→ R: I'd do that even if I didn't want to.

G: Hm

→ R: Whenever I go into anyone's place automatically

G: ⌊ <softly laughing>

→ R: my eyes look everywhere.

G: Pau⌈l! [The conversation occurs in Paul's apartment]

H: ⌊ Have you checked out the corners in Paul's pla⌐ce=

?:   ⌊(   )⌋

H: Hahahaha⌐haha

G: ⌊Hehe

P: So, when the (—) welfare wor⌐ker comes tomorrow

G: ⌊Hehe

P: ⌐I'll know the reason why.

R: ⌊Hahahahahaha⌐ha

G: ⌊Hahahaha

P: Hehehehe

To support the credibility of her presentation Mrs. R emphasizes that we should not be deceived by outward appearances but should try to look beneath the surface. But she notices right away that this rule, insofar as it implies a deliberate investigation and disclosure of a concealed reality, is problematic precisely where it is concerned with information about the private affairs of others. With the admission that she would not deliberately, only unintentionally, "automatically" scrutinize and expose her neighbors, she tries, to be sure, to save her position. But she really only gets herself in deeper. Her partners now—even if only jokingly—toy with the idea that she spies on the private spheres of other people and in her "concern" denounces those who do not meet her standards of sobriety.

This episode is instructive in different respects. On one hand, it clearly shows *that gossip-information has to be passively or accidentally acquired*—which also holds for other societies. In his ethnography about the Tahitians on the Society Islands Robert Levy writes that, "Although gossip is an important part of 'shame control,' the words designating gossip have a pejorative tone, and gossiping is said to be a bad thing to do. Ideally, the behavior which would produce shame on becoming visible has to spontaneously force its way into visibility; people are not supposed to search out shameful acts. Such searching out is in itself a *ha'amā* thing."[45] Therefore, gossip producers are as a rule careful to characterize their information as passively acquired.

Through mentioning situational details in segments [12] and [13] the gossip producer makes clear that the events she will depict were heard by her and that it was impossible for her to avoid overhearing them. Nevertheless, in segment [16] the gossip producer gets herself into a precarious situation as a result of emphasizing the need to perform an active visual scanning of the neighborhood for "blemishes." This shows *that the passively receptive ear is better suited to authorize gossip-information than the actively perceptive eye.* Georg Simmel had called the ear the "egoistic organ simpliciter," which in contrast to the eye only receives and does not give. And regarding this difference he went on to remark that, "It suffers for this egoism, in that it cannot turn away or close like the eye but, since its nature is merely to receive, is also condemned to receive everything that comes within its range."[46] As an instrument of permanent recording, the ear enables the hearer to prove that unintentionally, indeed involuntarily, he has acquired knowledge of things that did not concern him.[47] Of course, the ear can be used just as actively as the eye as a spying instrument—but in a significant way it thereby also loses its innocence:

[17]   [*High-Life*: GR: 42]

H: . . . So at night (   ), when he's in her apartment, Mrs. Jungblut, teapot in hand, stands in front of the door and listens.

→   Of course! "The eavesdropper hears his own shame!"*
         She gets a lot of information this way . . .

* Mrs. Hein is using a German proverb—translator.

Even the appeal to the fact that an event to be reported was only acoustically perceived does not automatically protect the gossip producer from the suspicion of having acquired his information through spying.

The above difficulties that confront gossip producers in the authentication of their information can now be focused as a *structural problematic of gossip production*. Since factual events are transacted in gossip, gossip producers have the duty to provide proofs of the credibility of their information and the truthfulness of their presentations. If—either through seeing or hearing—they have firsthand information about the event to be reconstructed, they are faced with an essential dilemma: the more detail they present in their story and the more they are forced to justify the accuracy of their presentations, the more they are open to the suspicion that they did not acquire the information passively or accidentally but have secured it through the active invasion of the privacy of the subject of the gossip.

In this situation, where *detail is purchased at the price of reputation*, a possible way out for the gossip producer is to repeat the stories that were told to him rather than to provide firsthand information. A series of ethnographies refer to the fact that children and individual occupational groups in particular play an important role in a social community as intermediaries of information.[48] But for the gossip producer such second-hand information is always burdened with specific drawbacks. Above all, the gossip producer in this case cannot demonstrate an exclusive relation with the subject of gossip through the repetition of his information. His story no longer possesses the excitement of an "original" but the value of a worn-out coin into whose circulation it is placed.

For the gossip producer, second-hand gossip-stories are only shallow copies of original presentations. Therefore, he will prefer personally witnessed events. This statement is supported by the observation that it is only in lengthier conversations that second-hand stories appear, when information about personally witnessed events is exhausted. The gossip producer, then, can counter the suspicion of having obtained his information through spying in a different way, namely, by keeping a relatively low level of detail in his presentation and only raising the level at specific points. And so this produces that peculiar mixture of precise information and sweeping paraphrase, of detailed proposals and vague indications, that is so characteristic of gossip-communication.

The Quotation as an Element of the Reconstruction
of Events That Is Specific to Gossip

A problem in the production of gossip similar to the one just indicated is to discover if one is himself directing his attention to the process of the reconstruction of events. In what follows one of the numerous presentational techniques by means of which the gossip producer transforms his information into language will be selected and analyzed more closely. This restriction is justified by that fact that it fulfills several functions for the communication of gossip and to this extent is a "pivotal phenomenon"[49] of the reconstruction of events that is specific to gossip. The phenomenon on which the following observations and considerations focus is found somewhat thrown together in the following segment:

[18/6]   [*Sicilian*: AK: EM 14B]

J: And Aunt Bertha really liked it;

M: Oh, ⌐and how!

A: ⌊*Her*! Oh my God=er=God. Sunday morning I thought
→   "you can't call her yet because
       she probably didn't get home till
       late last⌐night." But PROMPTLY ten minutes

J: ⌊hm

A: later the telephone rings. She got home
       at *1:30* A.M. and at 8:30
       ⌐she's all right again

M: ⌊all=right=⌐again

L: ⌊all right again.

→ A: So=I say, "why don't you *sleep* some more"
       but she says "Oh, I've slept *enough* and
       it was⌐plenty."

J: ⌊ehhhhhhhh (_____) I have to go.

A: Ha—she was. . . . she

→ M: Only at night, she says, "when I wake up
       at night and °I know I °°sometimes have to
       go [to the bathroom]°° I don't know where I am,°

→ A: said⌐to her—"hey, take the key with you."=

M: ⌊=so now she's LOCKED OUT;

A: take it—or let someone give you a key-=

M: =so now she's⌐locked out for good;⌐

A: ⌊   So yeah, what⌋ is she thinking about

L: =ha: yeah:!

→ M: "at *their* place there were *at least* as many
       doors as you have at your place"

L: Hihihihihihihihihi

→ M: "I went out, but I still don't
       know hhh which door led to the john,
       so that I ended up in Salvatore's
       room°hhhn in the middle of the night".

A: *Hhhhje⌐hhh*
L: ⌊*hhhn*

In this segment A and M dispute large parts of their presentation in the form of a literal repetition of their own or others' utterances (and thoughts). This *use of quotes in the reconstruction of events* is a highly characteristic phenomenon of gossip. The following remarks will explore this in more detail.

Segment [18] already describes two characteristic structural features of this presentational technique. A speaker can accentuate the words he speaks because he places a *verbum dicendi* (indicative word) in the first or second person before them, among them, or at their end. Such *verba dicendi* make clear that a bit of—someone else's or one's own—discourse is being repeated, which occurred in another situation and at another time. However, a *verbum dicendi* can also introduce the repetitive format of indirect discourse—the lines quoted in [18] could have run instead, "I told you to go to sleep but you said you were all slept out." Therefore, for the most part a *verbum dicendi* is not the only accentuative element of "quotes." It is almost always supplemented by having the speaker clearly modify the discourse he quotes: through intonation and paralinguistic effects (for example, through changes in volume and cadence); by imitating it in situ and thereby lifting it out of the flow of the reconstructive presentation. This second structural feature of the production format of quoted discourse, *intonative-paralinguistic accentuation*, is often also found without an additional *verbum dicendi*—as in the following segment:

[19]   [*High-Life*: GR: 33]
H: In the beginning she overdid the beating of the kid.
→   When someone was around, though, then Ahhh, yes Ahhh
→   she'd act so loving <with affection> but oh my, when no one
        was around to see, well, then, (lots of luck!)

The few ethnographic studies that also contain detailed observations of gossip's form of production all refer to the fact that the means of reconstructive presentation by quotation are a significant feature of gossip-conversations. In her investigation of the life of Spanish villagers, Susan Harding remarks that, "Quotation marks in the form of 'dije' and 'dijo' ('I said' and 'he/she said') are surface indicators of the appearance of gossip."[50] And in his work on the gossip genre "talanoa," which he encountered on one of the Fiji islands, Donald Breinneis writes that, "A particularly striking feature of 'talanoa'-discourse is the unusual frequency with which the word 'bole' (literally: the present form of the verb 'to speak' in the third person singular) is used."[51] Why, we might now ask, is the quotation form such an attractive presentational technique for the gossip producer? What does it achieve that makes quotations superior to the other narrative forms of reconstruction in gossip?

To determine the functions fulfilled by quoting in gossip-communication three different aspects of these means of presentation, which, of course, are closely connected with one another, have to be differentiated. Valentin Vološinov had already drawn attention to the first aspect in his 1929 work *Marxism and the Philosophy of Language*.[52] In order to apply the "sociological method in linguistics" to a concrete phenomenon, Vološinov contends he has, "To take the phenomenon of reported speech (*Wiedergabe fremder Rede*) and postulate it as a problem from a sociological orientation." To be sure, Vološinov restricts himself exclusively to literary texts in his analysis. But he thereby obtains results that are also relevant to the analysis of texts of everyday interaction. In particular his remarks on the distinction between direct and indirect discourse are helpful in the investigation of gossip. The decisive point to which Vološinov refers in this case is "that all emotive-affective features of speech, in so far as they are expressed not in the content but in the *form* of a message, do not pass into indirect discourse"[53] (emphasis added). In the case of indirect construction, the emotive-affective elements of an utterance's expression that are realized through mimetic gestures or paralinguistic intonations have to be concretely designated and repeated by means of semantically equivalent adjectives or commentaries. But this is only possible at the cost of a certain depersonalization and trivialization of the speech to be repeated. This effect can be seen if we imagine the transposition of the literal quotations appearing in the following segment into indirect speech:

> [20/11]   [*High-Life*: GR: 29]
> H: I have my bathroom— and Dieter's below.
> →   And she's at it with Dieter, "You want me to
> →   spray you?" And then she sprays him with the
>   showerhead. And the water leaks into my place.
>   I run upstairs and scream at her to stop.
>   "Dieter would have called me a chicken."
>   \<She says affectedly\>
> G: \<laughing softly\>
> → H: And I say, "Man,⌐if Dieter says 'jump
> → G: ⌊\<continues laughing\>
> → H: out the window' you'll jump." \<derisively\>
>   well, ok!
>   An hour later (—) all the water leaks onto
>   the balcony.

R: Yeah

H: And I have a rug lying underneath.

?:   (hehehe)

H: And so::: I got angry.

      Angry, you hear.

→   And I screamed upstairs.

→   I yelled, "Damn it all, don't you have anything

→   better to do than to screw around!" \<angrily\>

G: \<laughing\>

This segment that, in addition to simple quotations, also contains the more complex form of quotations and indirect repeated speech within quotations, graphically reveals an essential function of quotations in gossip, namely, gossip producers can reconstructively reanimate the interactive dynamics and the affective "tone" of a past event by means of the direct repetition of speech. Instead of being narratively recapitulated, the past event is dramatically staged—not to say, restaged. Quotations thereby function as a decisive *stylistic means of scenic dramatization* because they permit the speaker to represent not only the words but also the emotive-affective elements of the expression of a past utterance without a discrediting paraphrase. (In transcripts this dramatic quality of quotations can be comprehended only with the help of a semantically equivalent paraphrase—see \<angrily\> or \<she says affectedly). Quotations are settings for expressive intonation that give gossip its characteristic emotional coloring—and not least of all an essential part of its entertainment value.

The second significant aspect of quotations—if we want to determine their functions in gossip-communication—concerns the status of what is repeated in a quotation. If a speaker characterizes an utterance as a quotation, he thereby maintains at the same time that this is a previous utterance that was only reactivated by him and not freely generated ad hoc. Thus the speaker who quotes does not appear as the inventor but as a transmitter of this utterance. But the quotation thereby acquires a character independent of its actual presentation. It is presented by the speaker as if it existed before. But this does not automatically mean that every quotation claims that what is quoted is exactly in the same form in which it was originally uttered. Quotations also appear in fairy tales, fables, and jokes. And in these cases fictive characters, animals, even inanimate objects are credited with uttering quotations (a somewhat remarkable formulation when we consider inanimate objects). But as soon as quotations are no longer used within the framework of fiction but, as in the case of gossip, refer to actors in the intersubjectively constituted everyday world, they claim to reproduce a bit of speech actually produced in this form. Only if (as in the case of carnival or a playful birthday speech) interaction occurs within the situational context of "enjoyment" or "play" is it possible in the everyday world (up to a certain point!) safely to attribute freely invented "quotations"—which then are no longer quotations—to another person.

This does not mean that in the communication of gossip quotations imply that the communicated utterances were originally uttered in the exact same syntactic, lexical, and prosodic form in which they are now quoted. (Even the conversational transcripts that fill the present text should be understood in this sense as "quotations." Even in their case such a claim to exactness can only be raised with certain reservations.) [This point applies a fortiori, of course, to the present English translation—trans.] The quotations of gossip producers cannot possess the "fidelity" of tape recordings. Therefore, the only decisive point is that the utterances reproduced in linguistic discourse by means of quotations are presented as authentic. That is to say, *quotations function as marks of authenticity in gossip-communication.* They demonstrate a reconstruction's authenticity and signal that the information the gossip producer disseminates to his listeners authenticates firsthand information, if it is not that itself.

A third relevant aspect of quotations for the determination of their function in gossip becomes clear when we follow the above idea in the opposite direction, namely, when we consider that the speaker who uses quotations appears only as the transmitter of such an utterance and not its creator. Following Vološinov, Erving Goffman made this aspect a theme of his later works and analyzed it with the help of conceptual differentiations.[54] Anyone who characterizes an utterance as a quotation is certainly "speaking." But by accentuating the quotation he makes clear that he himself is not speaking but someone else—through him. Thus the concept of the speaker contains (conceals) different capacities that, for the most part, coincide in speaking, but that in specific situations—as in quoting—are separate. For Goffman the speaker, in a certain way, is made up of three persons: (1) the animator who, like a "sounding box," enlivens the words through his acoustic activity; (2) the author who composed the expressed feelings and opinions in words; and (3) the "principal," whose position and opinion are articulated through the expressed words.[55] During the activity of quoting the animator of the words is distinguished from their author. Splitting the speaker in this way entails that the person who speaks can delegate the responsibility for the utterance he repeats to the person who cites his words and to whom these words "belong." But this only amounts to saying that by quoting the speaker can use expressions that he would not normally use in his own discourse for reasons of etiquette.

The fact that in quoting the speaker has greater freedom to use forbidden expressions than in his own discourse[56] makes quotations a particularly suitable means of presenting obscene jokes[57]—but also for gossip, which often enough is concerned with sexual themes, too. The following segments contain examples of how *quotations can be used as a means of relaxing the rules of censure and restrictions on expression in gossip*:

[21]   [*High-Life*: GR: 28]

[This segment begins at the end of a story about a drunken woman]

```
R:  It gets just as bad with us (      ).
H:                              [(When that)
G:  Hm
R:  You should have seen it. The Schüren woman was so tanked
H:                                               [O::h, my!
    <with conviction>
R:  Paul.
    yeah, she's standing there on the balcony
H:  Paul, you would have taken off. You would've
R:       [I look (up) at the balcony
H:  you really would've if you heard—
R:     [a::h, "I'm really—drunk"
R:  And I (                        )
H:          [But I was the cause of it.
R:  I'd just washed my hair, and had rollers
    in it. She was playing around with the water and
    it all came down on me.
→   And I heard her say, "Do you have a big
    dick?"
→   Ha chch
H:     [<laughing along>
R:  If he has one— and that coming from a woman!
```

[22/12]   [*High-Life*: GR: 30]

```
H:  That was at 8:15. A crime show was on=
R:                    =[ "San Francisco"
G:  <faint laughter>
H:  Suddenly, on the bal(cony) "Cheers! Wanna
    drink with me? Cheers!" <feigning drunkenness>
    And then the guys in the upstairs apartment
    answer that she's got every Tom, Dick, and Harry
    in her place. <vehemently>
P:  Hmhm
```

H: And then all hell broke loose.
→   "Hey, you greedy pig, you" <Singing>
          <everyone laughing>
H: <u>And in all</u>, all these different ways she was screaming.

As these segments show, quotations form a kind of free range for
gossip producers where they can use modes of expressions to transmit
their information that, if they themselves were the "authors" of this
discourse, would cast a poor light on them. Thus gossip's above-
mentioned vulgar language cannot immediately be generalized as a stylistic feature of this communicative genre, as is possible in the case of
other communicative genres, for example, the exchange of insults between black youths in America.[58] In gossip-communication, vulgar language is a presentational technique that is completely mediated and
controlled by the gossip producer and used only periodically. This can
be seen not least of all in the fact that gossip producers prefer to use
neutral terms or euphemisms when they refer to a linguistically taboo
subject in their own discourse:

[23]   [*High-Life*: GR: 33]
R: So Breckmann says, "Let's get her drunk.
      Then she'll strip for us."
P: <faintly laughing>
R: She was wearing those neat Yokohama-pants, <u>tsk, tsk</u>
P: <faintly laughing>
R: So there she sat.
      and we, uh, we were fooling around=
      =pretty soon she was lying on the billiard <u>ta—able</u>.
      The more she drank, the wilder she got.
      A guy goes over to her and opens his pants and
      puts his thing in her hand.
      But I (   ) <boasting>
P: <faintly laughing>
R: And without blinking an eye—she—when
      she's drunk she's so, well, so (loose)

It is striking that in describing a sexually provocative action Mrs. R in
this case shows remarkable restraint in contrast to her rather free-and-
easy mode of expression when quoting—see [21] "Do you have a big
dick?" As we can gather from her not exactly prudish language she also
possesses other, less moderate expressions for what she here quite
vaguely calls "his thing"—expressions that she would not hesitate to
use in a quotation. The fact that gossip producers actually are careful in

their own discourse—despite the freedom that can be taken in repeating the discourse of others—linguistically to maintain the "proper tone" can be seen most clearly where an "ordinary" mode of expression is corrected by a speaker himself as a linguistic lapse and replaced with a decent, innocent formulation:

```
[24]                    [High-Life: GR: 46]
R:   . . . Afterward she broke (            ) her engagement
     and now she goes out with Jungblut.
     and— and— and what I don't know
     and Marki now dates that—, that—
     that— Brecht woman, the one he's
     supposed to be fooling (around with).
H:                        Yeah, the one— the one
     Jochen went with before
→ R:                      The one Jochen had, uh,
→    went with before.
H:   hihihihihihihihihihi
G:   °hahahahahahaha°
R:   Oh boy, what a (situation        )
```

The subtlety of Mrs. R's utterance:

R: The one Jochen had, uh, went with

is twofold: on one hand, it continues the discourse initiated by Mrs. H

H: Yeah, the one Jochen went with before

according to the format of a collaborative utterance sequence,[59] and thereby implies that, with her formulation, she is not expressing her own but Mrs. H's linguistic intentions. On the other, Mrs. R brings the statement

H/R: The one [Jochen] had . . . went with before

to the point where it undoubtedly can be recognized by her partner in order, then, to interrupt and complete it with the euphemistic, harmless formulation, "went with." The effect of this self-correction is unmistakable, namely, Mrs. R uses it to demonstrate that through her own effort she resists the exciting and available possibility of presenting a delicate matter in an indulgent, common way. By playing with impropriety she shows that she knows what is proper. Provocatively and apparently without scruple, she approaches the line of "indecency" (R. von Jhering),[60] only to turn back at the last moment. This is another example of the semantic structure of teasing. On the verge of breaking a rule, the gossip producer interrupts his reprehensible activity and turns back, as it seems, to the path of virtue. This clever maneuver serves, on one hand, to protect the gossip producer himself. On the other, the recipients are snared in the unscrupulous game: When—as happens in segment [24]—they honor Mrs. R's delicate formulation with laughter, they show that they understand this utterance despite its incompleteness. But at the same time this also means that they have amplified and completed it through their own "dirty" imaginations. The recipients thereby brand themselves equally as responsible for this morally problematic interactive sequence as the speaker who initiated the sequence with her subtle utterance.

In the above case the gossip producer corrects a vulgar mode of expression in her own discourse and replaces it with a harmless formulation. The following segment, however, contains an example of how, in quoting, a gossip producer seeks to increase, rather than reduce, the degree of vulgarity in his mode of expression, that is, in the repetition of the discourse of others—by means of self-correction:

[25]   [*High-Life*: GR: 32]
H: You should listen sometime when
       she's at it with the little kid.
       "You old sow; You old, haaaaa!"
       The little one, who's sitting on the lawn
       screams up
       "Oh, shut your— kiss my arse! You old
       goat!"
       Hah, (—) if one of my kids ever
       said that to me. I'd kill 'im. <menacingly>
       I'd knock his block off.
       <faintly laughing>
G: mmmmm <faintly laughing>
H: Right, the woman's not normal.

The interpretation of the escalating self-correction in Mrs. H's quotation "Oh, shut your— kiss my arse!" leads to a final remark about the importance of quotations in the communication of gossip. As was shown, quotations function in gossip as a means of relaxing the rules of censure and the restrictions on expression, because the speaker is not the author of the the the utterance he quotes. The fact that Mrs. H's self-correction turns a rude "Shut your <trap!">" into a drastic "kiss my arse" creates the suspicion that gossip producers often use the free range they enjoy in repeating the discourse of others in order to exaggerate. Of course, so long as the original event was not accidentally recorded in any form, the suspicion cannot be factually confirmed or disproved. But notwithstanding factual proof or even the gossip producer's own motivation, there are valid grounds for saying that *for structural reasons quotations provide a field for exaggerations in gossip-communication.*

- Because of the *difference in the amounts of information that they respectively possess*, the presentations of gossip producers cannot be checked by the recipients for their accuracy and therefore are hard to doubt—which is true especially when the gossip producer indicates through the use of quotations that he possesses firsthand information about the event in question. But in such situations, where a speaker fancies himself the only participant in the interaction who has privileged information about a specific matter, minor deviations from the truth seem a seductive, because harmless, possibility.[61]
- To prove that their information is worthy of communication gossip producers generally tend to accentuate the extraordinary and to make a scandal of transgressions of rules. Quotations are particularly suitable for this purpose because on one hand, the prosodic reactualization of emotive-affective forms of expression enables a dramatization of the original event. And on the other, the relaxation of the rules of censure clears the way for a *scandalizing reconstruction.*
- With the help of reproduced transcript segments we can easily show that gossipers *enjoy* playing with taboo modes of expression and turns of phrase that offend good taste. Here, too, it is obviously true that the forbidden fruits are the sweetest ones. Quotations allow the gossip producers to eat of these fruits. They offer a welcome and socially sanctioned occasion for this juicy, because not entirely safe, diversion.
- If we choose to interpret the exaggeration at the same level as the event it exaggerates, then it becomes impossible, as Charlotte von Reichenau (1936) has shown[62] to designate "exaggerations as a sociological phenomenon." The exaggeration would be nothing more than a falsehood, a lie. But if we relate the exaggeration to thought processes, feelings, and ideas of the exaggeration, we can see that it can fulfill an important presentational function. Exaggeration can serve to express the heightened experience of an extreme situation for which there is no adequate possibility of communication—as when a child who has been frightened by a dog depicts it as much

larger than it "really" is. Accordingly, gossip-communication has to deal with the possibility that in the presentations of gossip producers the *emotion of indignation* (see for this the following section) finds its expression in exaggerations; for these quotations, with their extensive linguistic, prosodic, and mimetic expressive possibilities, constitute an ideal medium.

If we follow these remarks we see that they lead to a paradoxical situation, namely, that *while quotations in gossip-communication, on one hand, constitute a structural basis for exaggerations, on the other they still function as a means of authentication.* This is also the reason why quotations appear as the prevailing form of the paradoxical structure that the foregoing sections described as a principle of gossip-communication. *Gossip is always a matter of the simultaneous transgression and respect for boundaries*—of boundaries between the private and the public, between what is decent and what is indecent, between the moral and the immoral and—as has just been demonstrated—between truth and lies as well. Gossipers are border-runners who in their exciting excursions into the zones of the improper do not simply ignore the boundaries of the domains of virtue and vice, but recognize and disdain them at the same time—*must* recognize them in fact, in order to be able to disdain them. This is precisely what gives gossip its equivocal character. The quotation, which as a means of presenting a "true" event at the same time provides the possibility of fictionalization—and thereby also of the creation of literature,[63]—is additionally a mode of reconstruction that reflects and enhances this equivocal quality of gossip in a special way. As a rule, an event is not copied in quotations in the form of a document, but rewritten. The subjects of gossip are not exactly imitated but imitatively stylized:

[26]   [*High-Life*: GR: 42]

[Conversation about a couple and the ups and downs of their relationship]

H: And then he comes begging again.
     And sits himself just like this. <ironically>
     "Oh, Kathy, let's try it one more time.
     I'll try to be much better." <with feeling>
     Then his crocodile tears begin to flow.
     And then Kathy's so happy again.
     Everything (   ) is so peaceful again.
     And it works for a while (   ),
     but four weeks later he has to leave again.

R: Yeah, that's so—

H: That's—but it really doesn't matter.

The gossip producer's exaggeration, which is clearly visible in the above segment, is not the sort that tries to disguise itself. This kind of exaggeration wants to emphasize specific features of situations and persons that are viewed as characteristic. But this means that *the reconstruction of events in gossip—above all in quotations—is determined by the principle of caricature.* Gossip always aims at projecting a caricature of an absent third party through redrawing his distinctive features—most of the time in not a very flattering way. (More on this below.)

As mentioned at the beginning of this section, quotations, of course, are not the only presentational technique that is used in gossip to reconstruct events. The segments included in the text have shown that gossip-information can also be repeated in the relatively ordinary form of brief reports

[24]

R: and Marki now dates that— that—
     that— Brecht woman, the one he's
     supposed to be fooling around with.

in which case the issue to be decided is not whether these *gossip reports,* if they had been registered thematically by the recipient, would have been developed into longer stories. Such information can also be narratively transmitted, that is, in the form of stories in which the gossip producer does not use quotations as a means of presentation. The story teller's possibilities of restaging dramatic events, offenses, surprises, and the like in the actual situation are restricted in this case, which can mean that the story does not have the effect the speaker desires. This is the underlying reason for the observation that in some cases a story that was initially presented in a purely narrative form and that did not produce any (desired) reaction in the recipients is presented a second time by the gossip producer, but now in a more dramatic version, using quotations:

[27]   [*High-Life*: GR: 27]

R: I was there- I saw how they
     lived, uh, (   ).
     Hansi was sleeping at the bottom
     of a kitchen closet.

```
        It's true.
        He—┌took the doors off and there┐
H:      └(                            )┘
R:      ┌there were a blanket and pil┐low inside
H:      └(                          )┘
G:      He stayed there briefly— while— she
        was already in jail:┌he was there with the kids
R:                         └No::
R:      Earlier=
G:      =(Oh) in the smaller housing project?
R:      Yeah, in the smaller one.
        I wasn't living there yet, (        )
        I came in (—) with the Conrads,
        she was friends with them.
        I thought, "Where could he be?"
        And there he was, lying at the bottom of the kitchen closet.
        Was he sleeping?
        I said, "What are you doing there?"
        (              ) on the couch, the kids were on
        mattresses.
?:      Hm
R:      It's not worth┌it, such a mess (confusion)
?:              └That too-
R:      and, uh, internationally. They're loonies.
H:      Loonies?
R:      They don't even wash themselves (          ).
```

In this case Mrs. R depicts the strange sleeping habits of a family she has initially observed in a descriptive-narrative way. In his reaction to her presentation, however, G does not show a concern with the eccentricities of her depiction but is interested only in a clarification of the time of her observation. She thereupon reconstructs the occurrence anew (17–24). But this time she emphasizes what is surprising about her observation by inserting self-quotations ("I thought . . . ," "I said. . . ."). Even if there is no (appropriate) reaction this time, the increased repetition emphasizes the important dramaturgical function that belongs to quotations as an element of the reconstruction of events in gossip.

MORAL INDIGNATION AND SOCIAL TYPING IN GOSSIP

In principle, gossip is not restricted to the reconstruction of events and facts that concern the private affairs of a mutual acquaintance. Gossip not only talks *about* the extraordinary or offensive behavior of another person but also *about* the person himself, about his character and what is typical of him. As interesting, exciting, and scurrilous as the behavior of the subject of gossip may be, when it relates to his entire person, it acquires the status of a specimen or even of something puzzling, about whose background it is hard to speculate. Action and person are hard to separate in gossip. What is worth reporting about the subject of gossip is interpretively introduced and situated by the gossipers in terms of what they already know about their mutual acquaintance as well as their prejudices about him. A conversation becomes gossip only because, over and above merely reconstructing an event, the participants combine a person's particular behavior with a social type.

In addition to social typing, a second interpretive component can be identified as of constitutive importance for the "logic" of the communication of gossip. It, too, begins with the behavior of the subject of gossip that is depicted in the reconstruction of events. But it does not relate this behavior to a personal type. Instead, it relates it to values and rules that the gossipers honor as determinative parts of a moral order. All gossip contains commentaries, positions, and evaluations of the gossipers toward what is known about the behavior of the subject of gossip in the reconstructive presentation. Thereby the moral rules and values that are assumed as valid are hardly ever explicitly formulated. Instead, they serve as a foil to judge the behavior presented.

To be sure, *the reconstruction of events, social typing, and moralizing* can be isolated as three structural components of gossip-communication. But we quickly see that among the components there is an essential interdependence that can only be separated analytically. This interdependence resides in the fact that the reconstruction of events in gossip does not occur as "ethically neutral." That is to say, it does not report only the "facts" but always contains an "evaluation" of these facts too. From the very beginning the story is replete with more or less clear references by the gossip producer to the fact that his presentation is based on a moral judgment. The gossip producer can present this moral indication by using, as R does in the following cases

[21]   [*Detail/Simplified*]
R: It's going to get just as bad with us (   ).
     You should have seen that Schüren woman. She
     was drunk, Paul . . .

       R: I was there—I saw how they
→   lived, uh, (   ).
            Hansi was . . .

an evaluative term ("bad," "lived") very early in his remarks that unmistakably expresses his attitude toward the issue that he will reconstruct in what follows. A somewhat different technique of moral indication consists of the gossip producer expressing, as do G and R in the following cases,

[4]   [Detail/Simplified]
G: How long ago did they move
    from Oswald Street?
→   R: Gunther! The moving van came.
    What gloves the workmen had . . .

[7]
R: And the Dischingers actually got themselves
    a dog.
→   G: Really, they're putting everyone on. A poodle . . .

his moral indignation through the form of address ("Gunther!") as a "reflex utterance of sensations"[64] or through negative global judgments ("they're putting everyone on") before he presents the criticized behavior itself. By establishing such moral indicators very early the gossip producer achieves two things. On one hand, the recipient is informed and alerted to the fact that the story he is about to hear concerns the improper behavior, rule transgression, or impropriety of a mutual acquaintance. On the other, the gossip producer also makes clear that he is making a topic of a third party's sins and shady side, not for their own sake, or even out of schadenfreude; rather, that the repetition of his information has an honorable motive: the disapproval of deviant or irrational behavior and, thereby, indirectly, compliance with norms and values. From the very beginning, reconstructions of events in gossip appear as *biased presentations* in which gossip producers take sides against the nonconforming behavior of the subject of gossip.

Even more drastically than at the beginning of their presentations, gossip producers, as a rule, express their disapproval and moral indignation *after* their gossip stories. In this postreconstructive phase the structural components of the moralization, which had already given the reconstruction of the events its specifically "indignant" coloring, can establish themselves as the thematic focus of the conversation. Here the presented behavior of the subject of gossip can be evaluated, his deviant character emphasized, his true motives disclosed, he can be typed, and, in addition, indignation and disgust can be given free rein. If we observe more closely how the gossipers "treat" the subject of gossip in this phase, which in contrast to the reconstruction of the events itself can possess an even more pronounced dialogical character, a *spectrum of forms of disapproval* emerges. Some of these forms will be briefly described in the following—arranged according to the intensity of the disapproval they express.

We rarely find a moderate form of disapproval where the gossip producer disposes of the behavior of the subject of gossip with a vague, global evaluation, but as yet decidedly inappropriate or irrational:

[26]

H: And then Kathy's so happy again.
Everything (   ) is so peaceful again.
And it works for a while (   ),
but four weeks later he has to leave again.
R: Yeah, that's so—
H: That's— but it really doesn't matter.

Mrs. H comments here on her depiction of a married couple, who have a history of separation and reconciliation, with a simple "but it really doesn't matter." Quite obviously she believes that her reconstruction of the marriage relation speaks for itself and that her critical evaluation does not need any further justification. She assumes that her recipients also agree with the rule that a constant interplay of separation and reconciliation is not a good basis for a marriage. In the following segment a depicted behavior is at first disapproved of globally—see the anaphoric "That's"—but then later the critique is supplemented with an explanation:

[28]   [*High-Life*: GR: 51/*Simplified*]

(H. explains how one woman brags, in front of her husband, how other men are interested in her.]

H: Well, to start with. She babbles about
every little detail. And adds—
"Oh, today I met a terrific guy.
He was really good looking, Bernd!
Really great.
He sent me a love poem
on a coaster" <affectedly>
→   That's no way to act! <emphatically>
She makes him very jealous this way.
And then he starts in.
I wish men weren't like that.

In this segment the gossip producer continues her discourse immediately after a reconstructed quotation with a commentary that consists of a vague formula of disapproval ("That's no way to act!") and a subsequent justification. The production format of this commentary, namely, formula of disapproval + justification is frequently encountered in gossip-communication (although it is not specific to gossip).[65] In the justificatory part of the commentary the gossip producer as a rule presents his reason for believing that the behavior of the subject of gossip is reprehensible and why he disapproves of it—in the above case perhaps because the depicted behavior of the wife leads to marital discord. Here, too, the general rule to which the justification appeals remains unexpressed. Yet the argumentation makes a point to disclose, rather than simply—as in segment [26]—to assume it.

Another widespread technique of showing disapproval consists of the gossip producer placing himself in the situation of the subject of gossip and showing how he would have behaved in his place:

[29]   [High-life: GR: 39]

[H. explains why Mrs. J. is responsible for her marital problems; all remarks are harsh and disapproving]

H: What's the matter? It's her own fault:
     What is— What did he do!
     He collected sick pay from Krysmanski,
     took a powder for three days and didn't
     come back until all the money was gone.
     Then he, uh, got a job as a waiter.
     And then he got himself, uh, a girlfriend,
R: Hah aha
H: ⌊then he packed his stuff, took
     the TV and moved in with her.
     Yeah, then Mrs. Jungblut goes there, runs
     after the broad (asking).
     What she— what she wants with her husband!
     since she's still married to him!
→   Man, oh man, I would have thrown the rest
→   of his stuff after him!
                         (1.5 secs.)
     Yeah!
     You shouldn't try to stop a moving train!
     And—, and— and when he finally tired of her,
     a taxi shows up and delivers him and
     his suitcases at the front door.

→   I would have taken his bags
→   and thrown them out the door!
→   I certainly would not have taken them in!
   G: Hm
   H: Then at night, he climbs in through her window.
       Apparently, she put her wallet on the washing
       machine under the window.
       He stole a hundred marks from it.
                     (2 secs.)
→   That's pretty rotten—I would've made mincemeat
→   of a guy like that long ago!
                     (2 secs.)
   (Yeah)

This segment shows quite clearly how a gossip producer, after her reconstruction of individual sections of events and episodes, often abandons the narrative perspective and goes over to evaluating the behavior of the subject of gossip that she presented. The model she follows is always the same: she exaltedly proclaims that she, had she ever been in the situation depicted, would have acted quite differently from the way the subject of gossip did. This model of *contrasting one's own behavioral option with another's actual behavior* can in principle be used as a technique of showing disapproval (in which case intensity of contrast is a direct measure of the intensity of disapproval). For whatever a speaker formulates—even in the subjunctive mood—as his preference (and thereby asserts, for example, as rational, moral, etc.) implicitly turns its opposite into something undesirable (irrational, immoral, etc.).

Formulas of rejection ("That's no way to act!") and preferred behavioral alternatives ("I would have taken his bags and thrown them out the door!") acquire their disapproving character via the principle of negation, namely, the reconstructed behavior of a subject of gossip is characterized as not acceptable. Nevertheless, gossip producers can now express their disapproval more fully because they can name and hold specific character flaws, moral shortcomings, or other deficiencies of the subject of gossip responsible for the behavior they incriminate.

   [30]   [*High-Life*: GR: 50]
   [The subject of this conversation is, once again, the couple J.]

   R: Gunther, she could have—
           (—)
      lived like a queen with him.
   H: [She could manipulate him! Because Jungblut=
   R: [She could do it.

H: =can manage a household.
G: Hm
R: ⌐She could do it.
H: ⌊He can do it all.
    He can set up a—, uh, uh, birthday
    party. Sandwiches, little plates, and
    everything. He's got a real knack for it!
R: (   )
H: *He's* the housewife. (   ) More than her.
    Better than I, in fact!
    If one⌐omits.
G: ⌊Hm
H: I don't bother with such
    nonsense. <flippantly>
    But *she* could pull the wool over his eyes.
R: Yeah,⌐she—
H: ⌊She could have had some life.
→ R: She's too stupid to realize it.

[31/13]   [*High-Life*: GR: 31]
H: And Sunday morning I'm sitting on the toilet.
    Suddenly, I hear her again upstairs
    "Ha, help, help, it's too much, I can't
    anymore, ha, ha" <loud and breathlessly>
    What a big deal she makes out of— <grinning>
    I think, "This can't be happening."=
→ R: =Yeah, she's nuts.
→ H: She's got serious brain⌐damage.
   G/P: ⌊<laughing faintly>
→ H: She's touched.
→   She's got a <u>screw loose</u>.
       And her old <u>man</u> . . .

In segment [30] a preferred behavioral alternative is at first expressed
("She could have lived like a queen with him"), and then an explanation
is given for why the subject of gossip does not grasp the possibility so
subtly presented by the gossipers, namely, "She's too stupid." The explanation of the mystery of why anyone would overlook or refuse such
an advantageous behavioral alternative is not sought by the gossipers in
the social circumstances of the action but included in the person as a
mental disposition. In this way the admonished behavior does not appear as a one-time slip or an accidental mistake. Instead, it is reduced to
an essential *personality flaw in the subject of gossip*. This flaw is often seized

upon, as segment [30] shows, by the gossipers with drastic if not abusive formulations and becomes a continual occasion of scorn, derision, and degrading utterances for them.

As far as the gossipers are concerned, the personality flaw of the subject of gossip constitutes as a rule, behind the censured behavior, a reality of its own, a kind of essence behind the appearance. Thus its existence can still be maintained, even when there is nothing in the behavior of the subject of gossip to warrant calling it a personality flaw at any particular time.

>   [32]   [*High-Life*: GR: 32]
>   G: What's with Mrs. Schüren?
>   She wasn't always like this.
>   H: Yes she was.=
> →   =Only it wasn't so obvious.

>   [33/23]   [*High-Life*: GR: 34]
>   R: When she's been drinking she's—
>   so, so, well so (weird)⌐
>   P: <faintly laughing> |
>   H: ⌊That's when—
> →   it all comes out—
> →   the weirdness <seriously>
>   R: Ha (_____) yeah, it's true—, that's
>   why her husband . . . .

This case shows how the structural components of moralizing, which reveal themselves in different forms of disapproval, are connected with the structural components of *social typing*. For from the practice of attributing to the subject of gossip—independently of his behavior—a personality flaw as a "typical" characteristic,[66] it is only a short step to subsuming the entire person under the flaw, that is, to type him socially. A subject of gossip, then, for example, is no longer merely "nuts," but belongs to the group of "nuts."

>   [34/25]   [*High-Life*: GR: 32]
>   H: Yeah, that woman's not normal anymore.
>   And her old man is crazy too.
>   R: On our block, in every house, there's
> →   a nut.
>   P: <laughing faintly>
>   R: It's true

```
    H:   There's that flat-footed floo  zy the—, the Schüren woman
    R:   Yeah                         ⌈(                              )⌉
    R:   Flat-foot floozy
   (P):  <laughing faintly>
    H:   Further down the street there's
    R:   Bröllo.
    H:   Bröllo doesn't have all his
         marbles either.
    R:   And then there's—, the—
    H:   the Jaspers woman
    R:   the Jaspers woman and then there's—, the—
    H:   Krysmanski?
    R:   Krysmanski
    H:   Yeah  (that's)
    R:         ⌊And all five on one (block).
```

In this segment we can follow how, after the completion of a gossip-story, and in reference to the subject of gossip, the social type of "nuts" is introduced, and how, through this type, still other persons from the neighborhood of the gossipers are identified as "cases" and dispatched to this group. In social typing the individual differences of the typed person are erased—that is, as far as the typed person is concerned, all that is relevant at the moment is what makes him a "case" of a specific social type. This reductive effect is increased within the context of gossip even more when the social types under which the subject of gossip is grouped essentially imply a negative evaluation of his social worth. The typing of the subject of gossip that turns him into a "nut," a "chauvin-ist," a "phony," a "Philistine," an "arse-kisser," a "loony," and the like thereby forms a focused expression of disapproval. The subject of gossip whose "moral identity"[67] is unified through this typing falls as a whole into a degrading social category—he is literally left not one shred of decency.

Taken together, moralizing and typing ensure that the discourse appears harsh, virulent, apodictic, disapproving, and intolerant. Gossip ignores its subject's own view of himself and the way he presents it. It is not deceived by the illusion, the facade with which the subject of gossip surrounds himself. Relentlessly and remorselessly it penetrates its subject's private mistakes and flaws. Gossipers indignantly refer to the seedy side of the lives of others in order to try to present themselves in a better light. But no matter how much they claim that their indignation results from an interest in preserving the moral order, their talk is never righteous, only self-righteous. This self-righteousness has its price: gos-sipers not only have to live with the fact that they are viewed as gossipers but also that they acquire a reputation as slanderers who malign, defame, smear, and cut other people to pieces. These descriptions clearly convey that others view gossip as a threat.

The threat gossip possesses for others lies simply in the fact that it can damage the stature, reputation, good standing, and name of the person who is its victim. If we examine this threat a bit more closely, we can see that two different, complementary mechanisms are interconnected in it. One of these mechanisms operates through *concretion*. In the reconstruction of an event, a "reprehensible" action from the private sphere of another is brought to light, and this concrete "datum" by itself is enough to undermine and destroy another's self-presentation. The concreteness of the story, in a way, "overindividualizes" and "detypifies" the subject of gossip. He is depicted in close-up and without a soft-focus lens, fragmented in his crude existence, reduced to his naked individuality, and at least incipiently denuded of his status and self-presentation.[68] (Perhaps this provides a special motive for the gossip about well-known people and superiors.)

The other mechanism operates through *abstraction*. Instead of isolating the concrete datum of a "mistake" and trivializing it as a unique faux pas, abstraction interprets it as a manifestation of a characteristic property that symbolizes the subject of gossip as a whole. The behavioral mistake is elevated to a type, and in the process the subject of gossip is, as it were, "deindividualized" and "overtyped." Thus, on one hand, the subject of gossip's moral identity is decomposed through the abstractive behavioral datum and, on the other, recomposed in a new form through abstractive typing.[69] Perhaps what is threatening about this process is not so much that the single action of a person is generalized but instead how gossip determines his reputation in the social community as a type and how this influences the interpretation of all his future actions.[70] Against this background we can see why for the gossipers themselves, such information, even when it is new to them, is often not surprising. It only confirms the reputation that the subject of gossip already "enjoys" for them.

In the light of the above segments, however, it must appear puzzling at first why the gossipers express their moral indignation so strongly and harshly and disapprove of the behavior of the subject of gossip. Why this vehemence when the mistake has occurred in someone's private sphere, where the gossipers have no business? Why this intolerance, since it is "only" about the rule of sobriety and other apparently marginal questions of decency, propriety, good taste, manners, and moral conventions? Why this brusk reaction to behavior that often does not even constitute a violation of a norm but is only perceived by the gossipers as irrational and indecent—as, perhaps, the fact that the Dischingers have bought a poodle? Why the indignation about transgressions that do not concern the gossipers directly?

We can answer this by referring to the sociological theorem of "moral indignation" (Svend Ranulf).[71] A sociology of deviant behavior is generally faced with the problem of explaining why those members of a society who do not suffer any direct damage through the violation of a norm react with repudiation and animosity to deviant acts. Sociology usually explains this by saying that the members of the society have internalized these moral norms and therefore perceive deviant actions that do not directly affect them as an attack on their validity and reply with appropriate reactions. Following Ranulf, Robert Merton writes that, "The form which such reprisals take is best described as 'moral indignation,' as a disinterested attack on those who depart from the norms of the group, even when such departures do not interfere with the performance of one's own roles, since one is not directly socially related to the deviant. Were it not for this reservoir of moral indignation, the mechanisms of social control would be severely limited in their operation. They would be confined only to the action of people who are *directly* disadvantaged by nonconformist and deviant behavior."[72] Viewed from this perspective, gossip is nothing more than an indirect form of social control. The moral indignation that so colors the tone of discourse in gossip is interpreted as the gossipers' indignation toward the violation of a norm that does not immediately affect them but that offends internalized norms and disdains moral order. Thereby gossip can be explained essentially by its function of confirming the validity of moral norms and controlling and dissuading (prospective) deviants through the loss of reputation— in any event, the major part of the sociological and ethnological literature about gossip can be reduced to this (for more on this, see Chapter 5, Section 1).

This functionalist argument appears to be initially supported by the above-mentioned finding that gossipers in fact indignantly disapprove of the mistakes of the subject of gossip and in their social typing rake him over the coals. Yet on closer inspection of conversational recordings we discover a series of details that give rise to considerable doubt whether it makes sense and is appropriate simply to subsume "gossip" under the theoretical concept of social control. Thus we would have to ask, why is gossip, when it is directed against dangers to moral order, itself a morally discredited practice? Or, how can the supposedly norm-preserving function of gossip be combined with the fact that the communicative reconstruction of a norm-transgressing action gives the gossipers so much enjoyment? Two other observations show, even more clearly than these skeptical questions, that the functional "explanation" that equates gossip with social control is essentially inadequate.

First, the analysis of gossip-conversations is always accompanied by

the remarkable finding that the gossipers suddenly express sympathy
and understanding for the subject of gossip that is the target of their
criticism and indignation:

[35/33]   [*High-Life*: GR: 34]

R: When she's been drinking she's—
     so, so, well so (weird)
P: [<laughing faintly>
H: That's when—
     it really comes out—
     the weirdness <seriously>
R: Ha (   ) yeah, it's true—, that's
     why her husband . . .
     For every escapade the excuse was, "I have
     to see some students" or "I have a meeting"
     when there was no meeting at all.
H: [Nah, she doesn't get
     much out of life.
     He goes out, uh, uh, except for Saturdays.
     But he goes out every week. To Wolters
     For a drink.
     But she always sits at home
P: [Hm
G: Hm
H: She never goes anywhere.
     Sure, but she (   ) he's—
R: [(   )
H: no better. <disapprovingly>
     In the beginning, when they first moved in, Paul,
     he was so . . .

[36]   [*Quite Sociable*: AK: EM20]

[Sonya has just finished a story about her boss's chauvinism]

S: Yeah, and the=the=the—
                 (1.5secs.)

     chauvinists=
     =(   ) are unbelievably grabby
     and they (—): for example, as soon as you give
     'em an inch, they grab on tight

S: . . . on the other hand, when I arrive in the morning, he's
     made *tea*

(—)
First he makes his *coffee* and then puts
on the tea.

.

.

.

S: I think that's pleasant, I mean nice—

In segment [35] Mrs. H begins by establishing (once again) that Mrs. S is "weird" and almost immediately thereupon expresses her sorrow and understanding for her unhappy marital situation ("Nah, she doesn't get much out of life"). In [36] S classifies her boss as belonging to the social type "chauvinists" in order only a little later to refer to his pleasant habit of preparing tea for her every morning. Both segments make clear that the condemnation of the subject of gossip who is the focus of the indignation and social typing is elsewhere softened, if not essentially revised, by the gossipers. Even the structural component of disapproval does not appear in its pure form but is characterized by the contradictoriness that already was observed in other elements of gossip. John Berger provides an example of this condemning/understanding quality of gossip in the following passage of his literary ethnography on life in a French village:

> Most of what happens during a day is recounted by somebody before the day ends. The stories are factual, based on observation or on a firsthand account. This combination of the sharpest observation, of the daily recounting of the day's events and encounters, and of lifelong mutual familiarities is what constitutes so-called village *gossip*.
>
> Sometimes there is a moral judgment implicit in the story, but this judgment—whether just or unjust—remains a detail: the story *as a whole* is told with some tolerance because it involves those with whom the storyteller and listener are going to go on living.[73]

To be sure, in contrast to Berger's observation, the data analyzed here show that a moral judgment about the subject of gossip is often explicitly expressed. (This refers to the fact that there is a range of variation within gossiping that extends from hateful/denouncing to friendly/well-wishing). Yet no matter in what guise the gossipers clothe their moral judgment, they must recognize that they themselves are acquainted with the subject of gossip. That is to say, each gossiper is faced with the situation that the person who functions today as the subject of gossip may tomorrow be his interaction, indeed gossip, partner. This situation prevents the gossipers from totally breaking with the subject of gossip, of condemning him finally. For, on one hand, it is always possible that the gossip will get back to the subject of gossip.[74] On the other, such inconsistent behavior might lead the gossiper to endanger his self-identity and forfeit his credibility. *Thus, to be sure, it is the gossip triad's particular personal constellation that makes the "sins" of an acquaintance socially relevant to it, but, at the same time, it also prevents this acquaintance from being morally condemned in gossip mercilessly.*[75] Gossipers are never merely accusers and judges but also defenders and witnesses in behalf of the subject of gossip. The simultaneity of condemnation and tolerance, of disapproval and understanding, of indignation and compassion is a constitutive structural feature of gossip. Therefore, the functional argument, which says that the mutual condemnation of a malefactor is a confirmation of collectively shared values and norms, is already evident from the perspective of its substantive conditions and thereby doubtful in its validity.

Second, if in analyzing the data we ask which "lapse" is censured by the gossipers, we will see that the explanation that gossip should be understood as an expression of "moral indignation" about the violation of internalized norms is wrong from the very start. Instead of starting with the fact that a "lapse" has occurred, which makes the gossipers indignant, it seems more appropriate to reverse the explanation and determine the "lapse" as a result of the moral and selective interpretations of the gossipers.

This is clearly apparent in the segment [39] quoted, on p. 124. Here Mrs. H depicts events that show that Mrs. J herself is responsible for her sad marital state. Mrs. H's presentation is remarkable in that her indignation is directed primarily against Mrs. J. However, she deals with Mr. J—who has begun an affair with another woman, moved out of his house, stolen things, and committed other inconsiderate actions toward his wife—rather lightly. (Cf. the innocently warm expression "girlfriend" in [39].) Not that she would recommend Mr. J's behavior. Her disapproval does not primarily concern his flaws. It concerns, instead, the behavior of Mrs. J, who despite everything that has happened still stays with her husband. The anthropologist A.L. Epstein describes a similar case of selective indignation in a brief case study of the modes of gossip dissemination in an African city in the Copperbelt region.[76] A married woman had begun an affair with another man, and this story was then disseminated within various gossip circles. Although in this region marital fidelity was viewed as the norm, moral indignation in the gossip was not directed at the affair, but at the fact that the woman had married a man whose social rank in the system of prestige of the copperbelt society was lower than her own. To be sure, this observation was limited to the gossip among friends and the woman's family. Gossip from the social environment of the husband who was betrayed, however, was unavailable to Epstein.

Both these cases clearly show that the gossipers do not directly react to the "violation of a norm" but always situate, interpret, and thus transform it into something relevant to them, against the background of their own social position and interests. That is to say, gossip is not concerned with the disdain and preservation of social norms and moral principles in their universality, but, in interpreting the situational behavior of other members of the group from their own situation and with the knowledge of the specific behavioral rules of the group, conversely with specifying the kind of validity of social rules for individual concrete cases. That is to say, gossip is essentially a hermeneutic enterprise as far as its structure is concerned.[77] The fact that gossipers take part in this process of rule interpretation and application, that they always speak *pro domo*, is quite clear from the gossip-conversations. However, it is not always evident that only rules and expressed moral indignation make the subject's reconstructed behavior the "mistake" to which the gossipers appear merely to react. Georg Simmel writes that, "The poor do not emerge as a sociological category because of a specific lack or privation but because they receive support or are preserved through social norms."[78] And this idea also holds—in somewhat modified form—for the "malefactor" who is the victim of gossip. Viewed sociologically, it is not the case that the flaws of the subject of gossip are given and then the feeling of moral indignation follows, expressed in gossip as disapproval. The sequence is exactly the opposite. It is the expression of disapproval that gives form and direction to the feeling of indignation[79] and turns the behavior of the subject of gossip into a flaw. Scandal, caricature, and all the other elements that were described in this chapter are therefore of constitutive significance for the genre "gossip." They turn a private action into a publicly relevant flaw and thereby legitimize the indiscretion, which is so essential to gossip, through the reconstruction of events and through moralization.

THE TERMINATION OF GOSSIP AS AN INTERACTIVE PROBLEM: REMARKS TOWARD A SOCIOLOGY OF GOSSIP MANIA

It is part of our everyday understanding of gossip that it possesses an almost magical attraction for many people and that it fascinates those who indulge in it. We know, to be sure, that, as a rule, the morally disreputable interest in gossip has to be subordinated to other social obligations and activities. Yet experience shows that, on the other hand, gossip absorbs the attention of the actors to such an extent that they forget the time, their surroundings, and their work. Although gossipers appear as guardians of morality and order, gossip itself possesses a chaotic aspect. It disrupts order, disdains social boundaries, and entices the actors to neglect their social duties. For outsiders gossip is a *malum*, for the gossipers a *fascinosum*—this is what is meant by the everyday concept of "gossip mania."

How does it happen that, lost in gossip, we forget about the time? That we cannot tear ourselves away from it? That it often takes an external signal—a telephone call, a glance at the clock, the sound of the church bell—to bring the actors back from their gossiping to their work? In his story, "Conversations of German Refugees," Goethe has an old pastor sing a hymn of praise to gossip in which he also inquires why gossip is so fascinating:

> I have seldom seen people at a serious reading or a presentation intended to stimulate heart and mind look as attentive and thoughtful as when they listened to the latest gossip, especially if it was derogatory. Ask yourself and ask anyone: what makes news attractive? Not its importance, not its consequences, but its novelty. For the most part only what is new seems important, because without a clear context it arouses amazement, momentarily stirs our imagination, just grazes our emotions, and requires no mental effort whatsoever. Everyone can take a lively interest in such things without the least trouble to himself. Indeed, since a series of news continually pulls us from one subject to the next, most people find nothing more pleasant than this stimulus to ceaseless diversion, this convenient and never-ending opportunity to vent their malice and spleen.[80]

It is correct in at least one respect to say that *gossip mania is a form of news mania*. But this interpretation does not address the question, why do people develop such a pronounced desire specifically for gossip— and not for any other kind of news? Given a positive twist, this objection leads to the view that the conclusion—as well as the initiation—of gossip is a structural problem, which, if the gossipers cannot reach a conclusion, indicates that the problem is a part of the organizational structure of gossip itself.

The point of departure for the following remarks on the conclusion of gossip as an interactive problem is the observation that a gossip-story rarely occurs in isolation. In the overwhelming majority of cases the reconstruction of and commentary on an initial event is followed by another story that can originate with the same or another participant, and be about the same or another subject of gossip. As a rule, this continues to a second, third, fourth story, and so on, so that a series of gossip reconstructions emerges that under favorable conditions (coffee-klatsch!) can go on for hours. This *seriality of stories* is a typical gossip phenomenon, although not restricted to gossip. In his essay "Über Gespräche" Moritz Lazarus had already observed that, "When a fact is recounted [. . .] everyone will have memories of events that are similar to the recounted fact. That is the natural course of conversation. [. . .] If a brief story is recounted within twenty different groups, each with five people, in each case all of the persons will reproduce and communicate a story from their own experience identical or similar to the original one recounted."[81] Only recently has this theme been renewed in sociology by conversation analysis and investigated with respect to the question of the kind of similarity that exists between two stories that are produced within a conversation in immediate succession.[82] The fact that stories—jokes are an illustrative special case—do not occur in isolation but in series is also a universal principle of everyday conversations. Fritz Mauthner has found a striking comparison for this fact. For him, "the ubiquitous use of language as pleasure in gossiping (oral as well as reading) seems to be very similar to the game of dominoes, where the mental work consists of matching the value of one's own piece with that of one's opponent for as long as one can. Just as in a so-called conversation."[83] But this universal principle of the seriality of everyday conversations has become a specific structural feature of gossip-conversations for many reasons.

First, we must remember that gossip is viewed as a socially disreputable practice, and therefore, the participants in a conversation, as a rule are forced in initiating gossip to take specific precautions and secure their partner's willingness, so as not to discredit themselves. But as shown above, this is always connected with a certain interactive expense. Once a gossip-conversation is successfully initiated, such a securing effort is no longer required—at least no longer to this extent. The morally contaminated information can be repeated in a relatively safe form. This enables the gossipers to move quickly from one story to another, from one subject of gossip to another. That is to say, a conversation that was framed and intersubjectively ratified by a moral "keying" (Goffman) is already—from the perspective of its structural conditions—a communicative context that invites serial transmission of news and stories that have to be discreetly withheld within other contexts.

But the moral problematic of gossip exercises a much more direct pressure on the gossipers to produce successive stories. The gossipers find themselves in a kind of exchange relation, in which the gossip producer surrenders his knowledge of the scarce resource "intimacy" and thereby implicitly obligates the recipients to a corresponding action. A tells a story about X and expects that he will receive something about Y from B in return. Of course, this exchange of information cannot be managed and "deducted" simultaneously. Yet if in the course of the conversation—or even over several conversations—it becomes clear

Figure 3. "Ye Song of Ye Gossips," Drawing by H. Pyle, 1885 from R.L. Rosnow and G.A. Fine 1976. Reproduced by permission of the publisher.

that one of the participants only takes without giving in return, the others can clamp a boycott on him.[84]

But still more is involved in this case than the simple obligation to exchange information. Anyone who only listens to gossip without contributing something subjects himself to the suspicion of being a sponger, who profits from the others' "immoral" activity but who likes to keep his own hands clean. Thus the obligation to exchange, as well as the pressure to "comply," force the actors to participate actively in gossip-conversations and in this way stimulate the successive production of gossip-stories.

In principle, all of the gossipers' mutual acquaintances—with the exception of those who are intimately related to any of them—are potential subjects of gossip. To be sure, this reservoir of relatives, friends, neighbors, colleagues, associates and locally well-known figures is numerically limited. But what appears as worthy of communication, interpretation, and speculation about each and every one of them is inexhaustible. Even what is already known receives new relevance in the light of subsequent events. It seems as if the flood of information, reconstructions, extrapolations, and speculations could be bound together through social typing and formed into a figurative whole. Yet social typing does not stop the avalanche of gossip. It only evokes new character types of the subject of gossip. *In contrast to other communicative genres gossip seems to admit no internal terminating mechanism. Therefore, its termination occurs mostly as an interruption or simply exhaustion.*

For anyone who wants to prevent himself from being made a subject of gossip there is only one secure place—since gossip is only about absent persons, he must himself participate as an actor in the gossip. A study of a rural Spanish community reports that "any woman who observes her neighbors engrossed in animated conversation assumes that she herself is the subject of this conversation. She therefore joins in the group to inhibit gossip. 'No one wants to be left out,' one woman said, for fear of becoming the object of speculation among her peers."[85] What appears as gossip mania can therefore be a countermeasure to gossip. A concern with becoming a subject of gossip can bring people together to gossip—and of course, to stay together gossiping. For it is also an everyday experience that anyone who quits a gossip circle and thereby becomes an absent party almost immediately becomes the subject of a gossip-story. (Cf. illustration 3.) The reason it is so difficult to bring gossip to an end is precisely that each of the gossipers is afraid of being the first to leave the gossip circle.

Chapter 5

Toward a Theory of Gossiping

The following remarks toward a theory of gossiping do not form the focus or the apex of the present work. This needs to be said because the remarks could easily have the fatal effect of devaluing the significance of the preceding analysis of the internal structure and organization of gossip to a preliminary study for what "really" counts, namely, the theory. This should not be read, however, as an antitheoretical sentiment but as the conviction that sociology can survive as a scientific discipline only if it succeeds in establishing itself as a science of reality. "We all agree, I think, that our job is to study society," explained Erving Goffman in his Presidential Address (1982) to the American Sociological Association, and he then continued to say that, "If you ask why and to what end, I would answer: because it is there. [. . .] For myself I believe that human social life is ours to study naturalistically, *sub specie aeternitatis*. From the perspective of the physical and biological sciences, human social life is only a small irregular scab on the face of nature, not particularly amenable to deep systematic analysis. And so it is. But it's ours."[1] The fact that through its use of hypertrophic theories with all-encompassing explanatory claims sociology has blocked rather than opened access to social reality, "to the things themselves," is an opinion that for some time now has been openly expressed in the profession. It is no mere coincidence that in the same year that Erving Goffman presented his Presidential Address the chairman of the Deutsche Gesellschaft für Soziologie lamented a "degradation of descriptive knowledge in the social sciences" in his opening address to the twentyfirst German Sociology Congress and attributed the social irrelevance of sociological research basically to the impoverishment of descriptive sociological knowledge.[2] Of course, this irrelevance also has its positive side. It provides the possibility of developing new procedures of description and analysis that can comprehend social reality with a precision and detail hitherto unknown and analyze it into its elementary social processes. The development of such a methodology, which could only profit from looking beyond the boundaries of its own disciple to biology (behavioral research) and philology and the study of literature (esthetics), has, for a long time, been unable to get beyond the stage of proposals and experiment. It has frequently been ignored by the scientific mainstream so that we might easily get the impression that it was something entirely subsidiary. Therefore, the research that has been done within this context necessarily possesses—beyond the usual measure— a provisional and incomplete character and, because of self-imposed restriction and restraint, often appears inconsequential. Yet, we can correct this deficiency by forcing it—contrary to its own logic of research— to inflate itself into grand theory. Whether such a development will only produce a temporary change in the appearance of sociological research or, as Clifford Geertz[3] believes, a long-term fundamental change in theory cannot be predicted today with any certainty.

*   *   *

Allowing for a few exceptions, the sociological and anthropological literature on gossip is dominated by the attempt to fit the phenomenon of "gossip" into a theoretical context of explanation. The current positions can be summarized as three approaches—approaches that despite their differences and reciprocal criticisms possess a common feature, namely, they all employ an explicit or implicit functional argument. The following discussion of these approaches begins on the level of society as a whole then moves to that of a sociology of groups approach and ends with the explanatory approach of social psychology.

GOSSIP AS A MEANS OF SOCIAL CONTROL

The argument that gossip is an effective means of social control was already represented in the first works that systematically developed this sociological concept. E.A. Ross (1901) refers to gossip when he investigates the role that "public opinion" plays in the creation and preservation of social order.[4] In his monograph *Means of Social Control*, F.E. Lumley (1925) devotes an entire chapter to gossip.[5] Today the assertion that gossip functions as an important means of control in all primary groups is almost a sociological cliché. It is difficult to derive anything original from it any longer. At best it leads the quiet life of an "interesting" example in introductions to sociology.[6]

There is general agreement that gossip is *typically* an informal means of control and exercises its regulative function best in small, stable, morally homogeneous groups or societies. This interpretation is usually

combined with the argument that in the process of social development—increase in population, urbanization, pluralization of values and
of moral standards—the significance of informal controls has also, basically, been relegated to the background and that these informal controls have been replaced by the institutionalization of *formal* social
controls. As far as gossip is concerned, W.F. Ogburn and M.F. Nimkoff
maintain that, "In the large community of the modern city, contacts in
secondary groups tend to be impersonal, and escape into anonymity is
possible. Under these circumstances, gossip and ridicule are less effective instruments and their place is taken by the police and the courts."[7]
The argument that gossip's function in premodern societies was as a
means of social control explains why it has become a theme of the
ethnology and sociology of law.[8] This argument enjoys a particularly
close connection with the above-mentioned anthropological view that
gossip characterizes "primitive" societies. For if gossip possesses a much
greater significance for the system of social controls in these simple
societies than in ours, then it seems reasonable to think that the anthropologists found the ethnic groups they observed in their field work to be
rather "gossipy."

A closer examination of the argument that gossip functions in simple
societies as a means of social control, however, almost immediately produces doubt about its validity. On one hand, legal ethnologists themselves have convincingly demonstrated that preurban, illiterate societies
possessed laws with fixed behavioral rules and catalogs of different
sanctions.[9] In *Crime and Custom in Savage Society*, Malinowski, for example, uses the case of the suicide of a young man who had broken the law
of exogamy to show how the gossip of the other members of the tribe
about this transgression neither produced a sanction of it nor even required a punishment for it, but how the public abuse he received for the
crime was enough to bring him to punish himself.[10] Finally, we should
mention that even in our modern, "juridified" societies gossip has not
disappeared but blossoms and thrives unabated at the office, in the
neighborhood, and among friends. In light of these observations, sociology's way of implicitly turning gossip into a means of social control
seems, at the very least, in need of differentiation. Thus we have to ask
in what way is gossip one of those "influences that a group is able to use
to introduce order among its members—and in the extreme case, society
its groups and their members—and to prevent deviant behavior."[11]

The first answer is that gossip functions as a social control over the
gossipers themselves insofar as these refer critically and disapprovingly
to another's deviant behavior and thereby implicitly confirm the validity
of established norms and values. As already shown, the problem with
this answer, which defines gossip's function in the sense of Durkheim's
theory of punishment,[12] is that it projects a picture of gossip that one-

sidedly defines the latter as a negatively critical type of reaction. Based on the analysis of the material presented here as well as on ethnographic reports, we can maintain, however, that gossip is structurally stratified, in fact contradictory, namely, that it shows sympathy for transgressors, overlooks gross transgressions, but is merciless toward small mistakes. Not to mention that the gossipers themselves transgress a norm, namely, the proscription of gossip, and that therefore their behavior cannot simply be interpreted as an implicit confirmation of norms.

The second answer is that gossip functions as a means of social control because it exercises pressure on its victim to change his disreputable behavior and to make it agree with the expectations of his environment, namely, with the established code of moral norms and values. This answer suffers, of course, from the fact that it no longer refers primarily to the gossip itself but to reactions to the subject of gossip that were triggered by the gossip. Since the subject of gossip is excluded from the gossiping, the fact that the others are talking about him and his behavior can be concealed from him for a long time. Only if the gossip gets back to him or if the others openly or covertly express their disapproval of him does he know or sense that he was the subject of gossip. Thus it is not the gossip itself that exercises pressure on the "victim" but the sanctioning reactions to which it leads— reactions that formally can no longer be called gossip. Thus gossip is a kind of transfer station for a larger process of social control whose circular structure can be presented in the following way:

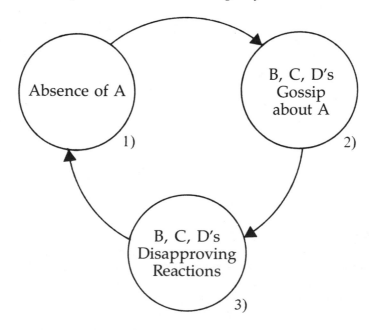

The disapproving reactions that can be triggered by gossip and are directed against its subject can differ greatly. Conversational hints and allusions as well as the avoidance of contact, are rather indirect measures that do not go as far—as in the case of gossip itself—as direct confrontation.[13] Teasing, clever remarks, and restricting social participation allow the "malefactor" to clearly see that he has done something wrong. Tricks that are played on the "deviator"[14] are another measure and constitute a preliminary stage to mockery and other customs of reproof described in legal folklore.[15] In some societies gossip even functions as an informal system of pre-judicial decision making ("gossip as adjudication") that can be finished by the police and the courts.[16] To be sure, all these reactions of disapproval can be triggered by gossip, but formally are no longer gossip themselves.

The third answer is that gossip functions as a means of social control because—as the mere threat of sanction—it pre-emptively ensures conformative behavior. Thus it must never actually come to gossip. The anxiety that accompanies the knowledge that people can gossip about one is enough to prevent people from acting deviantly. Fear of being discredited,[17] of having one's reputation soiled, of losing one's honor— this anxiety is often really nothing more than the fear of gossip. In her ethnography about a Taiwanewse village, Margery Wolf reports that, "We once asked a male friend in Peihotien just what 'having face' amounted to. He replied, 'When no one is talking about a family, you can say it has face'."[18] Therefore, gossip seems to function as a means of social control in those cultures that Ruth Benedict—in contrasting them with "guilt cultures"—calls "shame cultures."[19] Actually, however, gossip-communication itself is not the determining factor in this case either, but fear of gossip or more exactly the fear of the loss of reputation through gossip.

The fact that the fear of becoming a subject of gossip forms a separate complex, which to a large part is independent of gossip-communication, is clearly shown by a phenomenon that would certainly be worth an investigation of its own, namely, the interconnection of gossip and paranoia. It is characteristic for most patients who manifest symptoms of paranoia constantly to complain that others are gossiping about them.[20] For someone suffering from paranoia, loud laughter, an accidentally overheard remark, a group of people who are whispering, and other unseen and trivial events are proof enough of his conviction that they are talking about his shortcomings and saying negative things about him. The person suffering from paranoia is, as it were, the opposite of the gossiper. Whereas the gossiper constantly rails against the sins of another, the paranoid person believes that others are constantly talking about his sins.

The fact that it is not gossip itself but the anticipation of gossip that can prevent deviant behavior clearly reveals at one stroke the central problem of the original argument. *The argument that gossip is a means of social control is basically nothing more than a scientific reformulation and duplication of the common opinion that gossip can damage the reputation of its subject but can be checked by conformative behavior.* Thereby the argument does not provide a disinterested description of a social fact. Instead, it itself is an essential part of what it seems objectively to comprehend. In a somewhat extreme form we could therefore say that the argument that gossip is a means of social control possesses validity as long as the people in their everyday life believe in it and guide their action by it.

GOSSIP AS A MECHANISM OF PRESERVING SOCIAL GROUPS

The argument that, because it reinforces the validity of moral norms, gossip functions as a means of social control forms the point of departure for an explanatory approach that places the main accent on the stabilizing function of gossip. This explanatory approach is closely connected with the name of the social and legal anthropologist Max Gluckman whose 1963 article "Gossip and Scandal" has dominated the anthropological discussion of gossip for a long time.[21] The argument that Gluckman presents in this essay is essentially that gossip is by no means empty and meaningless prattle as is normally assumed in everyday experience but, on the contrary, fulfills important social functions for the preservation of a social group. This formulation already makes clear a basic deficiency in Gluckman's argumentation. Against the background of his positive determination of the function of gossip as a mechanism of group stabilization, he views gossip's normally negative standing only as an erroneous opinion. Instead of acknowledging gossip's social disrepute as an empirical feature and explaining it, he treats it as a scientific statement about gossip that needs to be disproved. Therefore, it is no accident that in Gluckman's explanation the social disdain of gossip is insignificant and simply overlooked.

If we consider Gluckman's argument more closely it becomes clear that it consists of a series of pieces.[22] The argument that gossip serves to delimit and preserve social groups is mainly justified by the following observations. *First*, gossip does not reinforce a code of universal rules through the disapproval of mistakes, but through the validity of the moral norms and values of a group. Village gossip has the effect of making the villagers conform to the ideas of morality and value that are valid in the village.[23] But this orientation toward a group's code of rules and values implicitly means that the gossipers obligate both themselves and the subject of gossip to their mutual membership in a social group and thereby recognize and strengthen the group as a binding social unit. *Second*, it is essential for gossip that it restricts itself to those who are members of a social group, that is, nonmembers are generally excluded from gossip-communication. The right to say negative things about other members of the group belongs only to those who are members of the group. "The right to participate in gossip is a sign of membership." But, because the members constantly talk about one another in their gossip, they make sure that the group is renewed and reinforced as a social system.[24] Therefore, membership in a group, says Gluckman, is also connected with "the duty to gossip." And *third*, aggression toward others is expressed[25] and conflicts between individuals or cliques are carried out[26] so that the appearance of harmony within the group ("the pretense of group amity") is preserved and the group's integration is not threatened by open dispute.

While on one hand Gluckman argues that gossip strengthens the identity and cohesion of a social group, on the other, he emphasizes that it fulfills this function only within social groups whose members are already integrated through a feeling of belonging.[27] If a social group dissolves and the members no longer recognize the group's ideas of values and goals as binding, the function of gossip is reversed, namely, it accelerates the process of disintegration. All these considerations finally lead Gluckman to formulate a "law" for the interconnection of gossip and social groups that says, "The more exclusive a social group is, the more its members will concern themselves with gossip and scandalous stories." Examples of groups with a high degree of exclusivity are professional groups (lawyers, anthropologists, etc.); groups that attribute themselves high social status and that try to keep out social climbers; as well as groups that are forced into exclusivity through spatial isolation, minority status, or other criteria.[28] The primary function of gossip in these groups is to demonstrate, through indirect disapproval of improper behavior, the validity of the group's ideas about values and moral laws and thus to solidify the group's identity and integration.

Even if in interpreting gossip many ethnographic studies appropriate Gluckman's argument, the weaknesses of his explanatory approach cannot be missed. This argument commits a category mistake that is typical of functionalist explanations because it implicitly foists its determination of the latent function of gossip on the gossipers as a goal, as when it suggests its function of eliminating a danger to group integration through the avoidance of open conflict as a gossip motive. But do group members really have the preservation of their group in mind when they avoid open discussion and, instead, gossip about another member behind his or her back? Don't we turn the actors into implicit functionalists when we impose the "duty to gossip" on them because gossip fulfills a positive function for group preservation? We may view this problem, which is introduced by these questions and which deals with the fact that the determination of the latent functions of social processes cannot be empirically confirmed, as not particularly important. Another deficiency that Gluckman calls gossip interpretation is more important.

Gluckman is so convinced that the function of gossip is to preserve the group that he has no interest in the details of gossip-communication. He already knows more about gossip than he really can. He does not realize that the gossipers' behavior reflects a completely broken relation with moral rules and values and that, in any event, a simple, unambiguous confirmation of valid norms is out of the question. He overlooks the fact that gossip, since it repeats the private affairs of others, is, and in principle has to be, a morally disreputable practice. Instead, in light of his functional argument, he calls for a "school for scandal." He not only ignores gossip's specific form and internal organization but also fails to distinguish between gossip and the disapproving reactions to its subject that gossip triggers. In summary we can say that a person does not learn much about gossip from Gluckman's work because we are always confronted with ever-new variations of the argument that the function of gossip is to preserve the group. This functional attribution obviously does not result from an analysis of the social phenomenon of "gossip." Instead, it is a continuation of Durkheim's argument that crime, because it evokes collective indignation and punishment from the social community, plays an important role in reinforcing the validity of law and of anchoring it in the social consciousness.

Undoubtedly Gluckman is correct in establishing an essential connection between gossip and social groups. Yet the kind of relation this is is more obfuscated than clarified by a functionalist approach. This was clearly seen by other anthropologists from among Gluckman's circle who were associated with the "Manchester School."[29] In any event, several studies were made by the members of this school that—at first quite cautiously and hesitantly—began by determining the interconnection of gossip and social groups with the help of network analysis, instead of working exclusively from its function.[30] In this case the focus of interest was no longer social function but transaction, no longer the group but the individual.

GOSSIP AS A TECHNIQUE OF INFORMATION MANAGEMENT

If Gluckman had focused the general argument of gossip's function as a control on the role that it plays in the preservation of social groups his critics would have restricted the significance of gossip almost entirely to the acting individual. "It is the individual and not the community that gossips," says Robert Paine in an essay that, in critically distancing itself from Gluckman, developed an alternative hypothesis to explain gossip.[31] This alternative explanatory approach begins with the observation that gossip is to be determined primarily as a model of informal communication that is basically concerned with the exchange of information. This information is relevant to the participants because it concerns persons and events in the social community to which they belong. As members of this social community, the gossipers are themselves involved, which means that the exchange of gossip-information is essentially determined by the interests of the participants. Even more, gossip itself can be viewed as an institution to effectuate and distribute individual interests.

It is clear that within this explanatory framework gossip is conceived as a form of strategic action whose primary goal is to validate the respective interests of the gossipers. Building on Erving Goffman's concept of "impression management," Robert Paine coined the concept "information management" for this interest-oriented handling of information in gossip.[32] The interests that determine the behavior of the gossip participants work in three ways: it is the urgent interest of every gossiper to receive information about what is going on around him. Therefore, he is anxious to maintain the flow of information that provides him with messages and news about relevant events. On the other hand, however, gossipers are also interested in repeating information that, as far as they can tell, is of interest to others. They not only try to get their interpretation of a social fact accepted, but they also calculate, in accordance with the principle of *do ut des*, that their repetition of information will return an even greater informational gain in the short or long run. And finally, gossipers always pursue the goal of exploiting the values and moral ideas to which they implicitly or explicitly refer in their information in order to promote their own interests and of adapting them to their interests through appropriate interpretations. If gossipers appeal to moral norms and rules, then it is not to solidify the social community but in the interest of raising their own status.

Because of their rigid theoretical premises and their circularity, both explanatory approaches that conceive gossip as a means of social control or as a mechanism of the preservation of social groups hardly leave any room for new, empirical knowledge about gossip. However, Paine emphasizes for his transactional approach that, "beyond this basic conceptual framework, assumptions should not be included at the outset of the investigation of gossip regarding the distribution, strength, and character of social alignments in a community. These features should be constructed from the data collected about the lines of communication and the flow of information (of various kinds) in the community."[33] In fact, the approach that focuses on the informational aspect of gossip is much more empirically open than the other two approaches. This is shown quite clearly by a series of studies that have empirically worked out individual aspects of information management in gossip.[34]

The conception of a research approach based on the idea that gossip can be determined as an interest-bound exchange of information about others was, from the very beginning, expressly directed against the functionalist explanation of gossip as it had been presented before Max Gluckman. The antagonism that was perceived as such by both sides turns out, however, on closer examination to be a pseudo-conflict for at least two reasons. On one hand, both explanations of gossip work on two different levels—one on the level of groups and institutions, the other on that of individual processes. Therefore, they do not argue about the same social issues and conflict with each other, except in their claims regarding the scope of their explanatory approaches and not with respect to their substantive statements. In fact, their substantive statements are even complementary. On the other hand, there is no pseudo-conflict in this case because even the explanation of gossip as a technique of information management argues functionalistically against what it wants to be. According to this explanation, gossip is instrumentalized as a technique that makes it possible for the interactors to acquire and distribute information and thereby promote their individual interests.[35] We can simply say that the two so seemingly opposite explanatory approaches are complementary insofar as one seeks to comprehend the latent functions of gossip for group preservation, whereas the other seeks to comprehend its manifest functions for the interests of the individual gossipers.

If we examine these explanatory approaches once again in retrospect we see that each of them focuses on a different social element that it then functionally relates to gossip. The first focuses on "morality," the second on the "group," and the third on "information." This may be surprising (or not surprising) insofar as the preceding material has shown that, in the communication of gossip, morality (in the form of moral indignation and social typing), the group relation (structured as the gossip triad) as well as information (as news) play a constitutive role. Does this now mean that our painstaking analysis of the material only confirms what previously was already known in the scientific literature? Was the entire effort possibly for nothing? If we omit the fact that none of these three approaches even begins to appreciate the decisive point, namely, that gossip-information is morally contaminated and that gossip is viewed as a morally reprehensible practice, *the decisive flaw of these approaches is that each isolates one of these social elements for itself and universalizes it as the sole functional variable of gossip.* Gossip preserves its dynamics and contradictory character because these different social elements occur simultaneously, intersect, and neutralize themselves in gossip-communication. Gossip rests on a basic paradox that none of these approaches can detect, conceptually or methodologically.

GOSSIP AS THE SOCIAL FORM OF DISCREET INDISCRETION

Gossip is characterized by a structural feature that is like a collection of nesting dolls—it not only characterizes the gossip-conversation as a whole but is also found in smaller conversational units. It occurs in sequences and individual utterances and is finally reproduced even in the minimal form of self-correction. This feature is its equivocal-contradictory character (gossip is publicly despised and at the same time practiced in private with great delight). It is precise and detailed and remains, however, vague and allusive. Authentic presentations are suddenly transformed into exaggerations. Indecency is mixed with decent restraint. Indignation about transgressions is paired with amusement. Disgust with compassion, disapproval with understanding. Morally contaminated information is presented in an innocent wrapper. Ingenuous sociability is mixed with calculated backbiting. Shameful affectation and coyness interchanges with shameless directness. Gossip is like a moral balancing act, a boundary crossing that is undone with the next step. This equivocal-contradictory quality is so characteristic of gossip that we have to suspect that there are reasons for it that are a part of its very structure. What kind of reasons are these?

In everyday life it is, as Georg Simmel says, unavoidable, "that one learns more from another than the latter willingly discloses, and many times something that the other, if he only knew about this, would not want to reveal."[36] In the case of a stranger, however, the indiscreet information that we acquire through paying careful attention to intonation, slips of the tongue, mimicry, and anything that a person unintentionally reveals about himself, does not extend far into the stranger's private sphere. About friends and acquaintances, on the other hand, we acquire, even without trying, information that often concerns intimate things—things that, if they became public, could have unpleasant, if not downright dangerous consequences.

We could perform a thought experiment about someone who acquires such indiscreet information. Let's suppose that he has information about something significant or sensitive to a friend, for example, he sees Petra, who is presently unemployed, coming out of an expensive boutique with things she bought. Or Peter tells him that last week he "borrowed" two books from a bookstore. What kind of a situation does such information place him in regarding his friends? What possibilities for action are open to him?

At first glance it seems that the information about another's personal affairs are in good, namely, a friend's, hands. Ultimately, friendship also means trust. And to repeat private things would be a breach of such trust, an act of indiscretion and can, under circumstances, put the friendship in jeopardy. But Nietzsche with his characteristic psychological penetration already observed that, "there are few who when they are confused about a subject for conversation do not disclose the more private affairs of their friends."[37] This leads to the sociological question whether a structural explanation can be found for this observation, instead of the mere tautology that people gossip.

In answer to this question we can argue that just as a secret always contains the possibility of betrayal, *the tendency to gossip is a structural part of private information*. By modifying and supplementing Simmel's argument on secrets[38] our argument could be justified in the following way. If someone has learned something about Petra/Peter's private affairs then, as a rule, he not only conceals *what* he knows about Petra/Peter from his neighbors but also *that* he knows something about their private lives. Thus he alone knows that he knows something. And structurally this is a very unstable situation that, for different reasons, can cause him to disclose his information.

To begin with a psychological reason, the knowledge of another's personal affairs can tempt the possessor of this information to repeat it as gossip because as concealed information it remains socially inactive. Only when the information is repeated can its possessor turn the fact that he knows something into something socially valuable like social recognition, prestige, and notoriety. As long as he keeps his information to himself he may feel superior to those who do not know it. But knowing and not telling does not give him that feeling of, "superiority that, so to say, latently contained in the secret, fully actualizes itself only at the moment of disclosure."[39] This is the main motive for gossiping about well-known figures and superiors. The gossip producer assumes that some of the "fame" of the subject of gossip, as whose "friend" he presents himself, will rub off on him.

Besides this psychological reason, to which others could be added,[40] there are many sociological reasons for maintaining that a knowledge of the private affairs of others induces gossip. Two of these reasons will be presented briefly. On one hand, there is the universal phenomenon of a clearly perceptible tendency to criticize, belittle, blame, and implicate absent third parties to one's present conversational partners. It is a universal principle of everyday conversation that one should avoid "face threatening acts" and if possible to agree with one's partner.[41] Yet, the range of this principle is restricted to those involved in face-to-face situations. If the protection of this principle cannot be assumed, then the conversational partners are suddenly freed to say negative things about another. The well-known precept "De mortuis nihil nisi bene," which is supposed to protect those who cannot help but be absent (the dead), clearly indicates that those who are absent are received with much less consideration and care than those who are present. It is a common experience that anyone who quits a conversation (even if for only a little while) is often made a subject of gossip immediately upon his departure. This refers to the same situation. It is clear that this principle, which protects those present from mutual criticism but which releases those absent to criticize, essentially nurtures the willingness to gossip.

But the second sociological reason, which determines why indiscreet knowledge about the private affairs of others provokes gossip, is decisive. Friendship and acquaintanceship relations imply (with different degrees of intensity) mutual trust, which means to bring someone "into one's confidence," to "entrust" him with particular things. If Peter has information about the personal affairs of his friend Paul, then Petra, if she is a friend of both, has, to a certain degree, a right to have this information given to her. To withhold it from her would mean not to trust her.

This is where *we find that contradictory, indeed paradoxical loyalty structure of friendship and acquaintanceship that counts as the main source of energy for the equivocal nature as well as the lasting success of the communicative genre "gossip."* Anyone who has information about the personal affairs of a friend is, on one hand, obligated to discretion toward this friend. And as a rule he honors this obligation insofar as he does not disseminate this information indiscriminately or pass it on to the general public. On the other hand, however, anyone who possesses this indiscreet information is obligated by loyalty to his other friends,[42] which as a rule means not to conceal or withhold from them information in which they are interested. It is precisely in this contradictory situation that the communicative genre "gossip" has developed and established itself. When the gossip producer repeats his information about the subject of gossip he commits an act of indiscretion. When he refuses to disseminate his information indiscriminately but, instead, repeats it intentionally (cf. *discernere*) to specific friends, and that means to mutual friends and acquaintances, he behaves once again considerately, carefully, in a word: discreetly. Gossip—so runs our central argument—*is the social form of discreet indiscretion.* This social form of discreet indiscretion[43] represents the institutionalized solution to a structural contradiction and in this way acquires its basic paradoxical structure, dynamics, and equivocal nature. Gossip violates the precept of discretion and respects it at the same time. To be sure, a secret may be revealed in gossip, but only insofar as a mutual friend is initiated into the secret and thereby a new secret created.

The designation of gossip as the social form of discreet indiscretion unites the social elements of morality, the group and information that were separate in the above explanatory approaches. This point needs to be discussed here once again no matter how pointless it may appear to correlate this designation in particular with the results of the analysis of the material. By way of example, only one possible consequence of gossip's basic paradoxical structure will be discussed. As soon as the gossip recipient has received the "trusted" information about the subject of gossip, he can, of course, advance himself to the position of a gossip producer. He is thereby faced with the dilemma, if he disseminates the information quickly, it can just as quickly—since it has gone public—lose it newsworthiness. However, if he sits on his information as on a treasure, the information—since it may be disseminated by others—may lose its market value. Not to mention that the withholding of interesting information can be interpreted as a lack of trust and repaid with appropriate reactions by those who, because of their friendship, can express a claim to the information.

These observations show that indiscreet information has a—we could say—short half-life. But, on one hand, this leads to the formation of *gossip chains* in which indiscreet information is disseminated rapidly and, on the other, to the well-known phenomenon of *backbiting* that consists of a large number of friends and acquaintances going through gossipy information in their conversation as fast as possible. When these mechanisms of the dissemination of gossip are functioning a bit of private information—for example, that a woman is pregnant—without being officially disclosed, can become known within the shortest period of time by the most possible friends and acquaintances and can thereby become what is called an "open secret." Even this expression reflects gossip's paradoxical structure as the social form of discreet indiscretion.

Furthermore, we can also see that the discrepancy between the public disdain and the private practice of gossip is directly related to its basic paradoxical structure. Without the disdain of gossip and indiscretion there would be no occasion for someone who had information about the private affairs of another to show care and consideration in his dissemination of this information. It is only the condemnation of gossip and indiscretion that leads to the activation of the social network of friends and acquaintances as the most appropriate-because-most-restricted system of information distribution. The social disdain of gossip and indiscretion also—functionalistically speaking—reinforces the social network of gossipers. Even more, when two persons gossip together and thus share their indiscreet information and their disgust about a mutual acquaintance they produce and reproduce between themselves a social relation with a high degree of intimacy. Thereby, gossip, as the social form of discreet indiscretion, is a mechanism of socialization of the first order[44]—of course, only under the condition that it is also largely subject to social disdain.

For some time now we have been able to observe how the collective public disdain of gossip has shown breaks in some spots and has begun to wear out. Gossip today is no longer viewed as a self-evidently disreputable practice from which one should distance himself, but to a great extent has been discovered and presented as a "homemade remedy" and celebrated as a kind of popular psychotherapy. "Gossip—a balm for the soul," such and similar headings have, for several years now, appeared in women's magazines and other journals with advice or comments that openly approximate a glorification of gossip.[45] It seems as if the moral discourse that had always dominated the public discussion of gossip is in the process of being transformed into a medical discussion of gossip. Yet insofar as it amounts to a public rehabilitation of gossip, this *process of therapeutic ennoblement* is characterized by a paradox. It must fail in order to succeed. With the elimination of its social condemnation gossip would no longer need to be conducted in secrecy. Indiscreet information would no longer need to be communicated discreetly. There would be no more whispering, no conspiring together, no more furtive "only for you!" That is to say, saving gossip's social honor would necessarily also destroy its socializing function, that is, the feature on which its therapeutic ennoblement is based. The socializing function of gossip is impossible without its social disdain. It is only as something bad that gossip can be something good.

Notes

Chapter 1

1. A. Schütz 1967, p. 74.
2. "The disorder [. . .] that consciousness produces," is demonstrated by Kleist 1964, in the well-known story of a young man who, observing his pleasing bearing in a mirror, immediately lost his innocence and tried in vain to repeat the movement.
3. G.W.F. Hegel 1830/1970, vol. 10, p. 80.
4. E. Durkheim 1895/1966, p. 128 (trans. from German text).
5. H. Plessner 1924/1972, p. 64.
6. Actually this is a quotation from the investigation of Elias's student. H.-V. Krumrey 1984, p. 233. To this day there have hardly been any studies of science parodies. See, however, Mulkay/Gilbert 1982, pp. 585–613.
7. M. Weber 1921–22/1978, pp. 21ff.
8. More recently, Hans-Georg Soeffner has energetically introduced these hermeneutic implications of social scientific methodology—which is very helpful because the interpretive approaches that since the 1970s have been imported into Europe from American sociology (and reimported by the Germans—through Alfred Schütz) largely lack a methodological, especially a hermeneutical, consciousness of tradition. See H.-G. Soeffner 1984, pp. 9–52.
9. The methodology of participant observation was introduced in the 1920s by the representatives of the "Chicago School"—although they did not use the term itself—for whom the anthropological method of ethnographic field research exercised a considerable influence. See J. Platt 1983, pp. 379–393.
10. For the significance and the personal and social background of Malinowski's works that initiated scientific ethnography, see Ph. Kaberry 1957, pp. 71–91, as well as F. Kramer 1977, pp. 82–92.
11. B. Malinowski 1922/1960, p. 7.
12. *Ibid.*
13. "The hasty field-worker, who relies completely upon the question-and-answer method, obtains at best that lifeless body of laws, regulations, morals, and conventionalities which *ought* to be obeyed, but in reality are often evaded. (. . .) But most modern scientific field-work has been accomplished by the rapid and precise, sometimes overprecise, methods built upon the technique of question-and-answer, and it suffers from over-simplifying and over-standardizing the legal constitution of native culture. Such material again has led unfortunately to the anthropological doctrine of the impeccability of native races, of

their immanent legality, and inherent and automatic subservience to custom." In Malinowski 1929, pp. 509ff.

14.   For the role of everyday understanding in conducting interviews and the problems connected with this, see A. Cicourel 1964, pp. 83ff. In connection with this one can ask whether the current forms of journalistic and social scientific interviews do not contain structural and semantic elements—however transformed—that even today still refer to their origin in the older interrogative forms of confession, counsel, and trial.

15.   See, for example, J. Rubenstein, 1973, pp. 200ff.

16.   See R. Rohr 1979, pp. 79ff (on the significance of "cultivating contacts" for local journalists).

17.   M.N. Srinivas 1976, p. 23. (The field research on which this study is based was conducted in the 1940s.)

18.   K. Elwert-Kretschmer 1984, p.25.

19.   R. Frankenberg 1957, p. 21.

20.   C. Bell 1968, p. 139. F. Schütze 1977, p. 21, had already referred to the danger that gossip possesses for the field researcher: "In no case should the field researcher, if he wants to improve his chances of having access to information sources, attempt to deal in the market of unoffical communication when he reports contents already raised in field research that were previously only dealt with on the unoffical market. This would endanger his role as a neutral authority and close off significant sources of information to him in the future." To be sure it is hard for the field researcher to avoid becoming a subject of gossip for those he observes. M.D. Murphy 1985, pp. 132–137, refers to this. He suggests collecting and interpreting the gossip about the field researcher as instructive ethnographic information.

21.   Aristotle 1962, p. 94, 1982, p. 225.

22.   Generally one begins, today, from the fact that three levels of social development can be distinguished: hunter-gatherer societies ("food-gathering"), segmentary societies ("food-producing") and centrally organized societies. Initially, such distinctions do not play a significant role in the investigation of gossip. There is no single ethnography that explicitly determines the absence of gossip for a society.

23.   P. Radin 1957 p. 77. For a more recent work, see M.S. Edmonson 1967, p. 191: "Middle American Indians (. . .) are inveterate and vivacious gossips."

24.   See A. Hahn, H.-A. Schubert, and H.-J. Siewert 1979, p. 19, "Methods and theories that were developed for research in Asia, Polynesia or New Guinea were still used [viz., in the 1920s] to study American communities."

25.   E. LeRoy Ladurie 1979, p. 276, (trans. from German text).

26.   C. Geertz 1984, p. 80.

27.   A presentation of the problem and a survey of the recent literature in which sociological, anthropological, methodological, literary, and rhetorical arguments intertwine can be found in G.E. Marcus and D. Cushman 1982, pp. 25–69. The problem has been developed sociologically by P. Atkinson 1982, pp. 77–105, who tries to avoid the obvious danger of relativism. The problem has been discussed from the anthropological side by J. Clifford 1983, pp. 118–146. The

problem has remained hardly undiscussed by the German scholarly community for a long time. See however F. Kramer 1978, pp. 9–27, who, of course, approaches the problem via a critique of ideology and reduces it to the "bourgeois ethnocentrism" of social anthropology.

28. C. Geertz 1980, pp. 165–179, shows a sense for this development, which possibly will influence the discussion of the self-understanding of sociology in the coming years. For the French—for example, the works of Michel Leiris or Lévi-Strauss's *A World on the Wane*—such a blurring of genre-boundaries seems less alien than for the Germans. For the interplay of ethnology, sociology and the surrealistic movement in France in the 1920's and 1930s, see J. Clifford 1981, pp. 539–564. For the German scholarly community, Hugo Fichte's literary and poetical ethnographies—for example, those about Afro-American syncretism—have been accepted for a long time in the literary but not the sociological context. See for this G. Dischner 1981, pp. 30–47.

29. L. Tiger and R. Fox 1971, p. 200.

30. L. Wylie 1957, pp. 270–273, with ommissions.

31. W. Benjamin 1938/1969, p. 39.

32. E.E. Evans-Pritchard 1970, pp. 29 and 49. In his last work, Evans-Pritchard expressly refers to the presentational shortcomings of his own works. "I have gotten the impression that in their writings about African societies anthropologists (if you want you can include me) dehumanize the Africans in systems and structures and thereby have forgotten flesh and blood." In Evans-Pritchard 1974, p. 9.

33. E.C. Parsons 1936, p. 386.

34. T. Gladwin and S.B. Sarason 1953, pp. 148ff.

35. In his study of a small American town, J. West 1945, pp. 99ff., has studied such intimate groups that spend a large part of their time in gossip and designated them as "gossip cells." (J. West is a pseudonym for Withers—there are many group studies that had to be published under a pseudonym. See, for example, W. Lancaster 1974, pp. 626–627, for the reasons why he had to publish his investigation of an English village under the name of C. Harris.) In his follow-up study of the same small town, "Plainville," A. Gallaher 1961, pp. 136ff., which is obviously a pseudonym, deals with the same clients J. West described.

36. The fact that among the Tchambuli, a small Pacific tribal culture, the men count as the gossipers has been described by M. Mead 1949/1958, pp. 79ff. The coordination of gossip with sex will be examined in detail in Chap. 3.

37. See L. Wylie 1957, pp. 274ff.

38. See R. Frankenberg, 1957, p. 20.

39. See S. Harding 1975, p. 300.

40. See M. Wolf 1972, p. 146.

41. A.L. Epstein 1961, p. 44.

42. B. Malinowski 1929, p. 31.

43. L. Bennett 1983, p. 3.

44. J. du Boulay 1974, p. 208.

45. Y. Murphy and R.F. Murphy 1974, p. 135.

46.   J.F. Embree 1939, p. 53.

47.   D. Gilmore 1978, p. 91.

48.   J.C. Faris 1966, pp. 238ff.

49.   J. du Boulay 1974, p. 122 and passim, for single women and widows as favorite targets of gossip in a Greek mountain village.

50.   M. Wolf 1972, pp. 48 and 146, reports that the women in a Taiwanese village gossip extensively about daughter-in-laws who must wait some time before they themselves can be accepted into the gossip-circle.

51.   W. Waller 1961, Chap. V, provides numerous examples of the teacher as a target of gossip in a small American town of the 1930s.

52.   From my own observations and those of R.L. Coser 1961, p. 38.

53.   A list of gossip themes can be found in F.E. Lumley 1925, pp. 222ff., as well as in D.E. Allen and R.F. Guy 1974, pp. 247ff.

54.   For a long time now ethnology has discussed the argument that in societies where women are segregated and excluded from public life a tight net of friendship relations exists among them. This network helps the women to attain a high measure of social control over the decisions and behavior of the men because the women can use this network to acquire and circulate information about the men as gossip. By means of threatening to disseminate gossip, the women in these societies—so the argument goes—exercise a tacit but effective power over the men. See for this E. Friedl 1967, pp. 97–108; C. Nelson 1974, pp.551–563; S.C. Rogers 1975, pp.727–756; L. Lamphere 1975, pp. 123ff. ("These informal women's groups exercise a different kind of informal pressure on men through gossip"). See for this also below Chapter 3, note 58.

55.   Y.A. Cohen 1971, p. 421, remarks that, "Gossip (. . .) is intimately linked with sorcery" and thereby addresses something that has often been confirmed by historians as well as ethnologists. See C. Kluckhohn 1967, pp. 92, 101, and passim, who functionalistically declares "witchcraft gossip" to be a form of the concealed expression of aggression. For a critique of Kluckhohn's mechanistic application of psychoanalysis in the interpretation of gossip, see E. Devons and M. Gluckman 1964, pp. 247ff. In connection with this, see also L. Lamphere 1971, pp. 91–114, who, in contrast to Kluckhohn's psychologistic explanation, emphasizes that the gossip in which others are accused of witchcraft primarily focuses on preventing uncooperative behavior. For the Paiute tribe in Oregon, see B.B. Whiting 1950, pp. 64ff., and for the Kwahu tribe in Ghana, see W. Bleek 1976, pp. 526–541, whose work also contains a detailed case study. A series of historical and anthropological references to the interconnection of gossip and witchcraft is contained in the volume by M. Douglas 1970 (p. 67, 91, 229ff.). W.I. Thomas and F. Znaniecki 1919/1958, p. 1060, ask, "whether the origin of the enormous significance which any bad gossip assumes in the eyes of the person gossiped about does not lie in the primitive magical belief in the real influence of words." In fact, both possibilities can almost always be observed: in gossip others are accused of witchcraft, but anyone who gossips a lot brings the suspicion of witchcraft upon himself. See for this E.E. Evans-Pritchard 1937, pp. 107ff.

56.   See A. Silbermann 1974, p. 254.

Chapter 2

1. Newspaper headlines generally form an interesting subject for the sociology of knowledge because, under extensive pressure to economize and attract attention, they play with the everyday understanding of the reader. In recent years, several conversation analysts have dealt with this aspect of newspapers. See, for example, the analysis of the headline "Girl Guide Aged 14 Raped at Hell's Angels Convention" by J. Lee 1984, pp. 69–73, as well as P. Elgin 1983. The critical distance of such studies from the usual sociological approaches is emphasized in D.C. Anderson and W.W. Sharrock 1979, pp. 375ff.

2. D. Lessing 1962, p. 9.

3. Such types of metacommunicative conversation are designated "formulations" by H. Garfinkel and Sacks 1970, pp. 350ff.; a specific placing and function of such "formulations" is analyzed by J.C. Heritage and D.R. Watson 1979, pp. 123–162. A good general presentation of such delimitations of units of discourse is provided by D. Schiffrin 1980, pp. 199–236.

4. See G. Ryle 1949, Chapter 2, and A. Schütz and T. Luckmann 1984, Chapter III.

5. K. Vossler 1923, p. 239.

6. In the following, C. Schmölder's 1979 excellent collection of texts on the history of the theory of conversation serves as the source.

7. Theophrastus 1953, p. 117.

8. Jesus Sirach 1979, p. 92.

9. G. della Casa 1558/1979, p. 124.

10. N.L.G. Zinzendorf 1723/1979, p.193.

11. See W. Martens 1968, pp. 344ff., 359, 377, 507, 519, and 536. Steele and Addison, who published the first number of the *Tatler* in 1709, viewed themselves as "censors of manners and morals." See for this J. Habermas 1989, pp. 42ff.

12. In the preface to a new edition of his book Knigge himself rejects a reductionist reading: "If the rules of association are not to be mere prescriptions of conventional civility or even a dangerous policy then they must be based on the theory of duties that we owe all men and that they owe us. This means that a system whose guidelines are *morality and intelligence* must be the foundation." See A. von Knigge 1788/1966, p. 6. Moreover, Knigge also warns against, "carrying news, intimate discussions, family conversations, remarks that you have made about the domestic life of the people with whom you associate from one house to another and to gossip about such things, (p. 28).

13. N. and D. Schäfer-Elmayer 1969, p. 56. See among others the following incisive warning: "Gossip! Have you already heard? Miss X and Mr. Y have separated. And she was very distraught about it! Oh, has it dawned on him yet? No, quite the contrary, he was simply snubbed. Her parents have forbidden it. But something must have caused it? Of course, and intimate things have been revealed. Don't you know? Didn't you hear? Buzz. . not to prevent this sorry flood of rumors neither she nor he had a hand in its 'justification.' Silence!" in H. Dietrich 1965, p. 272. "Gossip is not only cowardly because it is carried on behind someone's back so that its victim cannot even defend himself, but it also

sows deep enmity," in I. Wolter n.d., p. 91. A technique for stopping gossip is recommended by the following author. "Those who are absent are the favorite subjects of gossip because in this way one can criticize, gossip and spread rumors. And there is hardly any disagreement about the unlucky person. 'Have you already head . . . ,' 'And more recently. . . .' If you could only stop it! You don't have to jump up and give an impassioned speech against slander. I propose saying something like: 'But Irene, you? Yesterday I met you on the street, arm in arm with her. Besides, I thinks she's nice, it may only be a matter of taste. Who's up for a glass of Sprudel?'" in R. Harbert 1954, p. 26. The following expert recommends the avoidance of gossip altogether. "Gossip has caused the misfortune of many. [. . .] To tell someone something only after he has sworn 'a promise of silence' is impermissible even where it cannot be avoided. It makes a better impression on our partner if we forthrightly say, 'I am sorry but I can't talk about that,' than to impart something entrusted to us. People who do this are suspected of not being able to keep a secret." In R. Andreas-Friedrich 1954, p. 74.

14.   Volumes could be filled with artistic presentations of gossip scenes and gossipers in literature (from Bocaccio's *Decameron* through Jane Austen and Theodore Fontane to James Joyce), in drama (Shakespeare, Molière or in the eighteenth century salon comedies and comedies of intrigue—Beaumarchais), or in the plastic arts (Granville or Doré). Other presentations can be found in E. Fuchs 1906; K. Thiele-Dohrmann 1975, Chapter 2, provides some references.

15.   Ch. Thomasius 1710/1979, p. 184.

16.   See, for example, the article "Conversation, entretien," in D. Diderot, J.L. D'Alembert, and De Jaucourt 1801, pp. 94–96, or N. Trublet 1735/1979, pp. 194–198.

17.   See, for example, F.E.D. Schleiermacher 1799/1927, pp. 1–31.

18.   See W. von Humboldt 1827/1973, pp. 21–29, especially p. 21: "Language, however, is by no means merely a means of understanding, but the impression of spirit and the speakers' view of the world. *Sociability is the indispensable means of its unfolding.*" (My emphasis).

19.   Few remember that Moritz Lazarus and Heymann Steinthal, who founded the "Zeitschrift für Völkerpsychologie und Sprachwissenschaft" in 1859, were Georg Simmel's teachers, as W. Köhnke 1984, remarks. See also pp. 393–401 for Simmel's 1886 book review of Steinthal's *Allgemeine Ethik.*

20.   M. Lazarus 1878, pp. 233–265.

21.   *Ibid.*, pp. 237–238.

22.   R. Hirzel 1895/1963, pp. 2ff.

23.   A. Heller 1984 pp. 226ff. W. Benjamin 1931/1980, p. 397, calls gossip "the most petit-bourgeois" of all phenomena. E. Bloch begins his sociology of the declining bourgeoisie with a short piece on gossip. "Gossip trudges up and down the stairs, holds these persons together while it separates them. It is the distorted way of being discontented." See E. Bloch 1935/1962, pp. 25ff.

24.   B.F. Skinner 1948, p. 163. H. Lanz's 1936 work, pp. 492–499, whose goal is "to present the existence of the devil by means of an analysis of the phenomenon 'gossip,'" (p. 493), fits within this context too.

25.   M. Lazarus 1878, p. 242.

26.   E.B. Almirol 1981, p. 294.

27. J.A. Cutileiro 1971, p. 138.
28. Th. Gregor 1977, pp. 85ff.
29. *Duden Stilwörterbuch* 1963.
30. Viewed from the perspective of the history of science, this genre appears based upon and distinguished from its literary model in the 1930s in the research on the folklore of oral literature. P.G. Bogatyev and R. Jakobson's 1929/1972 essay, pp. 13–24, was very influential in this regard. Basically, both authors tried to distinguish oral literature or folklore from literature by using de Saussure's distinction of langue and parole. As the authors note, these efforts lead to a rehabilitation of the romantic conception of natural poetry—as in the contemporaneous 1930/1982 work by A. Jolles that shied away from abandoning the domain of written literature. On a broader front, the concept was discussed in folklore research in the 1960s. See, for example, the journal *Genre* that appeared in 1968, as well as H. Bausinger 1968/1980. (Bausinger's 1952 dissertation already concerned itself with the theme of "living narration'.) In the 1960s—inspired equally by anthropology and linguistics—D. Hymes 1964, pp. 13ff., introduced the concept of "communicative genres" into the "ethnography of communication." For a more recent presentation, see D. Ben-Amos 1976a, pp. 30–43.
31. See J. Ruesch and G. Bateson 1951, pp. 183ff.
32. M. Lazarus 1878, p. 240, already uses the history of botany as an analogy for the—for him still future—history of the science of conversation.
33. M. Weber 1904/1968, p. 53.
34. A. Schütz 1954/1973, p. 61.
35. O. Marquard 1981, pp. 117–146.
36. See A. Schütz and Th. Luckmann 1984, p. 13: "In all societies stylistic units of meaning are objectivated as communicative genres and form semantic traditions."
37. For the concept of "unproblematic problems," see P.L. Berger and Th. Luckmann 1966, p. 24.
38. To conceive communicative processes in this sense as the result of overlapping, partially contradictory ordering structures were the main point of departure for the analytic and reconstructive analyses of a research project of Thomas Luckmann and Peter Gross on the problem of the constitution of data. See the project report: J.R. Bergmann et al. 1986.
39. D. Hymes 1974, p. 443.
40. It is impossible even to approximate a reproduction of the fullness and diversification of the extant literature on individual communicative genres. See the extensive bibliography in Th. Luckmann and J.R. Bergmann 1982. An initial survey is provided by the anthology of R. Bauman and J. Scherzer 1974 and D. Ben-Amos 1976b.
41. See Th. Luckmann 1986, pp. 191–211.
42. R. Schott 1968, pp. 169ff.
43. O. Marquard 1973, p. 241.
44. See, for example, G. Albrecht 1972, pp. 242–293.
45. C. Ginzburg 1980, p. 12.
46. The concept of reconstructive genres presented here forms the guiding idea of the research project begun in 1984 entitled "Strukturen und Funktionen

von rekonstruktiven Gattungen in der alltäglichen Kommunikation" under the direction of Thomas Luckmann and J.R. Bergmann.

47.   For conversation as the dominant medium of modeling reality in Fontane, see W. Preisendanz 1984, pp. 473–487.

48.   L.N. Tolstoy 1973–76/1931 pp. 178 and 179.

49.   The problematic of the reconstructive quality of social scientific data is extensively discussed by J.R. Bergmann 1985, pp. 299–320.

50.   Th. Luckmann 1981, p. 518.

51.   The distinction of reconstructed and recorded preservation, as well as its significance for the problem of the constitution of social scientific data, is developed and clarified in J.R. Bergmann 1985, pp. 305ff.

52.   See especially the remarks on the concept of the text in H.-G. Soeffner 1982, pp. 9–48; as well as H.-G. Soeffner 1985, pp. 109–126.

53.   J.B. Haviland 1977.

54.   Whereas conversation analysis—in different ways—draws upon Schütz, ethnomethodology upon Goffman, and the ethnology and ethnography of speaking upon Wittgenstein, critical theory claims objective hermeneutics, structuralism, Piaget, and the tradition of the German Geisteswissenschaften as its own.

55.   A presentation of conversation analysis is found in J.R. Bergmann 1981a, pp. 9–51. For objective hermeneutics the most important—although already a little out of date—source text is U. Oevermann et al. 1979, pp. 352–434. Both approaches are discussed from the methodological perspective in J.R. Bergmann 1985, pp. 310–315.

56.   See K.W. Hempfer 1973, pp. 128ff.

57.   The fact that the recording of consciousness and the psychical pressure of providing a corresponding "performance" for a fee can lead to all kinds of artificialities and fatal consequences has become a truism for psychological and sociological methodology. C. Bell 1968, p. 7, reports of a woman who, on a moment's notice, invited her friend to a coffee-klatsch with the explanation that the next day a sociologist was visiting her.

58.   P.M. Spacks 1985.

59.   See G. Simmel 1908/1968c, pp. 287ff.

60.   See C. Giedion-Welcker 1966, p. 829.

61.   The ethnography of communication has concerned itself with a systematic description of the determinative elements of communicative processes. See, for example, D. Hymes 1972, pp. 35–71.

62.   Ch. H. Cooley 1909/1962.

63.   E. Goffman 1974.

64.   A. Kaplan 1964, pp. 3–11.

65.   E.O. Arewa and A. Dundes 1964, p. 70.

66.   In the more recent research conducted by the sociology of knowledge the organization of the form of introductory social scientific texts has become an important theme. See J. Gusfield 1976, pp. 16–34; J. O'Neill 1981, pp. 105–120; R. Edmonson 1984. See also footnote 26 in Chapter 1.

67.   As an example, see H. Sacks 1974, pp. 337–353.

68.   Spectacularly, U. Oevermann 1983, pp. 234–289.

69. A successful example is perhaps the analysis by E.A. Schegloff 1979, pp. 23–78, of the different types of identificatory and recognitional sequences that occur at the beginning of telephone calls.

Chapter 3

1. D. Sudnow 1967/1973, Chapter 6.
2. This interview passage was taken from R. Turner 1968, pp. 293ff. Turner analyzes this passage in regard to the question of the problems that arise for former psychiatric patients in talking or not talking about their psychiatric illnesses.
3. L. von Wiese 1924–28/1955, p. 310.
4. Quoted from S. Bok 1984, p. 94.
5. D. Handelman 1973, p. 213. See also M. Harrington 1964, p. 268, "Three women will gossip and joke about a fourth person, that fourth person will later join two of the first three in gossip about the third, and so on. When I was arranging one group meeting with Mrs. Young, in the presence of Mrs. Brown, one of them said, 'What shall we be talking about?' whereupon the other said at once with a guffaw, 'About the ones that aren't there of course.'"
6. See E. Goffman's 1963, pp. 112–123, remarks on the "institution of acquaintanceship."
7. G. Simmel 1908/1968c, pp. 264ff.
8. See the remarks on the social implications of "fame" in E. Goffman 1964, pp. 68ff.
9. For gossip about well-known people in journals, see K. Thiele-Dohrmann 1975, Chapter 7; J. Levin and A.J. Kimmel 1977, pp. 169–175; C. Lopate 1978, pp. 130–140; S.J. Zeitlin 1979, pp. 186–192; P.M. Spacks 1985, pp. 65–69; and H. Treiber 1986, pp. 140–159.
10. J. du Boulay 1974, p. 157. A similar account is provided by J.K. Campbell 1964, pp. 112ff., who, in his study of Greek shepherds of Sarakatsani, explains how the members of a family have the duty of countering village gossip about a relative, even if they themselves disapprove of the relative's behavior and *within* the family support his punishment. For a Taiwanese village, M. Wolf 1972, p. 38, remarks, "for a girl who gossips freely about the affairs of her husband's household may find herself labeled a troublemaker."
11. G. Simmel 1908/1968b, pp. 256–304.
12. *Ibid.*, p. 259.
13. Simmel's argument has been repeatedly discussed in different sociological and social-psychological theories—in a functionalist context, for example, by Robert Merton, "What is sometimes called 'the need for privacy'—that is, insulation of actions and thoughts from surveillance by others—is the individual counterpart to the functional requirement of social structure that some measure of exemption from full observability be provided for. [. . .] 'Privacy' is not merely a personal predilection; it is an important functional requirement for the effective operation of social structure." In R. Merton 1968, p. 429. In the spirit of Merton and Simmel, the interconnection of behavioral information and social

control is dealt with by H. Popitz 1968. Simmel's argument is discussed within the context of a general plan of a psychology of privacy by L. Kruse 1980, pp. 68ff.

14.   G. Simmel 1908/1986b, p. 272.

15.   As Sören Kierkegaard—using the example of the press—clearly recognized and severely criticized, this boundary-effacing effect is a characteristic of gossip. "What does it mean *to gossip*? It is the negation of the passionate either-or between talking and silence. Yet anyone who can essentially be silent is essentially abler to talk. [. . .] The less ideality and the greater externality, the more that conversation becomes an insignificant enumeration and reporting of personal names, of 'completely unreliable' private messages about what so and so said etc. [. . .] Gossip negates the distinction between the private and the public in a privately public garrulity." In S. Kierkegaard 1845/1954, pp. 104–107.

16.   This holds for conversations about another group of "family members"— for example, house pets—even more so than for conversations about little children. No one would feel that the numerous stories and conversations about the tricks and misdeeds of cats, dogs, hamsters, and other questionable family extras is "gossip."

17.   *Brockhaus' Konversations-Lexikon* 1894.

18.   For the etymology of "gossip," see A. Rysman 1977, pp. 176–180.

19.   This situation is described for a Middle Eastern village on the Turkish-Syrian border by B.C. Aswad 1967, p. 150; or for a Taiwanese village by M. Wolf 1972, pp. 144ff.

20.   A. Schütz 1946/1976, pp. 120–134.

21.   *Ibid.*, p. 122.

22.   For the concepts of "front stage" ("on stage") and "back stage" ("behind the scenes"), see E. Goffman 1959, pp. 128ff. In his study of the profane, political everyday life in the hallowed halls of science the anthropologist F.G. Bailey 1977, pp. 114ff., shows how this distinction has to be broadened insofar as it is not the "front stage" or the "back stage" but "under the stage (that) is the world where gossip and the dissemination of scandal takes place."

23.   For the connection between this market metaphor and gossip that will be addressed again later, see R.L. Rosnow 1977, pp. 158–163.

24.   For the distinction between actual and virtual social identity with respect to the effect of discrediting personal features, see E. Goffman 1964, pp. 2ff. and 65.

25.   M. Scheler 1915/1961, p. 61.

26.   C.F. Sulzberger 1953, p. 42. Other psychoanalysts—J.B. Rosenbaum and M. Subrin 1963, p. 830—view gossip as "a complex social-psychological phenomenon arising from unresolved intrafamilial and intrapsychic conflict, that is, from sibling rivalry and the oedipal relationship."

27.   See L. Tiger and R. Fox 1971, pp. 179ff.

28.   D. Breinneis 1984, p. 492.

29.   R.D. Abrahams 1970, p. 298.

30.   J. Levin and A. Arluke 1985, pp. 281–286.

31.   See W.I. Thomas 1928/1969, pp. 42ff. and 49; W.I. Thomas and

F. Znaniecki 1919/1958, p. 1060. (See W.I. Thomas's remarks on gossip in Chapter I, note 55.)

32. The literature on this has become quite extensive in the meantime. See the survey in J.R. Bergmann 1981a, pp. 30ff.; the classical presentation of the problem is found in H. Sacks 1972, pp. 325–345; a recent systematic presentation, development, and application are provided by L. Jayyusi 1984.

33. F.G. Bailey 1971a, p. 1. The observation that Bailey reports comes from Susan Hutson whose own study of the village of Valloire is contained in this anthology. The concept of bavardage is certainly—in contrast to its friendly and harmless meaning in Bailey—interpreted as a pejorative and discrediting label coined specifically for female gossip in A.-M. Waliullah 1982, pp. 93–99.

34. See, for example, similar presentations for the island of Désirade in the French Caribbean by J. Naish 1978, p. 246: "It is considered normal and acceptable for men to sit in loafing-groups and chat. If women go out and chat, they are labeled *macrelle*. . ." Or for a small American town, see A. Gallaher 1961, p. 138.

35. As sources, one can present J. Campe 1808; J. and W. Grimm 1873; A. Götze 1943; F. Kluge 1967.

36. Quoted from J. and W. Grimm 1873, p. 1011.

37. E.B. Almirol 1981, p. 294.

38. See footnote 35.

39. B. Althans 1985, p. 48, from whom I have taken the following reference, argues similarly.

40. J. Paul 1801/1975, p. 1095.

41. I will provide only a small selection: M. Weigle 1978, pp. 3ff.; V. Aebischer 1979, pp. 96–108; R. Borker 1980, pp. 31–37 (with many bibliographic references); D. Jones 1980, pp. 193–198; Ch. Benard and E. Schlaffer 1981, pp. 119–136; A.-M. Waliullah 1982; B. Althans 1985.

42. See, for example, M. Perrot 1981, p. 87: "The public washing place [. . .] is also a locale of conflict between women and state authority [. . .] When, during the Second Reich, laundries were established in order to prevent quarrels and gossip the women protested and boycotted them. They had to be removed."

43. A successful, well-documented and argued presentation of the ethnology of the battle between the sexes is provided by K.E. Müller 1984. Müller maintains that female communication, because it is outside the control of men, is denigrated by them as "gossip" (p. 318ff.). His remarks on the role that exogamy as well as the greater motility of men played in the development of two sexually specific spheres of interests and life are worth discussing. The men conquered the exo-sphere beyond the territorial boundaries of the tribe and the stories that they brought home with them "contributed to the emergence of fairytales and myths, of sagas, legends and miraculous stories of all kinds; what the women, however, told of life in the home, of children, neighbors and relatives appeared in comparison to be boring, banal and unimportant—was only "women's gossip" (p. 381).

44. E. Le Roy Ladurie 1975/1979, trans. Bray, p. 252.

45. Material and remarks on the interconnection of gossip and urban domestic servants in the eighteenth and nineteenth centuries can be found in R. Schulte 1978, pp. 902ff.; H. Müller 1981, pp. 201–205; D. Müller-Saats 1983, pp.

218ff. and 442; K. Walser 1985, p. 105; J.A. Cutileiro 1971, p. 139, refers to the fact that a servant girl could also, on the other hand, transmit to her "mistress" the gossip circulating in the village. The problem of the "betrayal of secrets" is discussed from functionalistic perspectives by L. A. Coser 1974, pp. 76ff. E. Goffman 1959, pp. 213ff. refers to the fact that the proverbial gossipy nature of servants was the background for the invention of the "dumb waiter" in the eighteenth century—a serving table, "which, prior to the dinner hour, was stocked with food, drink, and eating utensils by the servants, who then withdrew, leaving the guests to serve themselves."

46.   C. Viebig 1925, pp. 44ff.

47.   See D. Gilmore 1978, pp. 91ff., who reports the following experience: "I once tried to arrange an interview with a young man on a certain afternoon. He demurred, explaining that he would be unavailable for the entire day because he was going to have his hair cut at the neighborhood barbershop. Most of the time, of course, was to be spent in oral 'cutting' rather than tonsorial, as he sheepishly confessed under questioning. Men gossip as much as women in Fuenmayor." The fact that barbershops are viewed as gossip locations and at the same time that barbers are reputed to have effeminate behavioral features seems to be more than mere coincidence.

48.   G.C. Lichtenberg 1765–99/1983, p. 402.

49.   See for this R. Gold's 1952, p. 491, solid work.

50.   R. Frankenberg 1966, p. 67.

51.   C. Harris 1974, p. 55.

52.   R. Frankenberg, 1966, p. 67; A. Dieck 1950, p. 719; J.F. Embree 1939, p. 76.

53.   See for the proscription of gossip among doctors, lawyers, and so on U. Hannerz 1967, p. 37; a more general relationship of occupational secret-keeping and the social control of information is presented by R. Merton, 1968, p. 429. I.M.G. Schuster 1979, pp. 46ff., reports in her study of the social situation of women in modern Zambia that female students of the University of Lusaka are reluctant to go to the University Teaching Hospital to be prescribed contraceptives, "because young Zambian doctors and nurses, rather than honoring the western idea of doctor-patient privacy, gossip freely about unmarried female patients. A man who suspects his girlfriend is on the pill can easily check with doctors of his acquaintance who, as a favor, look up the girl's record and report its contents." Psychoanalysts surely do not form the only group from among these professions that sometimes has trouble with the proscription of gossip— they are merely the only ones who write about it. See, for example, S.L. Olinick 1980, pp. 439–445, as well as E.G. Caruth 1985, pp. 548–562.

54.   Unfortunately, there are not many studies of office gossip and of the gossip reputations of secretaries, probably because the sociology of organizations that is occupied with systems theory has little feeling for such empirical works. See, however, the survey article about informal channels of communication, office cliques, "grapevines," and so on by S.A. Hellweg 1987, pp. 213–230. See also N. Luhmann 1962, pp. 11–24; N. Luhmann 1964/1976, pp. 324–331; H. Grünberger 1978; H. Sutton and L.W. Porter 1968, pp. 223–230.

55.   See R.D. Abrahams, 1970, p. 297; J.K. Campbell 1964, p. 95: "A man [. . .] will not suffer in silence the public criticism of any of his kin."

56.   This observation has been reported in different ethnographies, for example, E.B. Almirol, 1981, p. 300; D. Breinneis, 1984, p. 55. M. Wolf 1972, p. 38, has observed in a Taiwanese village how the village women directed their conversations toward general themes when a young woman who had married into the village approached the washing place; this cautious and distrustful behavior of the women who initially treated her as an outsider changed only slowly.

57.   See C. Lazarus 1878, pp. 243ff.; G. Simmel 1908/1968c, p. 500.

58.   R. Frankenberg 1968, p. 79, reports that in the villages the women bring gossip home to the men, whereas the converse holds in the case of isolated farms. Here the home-bound women depend on their husbands and sons for gossip from the village and about their—often distant—neighbors. J.F. Riegelhaupt 1967, p. 125, writes: "Thus, in the agricultural patterns of the village, men work alone or in limited groups, while women during any given day are apt to congregate in large and diverse groups. Information generally flows from woman to woman and through women to their husbands." J. M. Boissevain 1972, p. 210, emphasizes the following aspects, "When her husband returns in the evening his wife fills him in on the news and comments of the day while she gives him tea. After his tea he goes out into the square or to his club. There he discusses the news and gossip about which his wife has briefed him. He discusses these with men whose own wives have briefed them on the same matters. They use the arguments they first heard from their wives. These are similar because their wives have already discussed the issues. They are left to take (sic.) the decisions, as is their right as holders of formal authority. But their wives by talking the issue out have already concluded what the decision should be, and briefed them accordingly." A similar model of the exchange of gossip-information among married couples in Sicily is provided by C. Cronin 1977, p. 79; and for the United States by O.E. Klapp 1978, p. 32. See also for this Chapter 1, footnote 54.

59.   The title of Bailey's anthology 1971a, which contains many contributions on gossip, plays upon this attractive/dangerous character of gifts. M. Mauss had already drawn attention to the double sense of the word "gift" that means "present" in English and "poison" in German. See M. Mauss 1925/1978, p. 120.

60.   See N. Luhmann 1964/1976, p. 326.

61.   "A slandered B to C. A's inimical action towards B is at the same time a personal advance towards C," remarks L. von Wiese 1924–28/1955, p. 310.

62.   See, for example, the observations on the dissemination of gossip in an African city by A.L. Epstein 1969, p. 119; in a Greek village by J.K. Campbell, 1964, p. 313, or on a Pacific island by Th. Gladwin and S.B. Sarason 1953, p. 149.

63.   J.C. Faris 1966, pp. 240ff.

64.   G.C. Lichtenberg 1765–99/1983, p. 376.

65.   See E. Goffman 1959, pp. 212ff.

66.   The better known social-psychological investigations of rumors only marginally touch on gossip. Whereas G.W. Allport and L. Postman 1965, p. 182, do not know what to do with gossip and resort to quite implausible statements and superficial examples, T. Shibutani 1966, pp. 41ff., provides a successful brief presentation. In both works gossip is treated as an uninteresting subclass of

rumor. The recent work by G.A. Fine 1985, pp. 223–237, in which—despite the framework of the analysis of discourse—gossip and rumor are simply interchanged, is disappointing.

67.   According to Horst Krüger in his 1967 work, p. 34.

68.   See M. Gluckmann 1963, p. 313.

69.   The concept of the "gossip cell" goes back to J. West 1945, p. 99.

70.   E. Bott 1957/1971, p. 67.

Chapter 4

1.   I refer here and in the following to W. Schivelbusch 1980, pp. 59–80 ("From the coffee house to the coffee circle".)

2.   See K.W. Back and D. Polisar 1983, p. 280.

3.   See for this G.S. Felton 1966, p. 446. The German term *Kaffeeklatsch* is also used in English. See, for example, M.R. Stein 1960/1972, p. 205. It is not entirely clear whether the specifically German "coffee-ideology," whose genesis is developed by Schivelbusch, plays a role here or whether this is simply a term that is facile in English because of its alliteration.

4.   J. West 1945, pp. 99ff., calls such groups "loafing groups" and writes, "while not rigidly organized, involves a central nucleus of membership, some communion of interest, and frequently an informal meeting place. The most visible loafing group in Plainville is that of the old men who 'put in their time' at loafing. They are called the 'Old Men,' the 'Club,' the 'Story Tellers,' the 'real loafers here,' or sometimes the 'Spit and Whittle (or Argue) Club.' [. . .] The club 'sits' throughout most of the long summer on two iron benches under a shade tree in one corner of the square. [. . .] The iron benches control a view of the street and everyone who enters it from any direction. The Old Men daily gather up all the threads of current events and gossip." The behavior of similar groups of "loitering" youths in Wales is described and interpreted by E.L. Peters in M. Gluckman 1972, pp. 109–130.

5.   W.H. Whyte 1956, p. 356.

6.   Bars, of course, can themselves acquire the reputation of being nests of gossip, especially when they are used by visitors and guests as "hangouts." See the case study of such an urban bar used by "bohemian-types" in P.A. Nathe 1976, pp. 86ff.

7.   The most interesting works on parties are still those that came out of the "sociability-project" that was conducted in the 1950s by David Riesman. For the design and—prototypically—changing course of this project, see D. Riesman and J. Watson 1964, pp. 235–321. In this project gossip as party behavior played only a subordinate role, among other reasons because the project conductors had observed that gossip was viewed by the hosts as behavior that endangered the party's "success" and therefore was blocked by them through different measures. See also D. Riesman, R.J. Potter, and J. Watson 1965, pp. 189 and 196, on gossip and "coffee-klatsch."

8.   The fact that a sauna is a place where gossip often occurs was told to me by many different informers.

9. Here I rely on my own observations of a weekly card game whose participants—although they must remain anonymous for obvious reasons—I would like to thank sincerely.

10. See E. Goffman 1963, p. 50.

11. These peripheral activities, which in everyday life often claim an enormous amount of our time, have, for a long time, remained a peripheral theme within sociology itself. See, for example, M. Wenglinsky 1973, pp. 83–100, who develops a—overflowing, to be sure—sociological conception of this marginal phenomenon; also L. Clausen 1981, pp. 307–322, who begins with observations of "ordinary" waiting lines and then goes on to speculations about sensationally long lines as "Super-signs of very long-term social processes."

12. On "self-engagement" in interaction, see E. Goffman 1963, pp. 69ff.

13. A personal communication from Ska Wiltschek.

14. G. Lomer 1913, p. 174, already mentions "office gossip" and views it as, "a kind of social revenge [. . .] for the many kinds of insufferabilities and discouragements that office life brings with it."

15. See, for example, the following segment of a conversation that will be presented and analyzed later in the text in detail. The section begins where G, after hearing many stories, asks where such conversations take place:

["*High-Life*": GR: 46/simplified version]

G: Where are people talking about it?

R: Everywhere, all the time, when—. Suppose you go shopping when a— When I go shopping I notice two women standing by the door, so I say "Hello." Then it starts: "Have you heard?" Bzz, bzz, bzz— then you (   ). Yeah, and when I hear that, then I start to get interested in everything. Then I ask "when?" "how?" and so on.

It is interesting that this information is presented in a largely typical coffee-klatsch conversation.

16. J. Boissevain 1972, p. 210.

17. D.F. Roy's classical 1960 case study, pp. 158–168, has in the meantime turned this expression almost into a symbol of informal interaction-based work breaks.

18. The early works of Harvey Sacks and Emanuel Schegloff on the social organization of the opening and concluding phases of conversations, where different interactive processes overlap in the narrowest of contexts, were crucially important for conversation analysis. See E.A. Schegloff 1968, pp. 1075–1095, as well as E.A. Schegloff and H. Sacks 1973, pp. 289–327. For the special interactive structure and significance of the opening phase of conversations within the specific context of action, see J.R. Bergmann 1980.

19. Many sessions analyzing data on gossip with Angela Keppler within the context of the DFG Project "Reconstructive Genres" (cf. Chapter 2, footnote 46) were very helpful to me. See also Angela Keppler's parallel investigation 1987.

20. A systematic presentation of the concept of the "presequence" that was developed by Harvey Sacks in the 1960s is found in S.C. Levinson 1983, pp. 345ff. Levinson shows how, with the help of this concept, the problem of indirect speech acts ("Is there any coffee?") that besets the theory of speech acts can

be solved in an elegant way. A brief discussion of many conversation analysis studies of different types of presequences is contained in W.A. Beach and D.G. Dunning 1982, pp. 170–185.

21. Clarifications of the modes of transcription and individual transcription symbols can be found in the frontmatter. The symbol "*High-Life*: GR:" indicates a gossip-conversation of several hours that was recorded and transcribed by Gerhard Riemann. Riemann himself had investigated parts of this conversation in his 1977 master's thesis in regard to models of action and value orientation as well as to the social typing of homeless people—that is, from the perspective of the analysis of content.

22. H. Sacks and E. Schegloff in Psathas 1979, pp. 15–21, show that personal reference in conversations is determined by two preferences: the preference of minimalization (that is, a single reference form should be used whenever possible) and the preference of "recipient design," that is, of tailoring expression specifically to the recipient (that is, a recognitional form should be used whenever possible). Both preferences are ideally fulfilled when a person is referred to by his first or family name. Both preferences, furthermore, refer to the central significance of presuppositions of social interaction that are the theme of E. Goffman's 1983 posthumous work, pp. 1–53.

23. This conversation segment—as well as others that are symbolized "AK"—come from a body of material that Angela Keppler collected during the DFG-Project "Reconstructive Genres" and that she kindly let me use.

24. For the social organization of related sequences, see G. Jefferson 1972, pp. 294–338, as well as E. Schegloff 1972, pp. 76ff., who speak of "inserted sequences." The structure of such related sequences, which focus specifically on the problem of the creation of reference, was investigated by J.C.P. Auer 1980. S.M. Yerkovich 1976, pp. 34ff., refers to the fact that gossip-sequences can also be introduced by "Do-you-know-X" questions, in which case acquaintanceship with the person introduced in this way has to be clarified initially in the form of a related sequence. In this case, however, mutual acquaintanceship of the gossipers is usually rather slight, with the result that the following conversation possesses the character of a mere exchange of information rather than gossip (a consequence Yerkovich completely overlooks in her work).

25. E.B. Almirol 1981, p. 300.

26. E.C. Cuff and D.W. Francis 1978, pp. 111–133, speak of "invited and non-invited stories."

27. See A. Pomerantz 1980, pp. 186–198.

28. The "fishing" character and the problematic implications of psychiatric utterances such as, "I have heard that things are not well with you" and "You have obviously become withdrawn lately" is investigated in detail by J.R. Bergmann in press.

29. A very similar effect is attained when a question is repeated in paraphrase by the asker before it is answered. See J.R. Bergmann 1981b, pp. 128–142.

30. The numbering of the segments [4/1] mean that the segment [4] continues segment [1]. In this way longer passages can be followed throughout the text.

31.   See the beginning of Doris Lessing's 1962 novel, p. 25, cited in Chapter 2 where a woman asks her friend, "Well, what's the gossip?"

32.   In the present case the contradiction announced by E is indicated by repetition with intonation of the question; hesitant pause; weakened disagreement; lower second evaluation. Such elements, that is, those that are preliminary to disagreements ("pre-disagreement"), are systematically investigated by A. Pomerantz 1984, pp. 57–101.

33.   This can also be formulated so that a speaker initially produces a kind of riddle that forces the recipient who cannot solve it to inquire how it is that the speaker comes to disseminate his information not of his own but at the request of the recipient. Of course, interaction sequences initiated by "riddles" can also be found outside of gossip. See J.N. Schenkein 1978, pp. 69ff.

34.   Such announcements of news are investigated by A.K. Terasaki 1976 in terms of the analysis of sequences.

35.   The same sequential format also characterizes the preliminary phase of "non-invited stories" in which initially the announcement of subsequent storytellers ("I am no longer afraid") provokes the recipient's inquiry that indicates his willingness to gossip ("what?") before the real story begins. See for this H. Sacks 1971, pp. 307–314.

36.   Basically, the intonative-paralinguistic and mimic-gestural forms of expression play an essential role in the maneuver of indirect invitation described here and in concealed proposals, because they do not restrict the speaker to the same extent as verbal expression and they also make it possible for him to give his formulations nuances, comments, and even to annul them.

37.   For the theme of "sequence expansion," see G. Jefferson and J. Schenkein 1977, pp. 87–103. The fact that the transition from the give-and-take order of succession in conversations to the actual telling of the story can occur economically as well as elaborately is demonstrated by G. Jefferson 1978, pp. 224ff.

38.   See for this E. Goffman 1974, p. 508: "The element of suspense is sufficiently important that often speakers make a special effort to establish the prospective hearer in this set. Thus the very common use of ritualistic hedges ('tickets,' as Harvey Sacks calls them), as when a speaker-to-be or a speaker-to-continue uses passing words or gestures to establish the listener's permission to go ahead: 'Do you know what I think?' 'Do you know what happened?' 'Listen to me,' 'Did you hear what happened to Mary Jane?' and so forth."

39.   See, for example, W. Labow and J. Waletzky 1967, pp. 78–126; or K. Ehlich 1980, with different works on storytelling at trials, in clinics, during psychoanalytic interviews, in the classroom etc., works that often run the risk of hypostasizing the story model because they only follow its successful or unsuccessful activation in different, externally defined contexts of action.

40.   See H. Garfinkel 1967, p. 33. "The policy is recommended that any social setting be viewed as self-organizing with respect to the intelligible character of its own appearances as either representations of or as evidences-of-a-social-order. Any setting organizes its activities to make its properties as an organized environment of practical activities detectable, countable, recordable, reportable, tell-a-story-aboutable, analyzable—in short, *accountable*." For Garfinkel's concept of "account," see J.R. Bergmann 1981a, pp. 9ff.

41. The sociological literature on "lying" is—qualitatively as well as quantitatively—meager. See, however, on lying as a superstructure for concealment W. Stok 1929, pp. 16ff, with some—not very helpful—differentiations ("covering lies," "purposeful lies").

42. Different types of such preventive denial are described by J.P. Hewitt and R. Stokes 1975, pp. 1–11, as well as by Ch. Baker, "This is just a first approximation, but . . ." in 1975, pp. 37–47.

43. H. Sacks 1974, pp. 340ff., refers to the special organizational effect of such preliminary phases in conversations that resides in the speaker's having the right to speak more than once and therefore being able to tell his story/report, his news, without running the risk of losing his right to speak to another speaker before the end of his story.

44. See the journal *Maledicta* (ed. Reinhold Aman) that concerns itself with graffiti, scatological words, culturally specific forms of obscenity, erotic vocabularies, and other practices of malediction. Of course, many of the contributions in this journal end up in psychoanalytic interpretations. See, however, the successful linguistic and social scientific investigation of different phenomena of malediction by R.M. Adams 1977.

45. R.I. Levy 1973, p. 340.

46. G. Simmel 1908/1968c, p. 487.

47. In a study of the sociology of communities Leo Kuper 1953, pp. 14ff. describes the consequences that result when apartments are visually, but not acoustically separated by thin, "non-soundproof" (!) walls. "Residents are aware of many 'vicinal' noises, extending from the unusual clamour of birthday celebrations to the sound of the daily routine. [. . .] In the connubial bedroom, the intimations from the neighbor may be shocking: 'You can even hear them use the pot; that's how bad it is. It's terrible'; or disturbing: 'I heard them having a row in bed. One wanted to read, and the other wanted to go to sleep. It's embarrassing to hear the noises in bed, so I turned my bed the other way round'." As Kuper (p. 45), later remarks, the information about neighbors that is obtained in this way is often turned into gossip. He quotes the following statement of a resident, "We've often had things repeated to us in the street or even down at the shops, that she, (the party neighbor) has heard us say to each other.'"

48. On children as intermediaries of gossip-information, see especially J.C. Hotchkiss 1967, pp. 715ff., who refers to the fact that children easily become double agents. They bring home information about third parties that is interesting to their parents, but, on the other hand, often are questioned by outsiders about family matters. On the theme of gossip and children, see also G.A. Fine 1977, pp. 181–185; G. Mettetal 1978, pp. 730ff., who in comparing three age groups of children (6–7, 11–12 and 16–17) found a lack of interest in gossip among the younger and a dramatic rise in gossip among the second age group. A close relationship with gossip also exists for another genre of "moral communication" that is widespread among children, namely, telling on others. In contrast to gossip, telling on others lacks the character of an end in itself (or at least the appearance of such). Because the person who tells on another generally repeats the information to a superior, he or she leaves the relational network that binds the children together.

49. For V.N. Vološinov the so-called "reported speech" that is the subject of the following is methodologically speaking a "pivotal phenomenon" that for a long time has been viewed as marginal but is of enormous interest to the sociologically directed scientific interest in language. For a literary treatment of the phenomenon of reported speech, see M. Sternberg 1982, pp. 107–156.

50. S. Harding 1975, p. 298.

51. D. Breinneis 1984, p. 494.

52. V.N. Vološinov 1929/1973, Part 3. Vološinov is perhaps not, as S.M. Weber believes, a colleague, but the pseudonym of Mikhail Bakhtin.

53. Vološinov, 1929/1973, p. 128.

54. See E. Goffman 1974, pp. 529ff. ("cited figures"); E. Goffman 1981, pp. 124–159.

55. E. Goffman 1981, pp. 144ff.

56. "In quoting another's use of curse words and other taboo utterances some license is provided beyond what the speaker can employ on his own behalf, but where does this license stop?" asks E. Goffman 1974, p. 539, but does not give an answer. The neutralizing effect of the quotational format is surely not unlimited. Nor can its extent be determined generally, but only in regard to situational circumstances.

57. See J. Streeck 1988, pp. 10ff.

58. See, for example, W. Labov 1972, pp. 120–169, as an example of the numerous studies that since the 1930s have concerned themselves with those (male) insult rituals, such as "playing the dozens," "sounding" and "signifying," and for which the competitive use of obscene expressions and abusive formulations is of constitutive significance.

59. Such a sequence always occurs when *one* speaking turn is shared by at least *two* speakers as a kind of division of labor; for example,

> A: If he squints his eyes in that way;
> B: then you have to be careful.

60. See R. von Jhering 1877/1905, p. 364. Even if von Jhering remained steadfastly bound to the idea of an "end" in law and if the jurist's analytical urge to systematize ultimately undid him, the consequence of his procedure remains impressive. His remarks on fashion, enjoyment, different customs, theory of acquaintanceship relations, manners, dress, the phenomenology and syntax of civility, tact, and other subjects are still not be found in a culturally oriented sociology of interaction.

61. See the analysis of such a lie believed to be "true" but immediately discovered in J.R. Bergmann in press.

62. See Ch. von Reichenau 1936, pp. 202–217.

63. The relation between gossip and the novel, to which many literary theorists have referred, may have its origins here. See for the empirically based critique of the false opposition of everyday talk and literary fiction W.-D. Stempel 1983, pp. 331–356. M. McCarthy 1962, pp. 264ff., writes more specifically about this relation: "Even when it is most serious, the novel's characteristic tone is one of gossip and tittletattle. [. . .] But the voice we overhear in their [Tolstoy's, Flaubert's, Proust's, Jane Austen's] narratives, putting aside preconceptions, is

the voice of a neighbor relating the latest gossip." Gossip can, as C. Rotzoll 1982, remarks, "grow into wisdom—and world literature. Two provincial women were unfaithful to their husbands. Both incidents became known and circulated as gossip. What a blessing! Without the grapevine of an earlier century we would never have met Effi Briest nor Emma Bovary." Gossip, like literature, creates a world of its own, according to M. Peckham 1972, pp. 86ff., and in gossip as in literature there is a differentiation of the roles of "entertainers" and the "public," according to D.W. Harding 1937, pp. 257ff. To be sure, in gossip's case the real speaker remains concealed. Gossip is anonymous, and yet everyone initiates it. "Gossip establishes an authority without an author," writes H.O. Brown 1977, p. 579. See also for this theme E.W.B. Hess-Lüttich 1984, pp. 91–96, where different gossip elements in Sheridan's "The School for Scandal" are described.

64.   See H. Wunderlich 1894, p. 41.

65.   Although agreements in conversation can transpire most of the time without the need for justification, denials, disagreements, and refusals generally require a justification and therefore expand the sequence—which also holds for scientific dialogues.

66.   In his "Kurze Apologie des Klatsches," 1963, p. 328, A. Mitscherlich says that in gossip, "the vocabulary of vulgarity [. . .] [is] adapted for handy prejudices: ambition, insidiousness, cowardice etc. become judgments about the person as a whole who thus becomes a target."

67.   See for this J. Katz 1975, pp. 1369–1390. More recently, it has also become clear that gossip involves a legal problem: insofar as "honor" is validly secured in law a bit of gossip can under circumstances very easily fulfill the conditions of slander, calumny, or abuse. The legal system has had problems with these kinds of utterances. Thereby, the main question has been whether one may say things about the private and intimate lives of others that jeopardize their honor but for which he can supply proof, or whether the protection of honor—in the interest of the potential victim—should be extended to such an extent that someone would commit an indiscretion even if he proved that his statements were true. See for this problem the classical, psychologically based work of E. Kern 1919. For the history of libel, see K. Thiel 1905. E.W. Roth 1927, p. 49, pleads for punishment only of public and not private indiscretion with the argument that, "One cannot prohibit private discussions about the private affairs of one's neighbor without robbing three quarters of humanity of three quarters of what it talks about." H.J. Hirsch 1967, p. 35, argues against the introduction of indiscretions by saying, "that talk—assuming it is true—fulfills an important social function. It presents one of the strongest guarantees for the establishment of social order and the morality of society, so that by allowing it we have a value-constituting and preserving factor of the highest order." See for the narrow problem of insults (in the form of viciousness) that "cannot be managed with a simple dogmatic recipe," K. Engisch 1957, pp. 326–337.

68.   This point is well developed in a study of a Turkish village by W. Schiffauer 1985, p. 289. Schiffauer believes that the exposing tendency of gossip presents a kind of counterweight to "impression management."

69.   This point clearly shows that gossip ideally fulfills the "conditions for successful ceremonies of degradation" analyzed by Harold Garfinkel 1956, pp.

77–83. For the interconnection of ceremonies of degradation, accusations of witchcraft, public trial, and gossip, see the study of the Pedi in the South African Megwang district by B. Sansom 1972, pp. 197ff. and 216ff.

70. See for this U. Wesel 1985, p. 321: "In small communities a consensus against a person forms rapidly, not, however, against his individual offenses but against the person as a whole. For more important than his individual deeds is the question of the kind of threat he poses for the future." Generally, says Wesel, local law is characterized by its unifying of the person and his action, while national law separates the two, that is, does not direct sanctions for an offense against the whole person. See for this E. Colson 1975, pp. 51ff.

71. See S. Ranulf 1938, p. 1, "Moral indignation (which is the emotion behind the disinterested tendency to inflict punishment) is a kind of disguised envy."

72. R.K. Merton 1968, p. 416.

73. J. Berger 1979, p. 8.

74. Insofar as information makes its way back to the subject of gossip the latter can make the gossip producer explain himself—a practice that is rare among adults, but not among children. See for this the studies by M.H. Goodwin 1980, pp. 674–695, as well as 1982, pp. 799–819.

75. See V. Vedel's 1901, p. 294, attempt to explain the tendency to moral rigor in medieval cities: "City-gossip also contains a social element of sympathy. It is true that this often belongs to very primitive kinds that have been called 'grudging sympathy.' The malicious pleasure in another's suffering and the jealous displeasure over his good fortune are, however, cultural advances vis-à-vis the dispassionate self-love that is totally indifferent to the suffering and joy of others." Quoted from Ranulph 1938, p. 47.

76. A.L. Epstein 1969, pp. 117–127.

77. Gossip is characterized as a "rudimentary hermeneutic act" by T.G. Pavel 1978, p. 147. The argument that gossip is basically an institution for the interpretation and application of social rules has been comprehensively developed—without specific reference to hermeneutics—in connection with Wittgenstein, Winch, Rawls, Garfinkel and others by J.B. Haviland 1977, Chapter 8 ("Rules of Gossip"), as well as by J. Sabini and M. Silver 1982, pp. 100ff.

78. G. Simmel 1908/1968c, pp. 371ff.

79. See for this Vološinov's 1929/1973 critique p. 85, of the linguistic dualism of internal and external: "It is not experience that organizes expression, but the other way around—*expression organizes experience*. Expression is what first gives experience its form and specificity of direction."

80. J.W. von Goethe 1989, pp. 25–26.

81. M. Lazarus 1878, pp. 251ff.

82. The phenomenon of "second stories" was first taken up by Harvey Sacks and—following his suggestions—empirically investigated by A.L. Ryave 1978, pp. 113–132. M. Moerman 1973, pp. 193–218, develops the argument that the juridical model of precedence cases can already be found in the structure of the sequence of stories in everyday conversations—an argument that directly refers to the function of such reconstructions for social typing in gossip.

83. F. Mauthner 1906/1982, p. 149.

84.   See as an example M.W. Hodges and /C.S. Smith 1954, pp. 112ff.

85.   See D. Gilmore 1978, p. 91. See also the remarks on gossip in the eth-
nographical monograph on the same rural community by D. Gilmore 1980, pp.
173 and 196ff.

Chapter 5

1.   E. Goffman 1983b, pp. 16ff. Because of advanced illness Goffman could
not present this inaugural address—which he reflected in a way typical of him,
"What I offer the reader is vicarious participation in something that did not itself
take place. A podium performance, but only readers in the seats." (p. 1).

2.   See J. Matthes 1983, p. 22.

3.   See C. Geertz 1980, pp. 165–179.

4.   E.A. Ross 1901/1929, pp. 89ff. See also J.S. Roucek 1947/1956, pp. 312ff.,
as well as G. Gurvitch 1945, pp. 278ff.

5.   F.E. Lumley 1925, pp. 211–236.

6.   As, for example, in P.L. Berger 1963, pp. 71ff., or A.M. Rose 1956/1965,
pp. 114ff.

7.   W.F. Ogburn and M.F. Nimkoff 1950, p. 115. References to the functional
loss of informal means of social control are already found in R.E. Park 1915, pp.
597ff. See, however, the observations of M.P. Baumgartner 1984, pp. 79–103,
who establishes a clear preference for informal, nonconformative modes of solv-
ing conflicts and reactions to rule offenses among the middle class in American
suburbia.

8.   It was above all Max Gluckman's 1963 essay, pp. 307–316, that made
gossip a theme of legal ethnology. For the literature, see the presentation and
discussion in S.E. Merry pp. 271–302. For an example from the sociology of law,
see P. Lewis 1976, pp. 276ff.

9.   See, for example, the successful presentation by U. Wesel 1985.

10.   B. Malinowski 1926, pp. 77–79.

11.   This definition is provided by F.H. Tenbruck 1962, col. 226.

12.   See E. Durkheim 1893/1964, pp. 85–110. The following remark is directly
relevant: "Crime brings together upright consciences and concentrates them. We
have only to notice what happens, particularly in a small town, when some
moral scandal has just been committed. They stop each other on the street, they
visit each other, they seek to come together to talk of the event and to wax
indignant in common. From all the similar impressions that are exchanged, from
all the temper that gets itself expressed, there emerges a unique temper, more or
less determinate according to the circumstances, which is everybody's without
being anybody's in particular. That is public temper." (p. 102).

13.   See for the sequence of escalating measures against the "deviator" F.G.
Bailey 1971c, pp. 286–290; a good example of the sequence gossip-indication-
direct confrontation is found in J.L. Briggs 1970, p. 222; for the close relation
between gossip and "teasing," see W. Lancaster 1974, p. 627; on the clever
technique of not addressing an utterance directly to the deviator but articulating
it so that it can be heard by him or her, see C.M. Kernan 1971, pp. 96–102, as well
as R.D. Abrahams 1974, pp. 259–261, about the techniques of "put-ons."

14.   See especially the work by E.L. Peters 1972, pp. 109–162, that shows how, in a small English town, information about deviators is fed to a group of youths through gossip and these then—with the approval of the community— are victimized by the group. S.E. Merry 1981, pp. 186ff., using the example of an ethnically mixed apartment building in a large American city, shows that gossip cannot function as a means of social control there because moral judgments are ignored by the person outside his or her own narrow social network and there are no informal groups to enforce sanctions. See for an entirely different cultural context, P. Riviere 1970, p. 249, "Gossip always precedes open accusations."

15.   For mockery, see G. Phillips 1860, pp. 26–92, as well as K. Meuli 1953, pp. 231–243.

16.   See A. Arno 1980, pp. 343–360; H.A. Selby 1974, p. 124, establishes that gossip plays an important role in the process of labeling of witches. "How then does a person finally come to be labeled a witch? Quite simply, through the social process of gossip." T.V. Smith 1937, pp. 24–34, considers custom, gossip, and law as three stages of social control and writes that, "Gossip covers the whole territory lying between what is taken for granted and the domain of law."

17.   See for this G. Lutz 1954.

18.   M. Wolf 1972, p. 40. W.I. Thomas 1928/1969, pp. 44ff., reports very similar formulations about Polish immigrants. The references in the literature to anxiety's capacity to steer behavior are so numerous that only a small selection can be given: D. Gilmore 1978, p. 94, reports that, "many young couples base their family planning decisions upon 'what people will say' rather than upon personal inclination." For similar observations in an Austrian village, see M.A. Heppenstall 1971, pp. 139–166. H. Lewis 1955, p. 193, refers to the fact that only those who have a reputation to lose are afraid of gossip. E.M. Albert 1972, pp. 87ff., reports about the Burundi's great fear of calumny. W.I. Thomas and F. Znaniecki 1919/1958, p. 1060, connect the fear of gossip with the fear of magic and primitive belief in the effect of words and curses in reality.

19.   See R. Benedict 1946, p. 223: "True shame cultures rely on external sanctions for good behavior, not, as true guilt cultures do, on an internalized conviction of sin. Shame is a reaction to other people's criticism. [. . .] But it requires an audience or at least a man's fantasy of an audience. Guilt does not. In a nation where honor means living up to one's own picture of oneself, a man may suffer from guilt though no man knows of his misdeed." For this distinction in connection with gossip, see, R.I. Levy 1973, pp. 326 and 340; S.H. Brandes 1973, p. 756. For "face" and "loss of face," see D.Y. Ho 1976, pp. 867–884.

20.   The case reports in E. Kretschmer 1950 contain continual complaints of paranoiacs about being gossiped about by others; similar positions are found in the case descriptions in K. Conrad 1966. G. Lomer 1913, p. 175, provides an early reference: "it almost seems as if certain psychoses are completely dominated by the element of (imagined) gossip. I have in mind the paranoiac's notions of persecution." R. Barthes 1977 also plays on the interconnection of gossip and paranoia. Of general relevance for the theme is E. Lemert 1967, pp. 33–60, who provides a structural description of the situation of outsiders—whether these are paranoiacs or victims of gossip.

21.   M. Gluckman 1963. Gluckman refers especially to the brief remarks on

gossip by M.J. Herskovits and F.S. Herskovits 1976, p. 185 and passim, and J. West 1945, pp. 99–107. Gluckman does not consider sociological works on gossip, by, for example, A. Blumenthal or F.E. Lumley.

22.   A presentation of Gluckman's argument is found, for example, in U. Hannerz 1980, pp. 186ff.

23.   See for this the similar remarks on gossip by L. von Wiese 1928, pp. 32 and 74ff.; by J.B. Loudon 1961, p. 347, or by W.M. Williams 1956, p. 143.

24.   This argument is, following Durkheim, developed by S.C. Heilman 1976, pp. 158–160, as well as by J.K. Campbell 1964, p. 314.

25.   Gossip is interpreted as concealed aggression by D.F. Aberle 1967, pp. 135ff.; by R.B. Stirling 1956, pp. 262–267; J. Dollard et al. 1950, p. 186, report about the Ashanti that they view gossip as a serious breach of etiquette, but that every year there are ceremonies in which everyone can safely express their anger to another's face—even to the king.

26.   See for gossip in connection with local and political group conflicts C.A. Dawson and W.E. Gettys 1929, pp.317ff., as well as B.A. Cox 1970, pp. 88–98.

27.   See for this N. Elias and J.L. Scotson 1965, p. 100: "To ascribe gossip an integrating function may easily suggest that gossip is the cause of which integration is the effect. One would probably be nearer the mark if one would say that the better integrated group is likely to gossip more freely than the less well-integrated group and that in the former case the gossiping of people reinforces the already existing cohesion." Similar also is E. Colson 1975, pp. 45–59.

28.   Gluckman himself refers to Colson's 1953a distinction, pp. 228 and passim. A lucid criticism of Colson's study can be found in P.J. Wilson 1974, pp. 93–102. Examples of investigations of gossip in groups with a high measure of exclusivity are F.G. Bailey 1977, pp. 114–120, 124ff., 203ff., with respect to gossip in the university and university groups; R.E.S. Tanner 1964, pp. 319–327; D. Koster 1977, pp. 144–165, on gossip in a restricted colonial situation (of a heterogeneous settlement group in northern Canada); S.C. Heilman 1976, pp. 151–192, on gossip in a Jewish community in North America; J.A. Henry 1963, pp. 149–159, on gossip among American teenagers.

29.   For Gluckman's central position, see R.P. Werbner 1984, pp. 157–185. Furthermore, it is astounding why Gluckman, in his essay on gossip, argues so consistently in a functionalist way, whereas in most of his other works, especially in those concerned with the sociology of law, he argues differently.

30.   For the network approach in general, see M. Schenk 1983, pp. 88–104, as well as B. Streck 1985, pp. 569–586, who develops a precise difference between the functional and the transactional approaches; and J.C. Mitchell 1973, pp. 15–35. Examples of works that emerged within Gluckman's orbit and concerned themselves with gossip, among other things, are, for example, E. Bott 1957/1971, pp. 67, 75–76, and passim; or A.L. Epstein 1961, pp. 45 and 58ff., and A.L. Epstein 1969, pp. 117–127. See also the extensive critique of Gluckman and functionalism in the classic network study by J.M. Boissevain 1974, pp. 9–23, especially pp. 21ff.

31.   See R. Paine 1967, pp. 278–285; Gluckman's reply is found in M. Gluckman 1968, pp. 20–34; a brief answer is formulated in R. Paine 1968, pp. 305–308.

32.   This concept is developed within a broader context in R. Paine 1970, pp.

172–188. Relevant here are also the remarks of J.M. Roberts 1964, p. 441, about gossip as a method of "informational storage and retrieval."

33.   R. Paine 1967, p. 283.

34.   See, for example, the works by B.A. Cox 1970; U. Hannerz 1967, pp. 35–60; J. Szwed 1966, pp. 434–441; G. McFarlane 1977, pp. 95–118; D. Handelmann 1973, pp. 210–227; see also the remarks on the function of gossip in courting by T. Tentori 1976, p. 279; the conception of gossip as a "running commentary" in F.O. Gearing 1970, pp. 102 and 114, and in S. Silverman 1975, p. 38.

35.   See, for example, the observations of U. Wikan 1980, pp. 57ff. and 130ff., about the significance of gossip as a means of increasing one's own moral status by interpreting and criticizing the behavior of others; as well as the remarks of Ch. C. Hughes et al. 1960, p. 302, about gossip as a technique of social distinction. Psychologists, in particular, support the position that gossip is used as a means of acquiring information in an indirect and safe way that is indispensable for the formation of opinion and identity. See for this G.A. Fine and R.L. Rosnow 1978, pp. 162ff., as well as J.M. Suls 1977, pp. 164–168, and Ph. Brickman and R.J. Bulman 1976, pp. 149–186. These psychological interpretations that attribute to gossip a comparative function likely refer to G.H. Mead 1934, p. 205ff.: "But there is a demand, a constant demand, to realize one's self in some sort of superiority over those about us. [. . .] There is a certain enjoyableness about the misfortunes of other people, especially those gathered about their personality. It finds its expression in what we term gossip, even mischievous gossip. We have to be on our guard against it. We may relate an event with real sorrow, and yet there is a certain satisfaction in something that has happened to somebody else but has not happened to us."

36.   G. Simmel 1908/1968b, p. 267.

37.   F.W. Nietzsche 1878/1968, p. 182.

38.   G. Simmel 1908/1968b, pp. 274ff.

39.   *Ibid.*, p. 275.

40.   In general, see R.B. Stirling 1956, pp. 262–267; as well as the psycho-analytic interpretations (gossip as a prelude) by S.L. Olinick 1980, pp. 439–445; also the attempts to relate gossip to phenomena such as isolation, feelings of self-worth, ambition, voyeurism, and empathy by G. Medini and E.H. Rosenberg 1976, pp. 452–462; or the (negatively proceeding) attempt to relate the willingness to gossip with introversion/extroversion by F.B. Davis and P.J. Rulon 1935/36, pp. 17–21.

41.   For the concept of "face-threatening acts" and its structural significance, see P. Brown and S. Levinson 1978, pp. 56–310, as well as W.-D. Stempel 1984, pp. 160ff. For "preference for agreement" in everyday conversation, see A. Pomerantz 1984, pp. 57–101.

42.   On "cross-cutting loyalties" and their consequences for the regulation of conflicts, see E. Colson 1953b, pp. 199–212. An argument similar to the one presented here is found in A. Blumenthal 1932. Blumenthal's argument is discussed in O.E. Klapp 1978, pp. 32ff.

43.   Similarly O. Kühne 1958, p. 578, who—still entirely within the tradition of L. von Wiese—writes, "*Gossiping* presents a social process of selection similar to indiscreet behavior. In it a—mostly concealed—unfriendly attitude of dis-

tance (thus with a negative selective character) is assumed vis-à-vis the subject of gossip which at the same time, is supposed to produce a friendly advance towards those who receive the gossip. The gossiper thereby can, of course, assume a cloak of 'discretion,' but the basic indiscreet behavior, however, remains unaffected by it."

44.   Thus gossip forms, as B. Malinowski 1923/1946, pp. 314ff., already established, the nucleus of what he calls "phatic communion."

45.   See, for example, E. Wolf 1984, pp. 131–132, or S.G. Schönfeldt 1983, p. 64.

References

Aberle, D.F. 1967. "The Psychosocial Analysis of a Hopi Life-History." Pp. 79–138 in R. Hunt. (ed.) *Personalities and Cultures: Readings in Psychological Anthropology*. Garden City, N.Y.: Natural History Press.

Abrahams, R.D. 1970. "A Performance-Centered Approach to Gossip." *Man* 5:290–301.

———. 1974. "Black Talk on the Streets." Pp. 240–262 in R. Bauman and J. Scherzer (eds.). *Explorations in the Ethnography of Speaking*. London: Cambridge University Press.

Adams, R.M. 1977. *Bad Mouth: Fugitive Papers on the Dark Side*. Berkeley: University of California Press.

Aebischer, V. 1979. "Chit-Chat: Women in Interaction." *Osnabrücker Beiträge zur Sprachtheorie* 9:96–108.

Albert, E.M. 1972. "Cultural Patterning of Speech Behavior in Burundi." Pp. 72–105 in J.J. Gumperz and D. Hymes (eds.). *The Ethnography of Communication*. New York: Oxford University Press

Albrecht, G. 1972. "Zur Stellung historischer Forschungsmethoden und nichtreactiver Methoden im System der empirischen Sozialforschung." Pp. 242–293 in P. Chr. Ludz (ed.). *Soziologie und Sozialgeschichte* (Special Issue 16 of the *Kölner Zeitschrift für Soziologie und Sozialpsychologie*). Opladen: Westdeutscher Verlag.

Allen, D.E. and R.F. Guy. 1974. *Conversation Analysis: The Sociology of Talk*. The Hague: Mouton.

Allport, G.W. and L. Postman. 1965. *The Psychology of Rumor*. New York: Russell & Russell.

Almirol, E.B. 1981. "Chasing the Elusive Butterfly: Gossip and the Pursuit of Reputation." *Ethnicity* 8:293–304.

Althans, B. 1985. " 'Halte dich fern von den klatschenden Weibern . . . ': Zur Phänomenologie des Klatsches." *Feministische Studien* 2:46–53.

Anderson, D.C. and W.W. Sharrock. 1979. "Biasing the News: Technical Issues in 'Media Studies.' " *Sociology* 13:367–385.

Andreas-Friedrich, R. 1954. *So benimmt sich die junge Dame*. Heidelberg: Kemper.

Arewa, E.O. and A. Dundes. 1964. "Proverbs and the Ethnography of Speaking Folklore." *American Anthropologist* 66:70–85.

Aristotle. 1962. *Nicomachean Ethics*. Cambridge, Mass.: Harvard University Press.

Arno, A. 1980. "Fijian Gossip as Adjudication: A Communication Model of Informal Social Control." *Journal of Anthropological Research* 36:343–360.

Aswad, B.C. 1967. "Key and Peripheral Roles of Noble Women in a Middle Eastern Plains Village." *Anthropological Quarterly* 40:139–152.

Atkinson, P. 1982. "Writing Ethnography." Pp. 77–105 in H.J. Helle (ed.). *Kultur und Institution*. Berlin: Duncker & Humblot.

Auer, J.C.P. 1980. "Referenzierungssequenzen: Ein Beitrag zur Ethno-Konversationsanalyse des Referierens." Master's Thesis, University of Konstanz.

Back, K.W. and D. Polisar. 1983. "Salons und Kaffeehäuser." Pp. 276–286 in F. Neidhardt (ed.). *Gruppensoziologie*. (Special Edition 25 of the *Kölner Zeitschrift für Soziologie und Sozialpsychologie*). Opladen: Westdeutscher Verlag.

Bailey, F.G. 1971a. "Gifts and Poison." Pp. 1–25 in F.G. Bailey (ed.). *Gifts and Poisons: The Politics of Reputation*. New York: Schocken.

———. 1971b. "Losa." in F.G. Bailey (ed.). *Debate and Compromise: The Politics of Innovation*. Totowa, N.J.: Rowman and Littlefield.

———. 1971c. "The Management of Reputations in the Process of Change." Pp. 281–301 in F.G. Bailey (ed.). *Gifts and Poisons: The Politics of Reputation*. New York: Schocken.

———. 1977. *Morality and Expediency: The Folklore of Academic Politics*. Chicago: Aldine.

Baker, Ch. 1975. "This Is Just a First Approximation, but. . ." Pp. 37–47 in *Papers from the Eleventh Regional Meeting of the Chicago Linguistics Society*. Chicago: The Chicago Liguistic Society.

Balikci, A. 1968. "Bad Friends." *Human organization* 27:191–199.

Barthes, R. 1977. *Roland Barthes*. New York: Hill and Wang.

Baumann, R. and J. Scherzer (eds.). 1974. *Explorations in the Ethnography of Speaking*. London: Cambridge University Press.

Baumgartner, M.P. 1984. "Social Control of Suburbia." Pp. 79–103 in D. Black (ed.). *Toward a General Theory of Social Control*. Orlando, Fla.: Academic Press.

Bausinger, H. 1968/1980. *Formen der "Volkspoesie."* Berlin: Erich Schmidt.

Beach, W.A. and D.G. Dunning. 1982. "Pre-indexing and Conversational Organization." *Quarterly Journal of Speech* 68:170–185.

Bell, C. 1968. *Middle Class Families: Social and Geographic Mobility*. London: Routledge & Kegan Paul.

Ben-Amos, S. 1976a. "The Concept of Genre in Folklore." Pp. 30–43 in J. Pentikainen and T.Juurika (eds.). *Folk Narrative Research*. Helsinki: Studia Fennica 20.

———. (ed.). 1976b. *Folklore Genres*. Austin: University of Texas Press.

Benard, Ch. and E. Schlaffer. 1981. "Männerdiskurs und Frauentratsch: Zum Doppelstandard in der Soziologie. Ein Beitrag zur Methodeninnovation." *Soziale Welt* 32:119–136.

Benedict, R. 1946. *The Chrysanthemum and the Sword: Patterns of Japanese Culture*. Boston: Houghton Mifflin.

Benjamin, W. 1931/1980. "Der destruktive Charakter." Pp. 396–398 in W. Benjamin. *Gesammelte Schriften*, vol. IV.1. Frankfurt: Suhrkamp Verlag.

———. 1936/1969. "Der Erzähler: Betrachtungen zum Werk Nikolai Lesskows." Pp. 33–61 in W. Benjamin. *Über Literatur*. Frankfurt: Suhrkamp Verlag.

Bennett, L. 1983. *Dangerous Wives and Sacred Sisters: Social and Symbolic Roles of High-Caste Women in Nepal.* New York: Columbia University Press.

Berger, J. 1979. *Pig Earth.* New York: Pantheon.

Berger, P.L. 1963. *Invitation to Sociology: A Humanistic Perspective.* Garden City, N.Y.: Doubleday.

Berger, P.L. and Th. Luckmann. 1966. *The Social Construction of Reality.* Garden City, N.Y.: Doubleday.

Bergmann, J.R. 1980. "Interaktion und Exploration: Eine konversations-analytische Studie zur sozialen Organization der Eröffnungsphase von psychiatrischen Aufnahmegesprächen." Dissertation, University of Konstanz.

————. 1981a. "Ethnomethodologische Konversationsanalyse." Pp. 9–51 in P. Schröder and H. Steger (eds.). *Dialogforschung: Jahrbuch 1980 des Instituts für deutsche Sprache.* Düsseldorf: Pädagogischer Verlag Schwann.

————. 1981b. "Frage und Frageparaphrase: Aspekte der redezuginternen und sequenziellen Organisation eines Äusserungsformats." Pp. 128–142 in P. Winkler (ed.). *Methoden der Analyse von Face-to-Face-Situationen.* Stuttgart: Metzler Verlag.

————. 1985. "Flüchtigkeit und methodische Fixierung sozialer Wirklichkeit: Aufzeichnungen als Daten der interpretativen Soziologie." Pp. 299–320 in W. Bonß and H. Hartmann. *Entzauberte Wissenschaft* (Special Edition 3 of *Soziale Welt*). Göttingen: Schwartz.

————. (in press). "Veiled Morality: Notes on Discretion in Psychiatry." In P. Drew and J. Heritage (eds.). *Talk at Work.* Cambridge: Cambridge University Press.

Bergmann, J.R., J. Bossi-Dünker, J. Fuhrmann, P. Gross, Th. Luckmann, J. Schmucker, S. Uhmann, and P. Winkler. 1986. "Zur Produktion und Konstitution sozialwissenschaftlicher Daten." Manuscript, University of Konstanz.

Bittner, E. 1967. "The Police on Skid-Row: A Study of Peace-Keeping." *American Sociological Quarterly* 32:699–715.

Bleek, W. 1976. "Witchcraft, Gossip and Death: A Social Drama." *Man* 11:526–541.

Bloch, E. 1935/1962. "Der Klatsch." Pp. 25–26 in E. Bloch. *Erbschaft dieser Zeit.* Frankfurt: Suhrkamp Verlag.

Blumenthal, A. 1932. *Small-Town Stuff.* Chicago: University of Chicago Press

————. 1937. "The Nature of Gossip." *Sociology and Social Research* 22:31–37.

Bogatyrev, P.G. and R. Jakobson. 1929/1972. "Die Folklore als eine besondere Form des Schaffens." Pp. 13–24 in H. Blumensath (ed.). *Strukutralismus in der Literaturwissenschaft.* Cologne: Kiepenheuer & Witsch.

Boissevain, J.M. 1972. "Some Notes on the Position of Women in Maltese Society." *Nord Nytt* 3:195–213.

————. 1974. *Friends of Friends: Networks, Manipulators and Coalitions.* Oxford: Basil Blackwell.

Bok, S. 1984. "Gossip." Pp. 89–101 in S. Bok. *Secrets: On the Ethics of Concealment and Revelation.* New York: Pantheon.

Borker, R. 1980. "Anthropology: Social and Cultural Perspectives." Pp. 26–44 in

S. McConnell-Ginet et al. (eds.). *Women and Language in Literature and Society*. New York: Praeger.

Bott, E. 1971. *Family and Social Network: Roles, Norms, and External Relationships in Ordinary Families*. London: Tavistock Publications [New York: Free Press, 1971].

Boulay, J. du. 1974. "Gossip, Friendship, and Quarrels." Pp. 210–229 in J. du Boulay. *Portrait of a Greek Mountain Village*. Oxford: Clarendon.

Brandes, S.H. 1973. "Social Structure and Interpersonal Relations in Navanogal (Spain)." *American Anthropologist* 75:750–765.

Breinneis, D. 1984. "Grog and Gossip in Bhatgon: Style and Substance in Fiji Indian Conversation." *American Ethnologist* 11:487–506.

Brickman, Ph. and R.J. Bulman. 1976. "Pleasure and Pain in Social Comparison." Pp. 149–186 in J.M. Suls and R.L. Miller (eds.). *Social Comparison Processes: Theoretical and Empirircal Perspectives*. Washington, D.C.: Hemisphere.

Briggs, J.L. 1970. *Never in Anger: Portrait of an Eskimo Family*. Cambridge, Mass.: Harvard University Press.

Brockhaus' Konversations-Lexikon. vol. 2. 1894. Leipzig: F.A. Brockhaus.

Brown, H.O. 1977. "The Errant Letter and the Whispering Gallery." *Genre* 10:573–599.

Brown, P. and S. Levinson. 1978. "Universals in Language Usage: Politeness Phenomena." Pp. 56–310 in E.N. Goody (ed.). *Questions and Politeness: Strategies in Social Interaction*. Cambridge: Cambridge University Press.

Campbell, J.K. 1964. *Honor, Family, and Patronage: A Study of Institutions and Moral Values in a Greek Mountain Community*. Oxford: Oxford University Press.

Campe, J.H. 1808. *Wörterbuch der deutschen Sprache*. Brunswick: Olms.

Caruth, E.G. 1985. "Secret Bearer or Secret Barer? Countertransference and the Gossiping Therapist." *Contemporary Psychoanalysis* 21:548–562.

Casa, G. della. 1558/1979. "Vom täglichen Gespräch." Pp. 124–127 in C. Schmölders (ed.). *Die Kunst des Gesprächs: Texte zur Geschichte des europäischen Konversationstheorie*. Munich: Deutscher Taschenbuch Verlag.

Cicourel, A. 1964. *Method and Measurement in Sociology*. New York: The Free Press.

Clausen, L. 1981. "Schlangen, Exkursion in den Quellsumpf der Theorien." Pp. 307–322 in H. von Alemann and H.P. Thurn (eds.). *Soziologie in weltbürgerlicher Absicht* (Festschrift for René König zum 75. Geburtstag). Opladen: Westdeutscher Verlag.

Clifford, J. 1981. "On Ethnographic Surrealism." *Comparative Studies in Society and History* 23:539–564.

———. 1983. "On Ethnographic Authority." *Representations* 1–2:118–146.

Cohen, Y.A. 1955/1971. "Four Categories of Interpersonal Relationships in the Family and Community in a Jamaican Village." Pp. 412–435 in M.M. Horowitz (ed.). *Peoples and Cultures of the Caribbean*. Garden City, N.Y.: Natural History Press.

Colson, E. 1953a. *The Makah Indians: A Study of an Indian Tribe in Modern American Society*. Manchester: Manchester University Press [Minneapolis: University of Minnesota Press, 1953].

———. 1953b. "Social Control and Vengeance in Plateau Tonga Society." *Africa* 23:199–212.

————. 1975. *Tradition and Contract: The Problem of Order.* London: Heinemann Educational Books [Chicago: Aldine, 1974].

Conrad, K. 1958/1966. *Die beginnende Schizophrenie: Versuch einer Gestaltanalyse des Wahns.* Stuttgart: Thieme Verlag.

Cooley, Ch. H. 1909/1962. *Social Organization: A Study of the Larger Mind.* New York: Schocken.

Coser, L.A. 1974. "Domestic Servants: The Obsolescence of an Occupational Role." Pp. 67–88 in L.A. Coser. *Greedy Institutions: Patterns of Undivided Commtment.* New York: The Free Press.

Coser, R.L. 1961. "Insulation from Observability and Types of Social Conformity." *American Scoiological Review* 26:28–39.

Cox, B.A. 1970. "What is Hopi Gossip About? Information Management and Hopi Factions." *Man* 5:88–98.

Cronin, C. 1977. "Illusion and Reality in Sicily." Pp. 67–93 in A. Schlegel (ed.). *Sexual Stratification: A Cross-Cultural View.* New York: Columbia University Press.

Cuff, E.C. and D.W. Francis. 1978. "Some Features of 'Invited Stories' about Marriage Breakdown." *International Journal of Sociology of Language* 18:111–133.

Cutileiro, J.A. 1971. *A Portugese Rural Society.* Oxford: Clarendon.

Davis, F.B. and P.J. Rulon. 1935–36. "Gossip and the Introvert." *Journal of Abnormal and Social Psychology* 30:17–21.

Dawson, C.A. and W.E. Gettys. 1929. *An Introduction to Sociology.* New York: The Ronald Press.

Devons, E. and M. Gluckman. 1964. "Conclusion: Modes and Consequences of Limiting a Field of Study." Pp. 158–216 in M. Gluckman (ed.). *Closed Systems and Open Minds.* Edinburgh: Oliver & Boyd [Chicago: Aldine 1964].

Diderot, D., J.L. D'Alembert, and de Jaucourt. 1801. "Conversation, entretien." Pp. 94–96 in D. Diderot et al. *Synonymes Francais.* Paris: Favre.

Dieck, A. 1950. "Der Weltuntergang am 17. März 1949 in Südhannover: Ein Beitrag zur Erforschung von Gerüchten." *Neues Archiv für Niedersachsen* 4–20:704–720.

Dietrich, H. 1965. *Menschen Miteinander: Ein Brevier des taktvollen und guten Benehmens.* Berlin: Deutsche Buch Gemeinschaft.

Dischner, G. 1981. "Das poetische Auge des Ethnographen." *Text + Kritik* 72:30–47.

Dollard, J. et al. 1950. *Frustration and Agression.* New Haven: Yale University Press.

Douglas, M. (ed.). 1970. *Witchcraft Confessions and Accusations.* London: Tavistock Publications.

Duden-Stilwörterbuch. 1963. Mannheim: Duden Verlag.

Durkheim, E. 1893/1964, *The Division of Labor in Society.* New York: The Free Press.

————. 1895/1966. *The Rules of Sociological Method.* New York: The Free Press.

Edmondson, M.S. 1967. "Play: Games, Gossip, and Humor." Pp. 191- 206 in M. Nash (ed.). *Handbook of Middle American Indians.* Austin: University of Texas Press.

Edmondson, R. 1984. *Rhetoric in Sociology*. London: Macmillan.

Eglin, P. 1983. "Readers' Work in Making News: A Study of a Newspaper Headline and a Direction for Research." Manuscript

Ehlich, K. (ed.). 1980. *Erzählen im Alltag*. Franfurt: Suhrkamp Verlag.

Elias, N. and J.L Scotson. 1965. "Observations on Gossip." Pp. 89–105 in N. Elias and J.L. Scotson. *The Established and The Outsiders: A Sociological Enquiry into Community Problems*. London: F. Cass.

Elwert-Kretschmer, K. 1984. "Zwischen Tratsch und Anpassung: Der Prozeß der Feldforschung in einem malaiischen Dorf." Working Paper No. 53, University of Bielefeld. Department of Sociology.

Embree, J.F. 1939. *Suye Mura: A Japanese Village*. Chicago: University of Chicago Press.

Engisch, K. 1957. "Beleidigende Äusserungen über dritte Personen im engsten Kreise." *Goltdammer's Archiv* 326–337.

Epstein, A.L. 1961. "The Network and Social Organization." *Rhodes-Livingstone Institute Journal* 29:29–62.

———. "Gossip, Normes, and Social Network." Pp. 117–127 in J.C. Mitchell (ed.). *Social Networks in Urban Situations*. Manchester: Manchester University Press.

Evans-Pritchard, E.E. 1939. *Witchcraft, Oracles and Magic among the Azande*. Oxford: Clarendon.

———. 1970. "Zande Conversation Pieces." Pp. 29- 49. in J.Pouillon and P. Maranda (eds.). *Éhange et communications. Mélanges offerts à Claude Lévi-Strauss à l'occasion de son 60ème anniversaire*, vol. 1. The Hague and Paris: Mouton.

———. 1974. *Man and Woman among the Azande*. London: Faber & Faber [New York: The Free Press 1974].

Faris, J.C. 1966. "The Dynamics of Verbal Exchange: A Newfoundland Example." *Anthropologica* 8:235–248.

Felton, G.S. 1966. "Psychosocial Implications of the Coffee-Break." *Journal of Human relations* 14:434–449.

Fine, G.A. 1977. "Social Components of Children's Gossip." *Journal of Communication* 27:181–185.

———. 1985. "Rumors and Gossiping." Pp. 233–237 in T.A. van Dijk (ed.). *Handbook of Discourse Analysis*, vol. 3. London and Orlando, Fla.: Academic Press.

Fine, G.A. and R.L. Rosnow. 1978. "Gossip, Gossipers, Gossiping." *Personality and Social Psychology* 4:161–168.

Frankenberg, R. 1957. *Village on the Border: A Social Study of Religion, Politics, and Football in a North Wales Community*. London: Cohen and West.

———. 1966. *Communities in Britain: Social Life in Town and Country*. Hammondsworth: Penguin [Baltimore: Penguin, 1966].

Friedl, E. 1967. "The Position of Women: Appearance and Reality." *Anthropological Quarterly* 40:97–108.

Fuchs, E. 1906. *Die Frau in der Karikatur*. Munich: Albert Langen.

Gallaher, A., Jr. 1961. *Plainville Fifteen Years Later*. New York: Columbia University Press.

Gans, H.J. 1962. *The Urban Villagers: Group and Class in the Life of Italian-Americans*. New York: The Free Press.

Garfinkel, H. 1956. "Conditions of Successful Degradation." *American Journal of Sociology* 61:420–424.

———. 1967. "What Is Ethnomethodology?" Pp. 1–34 in H. Garfinkel. *Studies in Ethnomethodology*. Englewood Cliffs, N.J.: Prentice-Hall.

Garfinkel, H. and H. Sacks. 1970. "On Formal Structures of Practical Actions." Pp. 337–366 in J.C. McKinney and E.A. Tiryakian (eds.). *Theoretical Sociology*. New York: Appleton- Century-Crofts.

Gearing, F.O. 1970. *The Face of the Fox*. Chicago: Aldine.

Geertz, C. 1980. "Blurred Genres: The Refiguration of Social Thought." *American Scholar* 49:165–179.

———. 1984. "Slide-Show: Evans-Pritchard's African Transparencies." *Raritan* III(2):62–80.

Giedion-Welcker, C. 1966. "Einführung zu James Joyce: *Ulysses*." In J. Joyce. *Ulysses*. Munich: Deutscher Taschenbuch Verlag.

Gilmore, D. 1978. "Varieties of Gossip in a Spanish Rural Community." *Ethnology* 17:89–99.

———. 1980. *The People of the Plain: Class and Community in Lower Andalusia*. New York: Columbia University Press.

Ginzburg, C. 1980. "Spurensicherung: Der Jäger entziffert die Fährte, Sherlock Holmes nimmt die Lupe, Freund liest Morelli—die Wissenschaft auf der Suche nach sich selbst." *Freibeuter* 3:7–19, 4:11–36.

Gladwin, Th. and S,B. Sarason. 1953. *Truk: Man in Paradise*. New York: Wenner-Gren Foundation for Anthropological Research.

Gluckman, M. 1963. "Gossip and Scandal." *Current Anthropology* 4:307–316.

———. 1968. "Psychological, Sociological, and Anthropological Explanations of Witchcraft and Gossip: A Clarification." *Man* 3:20–34.

Goethe, J.W. von 1989. "Conversations of German Refugees." Pp. 13–92 in J.W. v. Goethe. *Collected Works*, vol. 10. New York: Suhrkamp Publishers.

Goffman, E. 1959. *The Presentation of Self in Everyday Life*. Garden City, N.Y: Doubleday.

———. 1963. *Behavior in Public Places: Notes on the Social Organization of Gatherings*. New York: The Free Press.

———. 1964. *Stigma: Notes on the Management of Spoiled Identity*. Englewood Cliffs, N.J.: Prentice-Hall.

———. 1974. *Frame Analysis: An Essay on the Organization of Experience*. Cambridge, Mass.: Harvard University Press.

———. 1981. *Forms of Talk*. Oxford: Oxford University Press.

———. 1983a. "Felicity's Condition." *American Journal of Sociology* 89:1–53.

———. 1983b. "The Interaction Order." *American Sociological Review* 48:1–17.

Gold, R. 1952. "Janitors versus Tenants: A Status-Income Dilemma." *American Journal of Sociology* 57:486–493.

Goodwin, M.H. 1980. "He-Said-She-Said: Formal Cultural Procedures for the Construction of a Gossip Dispute Activity." *American Ethnologist* 7:674–695.

———. 1982. "'Instigating': Storytelling as a Social Process." *American Ethnologist* 9:799–819.

Götze, A. (ed.). 1943 *Trübners Deutsches Wörterbuch*. Berlin: Walter de Gruyter Verlag.

Gregor, Th. 1977. *Mehinaku: The Drama of Daily Life in a Brazilian Indian Village*. Chicago: University of Chicago Press.

Grimm, J. and W. 1873. *Deutsches Wörterbuch*, vol. 5. Leipzig: S. Hirzel.

Grünberger, H. 1978. "Formale Organisation und Soziales System: Soziologische Orte des Sprechhandelns von Mitgliedern—Die subcutane Gewalt des Klatsches." Manuscript, Frankfurt.

Gurvitch, G. 1945. "Social Control." Pp. 267–296 in G. Gurvitch and W.E. Moore (eds.). *Twentieth-Century Sociology*. New York: The Philosophical Library.

Gusfield, J. 1976. "The Literary Rhetoric of Science: Comedy and Pathos in Drinking Driver Research." *American Sociological Review* 41:16–34.

Habermas, J. 1989. *The Structural Transformation of the Public Sphere*. Cambridge, Mass.: MIT Press.

Hahn, A., H.-A. Schubert, and H.-J. Siewert. 1979. *Gemeindesoziologie: Eine Einführung*. Stuttgart: Kohlhammer Verlag.

Handelmann, D. 1973. "Gossip in Encounters: The Transformation of Information in a Bounded Social Setting." *Man* 8:210- 227.

Hannerz, U. 1967. "Gossip, Networks, and Culture in a Black American Ghetto." *Ethnos* 32:35–60.

———. 1980. *Exploring the City: Inquiries toward an Urban Anthropology*. New York: Columbia University Press.

Harbert, R. 1954. *Bitte so! Anstandsbüchlein für junge Damen und solche, die es werden wollen*. Recklinghausen: Paulus Verlag.

Harding, D.W. 1937. "The Role of the Onlooker." *Scrutiny* 6(3):247–258.

Harding S. 1975. "Women and Words in a Spanish Village." Pp. 283–308 in R. Reiter. *Towards an Anthropology of Women*. New York: Monthly Review Press.

Harrington, M. 1964. "Co-operation and Collusion in a Group of Young Housewives." *Sociological Review* 12(3):255–282.

Harris, C. 1974. *Hennage: A Social System in Miniature*. New York: Holt, Rinehart & Winston.

Hart, Ch. and A.R. Pilling. 1960. *The Tiwi of North Australia*. New York: Holt.

Haviland, J.B. 1977. *Gossip, Reputation, and Knowledge in Zinacantan*. Chicago: University of Chicago Press.

Hegel, G.W.F. 1830/1970. *Enzyklopädie der philosophischen Wissenschaften im Grundrisse. Dritter Teil*. In G.W.F. Hegel. *Werke in zwanzig Bänden*, vol. 10. Frankfurt: Suhrkamp Verlag.

Heilman, S.C. 1976. *Synagogue Life: A Study in Symbolic Interaction*. Chicago: University of Chicago Press.

Heller, A. 1984. *Everyday Life*. London: Routledge & Kegan Paul.

Hellweg, S.A. 1987. "Organizational Grapevines." Pp. 213–230 in B. Dervin and M.J. Voigt (eds.). *Progress in Communication Sciences*, vol. 8. Norwood, N.J.: Ablex.

Hempfer, K.W. 1973. *Gattungstheorie: Information und Synthese*. Munich: W. Fink.

Henry, J.A. 1963. *Culture against Man*. New York: Random House.

Heppenstall, M.A. 1971. "Reputation, Criticism, and Information in an Austrian

Village." Pp. 139–166 in F.G. Bailey (ed.). *Gifts and Poison: The Politics of Reputation*. New York: Oxford University Press.

Heritage, J.C. and D.R. Watson. 1979. "Formulations as Conversational Objects." Pp. 123–162 in G. Psathas (ed.) *Everyday Language: Studies in Ethnomethodology*. New York: Irvington Publishers.

Herskovits, M.J. 1937. *Life in a Haitian Valley*. New York: Knopf.

Herskovits, M.J. and F.S. Herskovits. 1947/1976. *Trinidad Village*. New York: Octagon Books.

Hess-Lüttich, E.W.B. 1986. "Klatsch als Kunstform. Lust und Lüsternheit des Lästern." in E.W.B. Hess-Lüttich. *Kommunkation als ästhetisches Problem*. Tübingen: Narr.

Hewitt, J.P. and R. Stokes. 1975. "Disclaimers." *American Sociological Review* 40:1–11.

Hirsch, H.J. 1967. *Ehre und Beleidigung: Grundfragen des strafrechtlichen Ehrenschutzes*. Karlsruhe: C.F. Müller Verlag.

Hirzel, R. 1895/1963. *Der Dialog: Ein literarhistorischer Versuch*. Hildesheim: Georg Olms.

Ho, D.Y. 1976. "On the Concept of Face." *American Journal of Sociology* 81:867–884.

Hodges, M.W. and C.S. Smith. 1954. *Neighborhood and Community: An Enquiry into Social relationships on Housing Estates in Liverpool and Sheffield*. Liverpool: University of Liverpool Department of Social Science.

Hoggart, R. 1958. *The Uses of Literacy: Aspects of Working-Class Life with Special Reference to Publications and Entertainments*. Hammondsworth: Penguin Books Ltd. [New York: Oxford University Press, 1970].

Hotchkiss, J.C. 1967. "Children and Conduct in a Ladino Community of Chiapas, Mexico." *American Anthropologist* 69:711–718.

Hughes, Ch. C. et al. 1960. *People of Cove and Woodlot: Communities from the Viewpoint of Social Psychiatry*. vol. 2. New York: Basic Books.

Humboldt, W. von 1827/1973. "Über den Dualis." Pp. 21–29 in W. von Humboldt. *Schriften zur Sprache*. Stuttgart: Reclam.

Hymes, D. 1964. "Introduction: Toward Ethnographies of Communication." Pp. 1–34. in J.J. Gumperz and D. Hymes (eds.). *The Ethnography of Communication* (Special Issue of *American Anthropologist*.) 66(6):Pt. 2.

———. 1972. "Models of the Interaction of Language and Social Life." Pp. 35–71 in J.J. Gumperz and D. Hymes (eds.). *Directions in Psycholinguistics: The Ethnography of Communication*. New York: Macmillan.

———. 1974. "Ways of Speaking." Pp. 433–451 in R. Baumann and J. Scherzer (eds.). *Explorations in the Ethnography of Speaking*. London: Cambridge University Press.

Jayyusi, L. 1984. *Categorization and Moral Order*. Boston: Routledge & Kegan Paul.

Jefferson, G. 1972. "Side Sequences." Pp. 219–338 in D. Sudnow. *Studies in Social Interaction*. New York: The Free Press.

———. 1978. "Sequential Aspects of Storytelling in Conversation." Pp. 219–248 in J. Schenkein (ed.). *Studies in the Organization of Conversational Interaction*. New York: Academic Press.

Jefferson, G. and J.R.E. Lee. 1988. "On the Sequential Organization of Troublestalk in Ordinary Conversation." *Social Problems* 35:418–441.

Jefferson. G. and J. Schenkein. 1977. "Some Sequential Negotiations in Conversation: Unexpanded and Expanded Versions of Projected Action Sequences." *Sociology* 11:87–103.

Jesus Sirach. 1979. "Unterricht über den Mund." Pp. 91–95 in Ch. Schmölders (ed.). *Die Kunst des Gesprächs: Texte zur Geschichte der europäischen Konversationstheorie.* Munich: Deutscher Taschenbuch Verlag.

Jhering, R. von. 1877/1905. *Der Zweck im Recht.* Leipzig: Breitkopf & Härtel.

Jolles, A. 1930/1982. *Einfache Formen: Legende, Sage, Mythe, Rätsel, Spruch, Kasus, Memorabile, Märchen, Witz.* Tübingen: Max Niemeyer Verlag.

Jones, D. 1980. "Gossip: Notes on Women's Oral Culture." Pp. 193- 198 in Ch. Kramarae (ed.). *The Voices and Words of Women and Men.* Oxford: Pergamon Press.

Joyce, J. 1922/1961. *Ulysses.* New York: Random House.

Kaberry, Ph. 1957. "Malinowski's Contribution to Fieldwork Methods and the Writing of Ethnography." Pp. 71–91 in R. Firth (ed.). *Man and Culture.* London: Routledge & Kegan Paul.

Kaplan, A. 1964. *The Conduct of Inquiry: Methodology for Behavioral Science.* San Francisco: Chandler Publishing.

Katz, J. 1975. "Essences as Moral Identities: Verifiability and Responsibility in Imputations of Deviance and Charisma." *American Journal of Sociology* 80:1369–1390.

Keppler, A. 1987. "Zur Verlaufsform von Klatschgesprächen." *Zeitschrift für Soziologie* 16:288–302.

Kern, E. 1919. *Die Äusserungsdelikte.* Tübingen: J.C.B. Mohr.

Kernan, C.M. 1971. "Loud Talking." Pp. 96–102 in C.M. Kernan. *Language Behavior in a Black Urban Community.* Monographs of the Language Behavior Research Laboratory No. 2. Berkeley: University of California.

Kierkegaard, S. 1845/1954. *Eine Literarische Anzeige.* Düsseldorf: Eugen Diederichs.

Klapp, O.E. 1978. *Opening and Closing: Strategies of Information Adaptation in Society.* Cambridge: Cambridge University Press.

Klein, J. 1965. *Samples from English Culture.* London: Routledge & Kegan Paul.

Kleist, H. von. 1810/1964. *Über das Marionettentheater.* Reinbek: Rowohlt.

Kluckhohn, C. 1944/1967. *Navaho Witchcraft.* Boston: Beacon Press.

Kluge, F. 1967. *Etymologisches Wörterbuch der Deutschen Sprache.* Berlin: Walter de Gruyter Verlag.

Knigge, A. von. 1788/1966. *Über den Umgang mit Menschen.* Berlin: Verlag Lebendiges Wissen.

Köhnke, K. Ch. 1984. "Von der Völkerpsychologie zur Soziologie: Unbekannte Texte des jungen Georg Simmel." Pp. 388–429 in H.-J. Dahme and O. Rammstedt (eds.). *Georg Simmel und die Moderne: Neue Interpretationen und Materialien.* Frankfurt: Suhrkamp Verlag.

Koster, D. 1977. "'Why Is He Here?' White Gossip." Pp. 144–165 in R. Paine (ed.). *The White Arctic: Anthropological Essays on Tutelage and Ethnicity.* Newfoundland Social and Economic Papers. No. 7. St. John's: Institute of Social and Economic Research, Memorial University of Newfoundland.

Kramer, F. 1977. *Verkehrte Welten: Zur imaginären Ethnographie des 19. Jahrhunderts.* Frankfurt: Syndikat.

———. 1978. "Die 'social anthropology' und das Problem der Darstellung anderer Gesellschaften." Pp. 9–27 in F. Kramer and Ch. Sigrist (eds.). *Gesellschaften ohne Staat I: Gleichheit und Gegenseitigkeit.* Frankfurt: Syndikat.

Kretschmer, E. 1950. *Der sensitive Beziehungswahn: Eine Beitrag zur Paranoiafrage und zur psychiatrischen Charakterlehre.* Berlin: Springer-Verlag.

Krüger, H. 1967. "Kleine Soziologie des Klatsches." *Streit-Zeit-Schrift*, VI(1):33–35.

Krumrey, H.-V. 1984. *Entwicklungsstrukturen von Verhaltensstandarden. Eine soziologische Prozeßanalyse auf der Grundlage deutscher Anstands- und Maniererbücher von 1870–1970.* Frankfurt: Suhrkamp Verlag.

Kruse, L. 1980. *Privatheit als Problem und Gegenstand der Psychologie.* Bern: H. Huber.

Kühne, O. 1958. *Allgemeine Soziologie: Lebenswissenschaftlicher Aufriß ihrer Grundprobleme*, vol. 1. Berlin: Duncker & Humblot.

Kuper, L. 1953. "Blueprint for Living Together." Pp. 1–202 in L. Kuper. *Living in Towns.* London: Cresset Press.

Labov, W. 1972. "Rules of Ritual Insults." Pp. 120–169 in D. Sudnow (ed.). *Studies in Social Interaction.* New York: The Free Press.

Labov, W. and J. Waletzky. 1967. "Narrative Analysis: Oral Versions of Personal Experience." Pp. 12–44 in J. Helm (ed.). *Essays on the Verbal and Visual Arts.* Seattle: University of Washington Press.

Lamphere, L. 1971. "The Navaho Cultural System: An Analysis of Concepts of Cooperation and Autonomy and Their Relation to Gossip and Witchcraft." Pp. 91–114 in K. Basso and M. Opler (eds.). *Apachean Culture History and Ethnology.* Tucson: University of Arizona Press.

———. 1975. "Women and Domestic Power: Political and Economic Strategies in Domestic Groups." Pp. 117–130 in D. Raphael (ed.). *Being Female: Reproduction, Power, and Change.* The Hague and Paris: Mouton.

Lancaster, W. 1974. "Correspondence." *Man* 9:626–627.

Lanz, H. 1936. "Metaphysics of Gossip." *International Journal of Ethics* 46:492–499.

Lazarus, M. 1878. "Über Gespräche." Pp. 233–265 in M. Lazarus. *Ideale Fragen.* Berlin: Wintersche Verlagshandlung.

Lee, J. 1984. "Innocent Victims and Evil Doers." *Women's Studies International Forum* 7:69–73.

Lemert, E. 1967. "Paranoia and the Dynamics of Exclusion." Pp. 30–60 in E. Lemert. *Human Deviance, Social Problems and Social Control.* Englewood Cliffs, N.J.: Prentice-Hall.

Le Roy Ladurie, E. 1975/1979. *Montaillou: The Promised Land of Error.* New York: Vintage.

Lessing, D. 1962. *The Golden Notebook.* New York: Simon and Schuster.

Levin, J. and A. Arluke. 1985. "An Explanatory Analysis of Sex Differences in Gossip." *Sex Roles* 12:281–286.

Levin, J. and A.J. Kimmel. 1977. "Gossip Columns: Media Small Talk." *Journal of Communication* 27:169–175.

Levinson, S.C. 1983. "Conversational Structure." Pp. 284–370 in S.C. Levinson. *Pragmatics*. Cambridge: Cambridge University Press.

Levy, R.I. 1973. *Tahitians: Mind and Experience in the Society Islands*. Chicago: University of Chicago Press.

Lewis, H. 1955. *Blackways of Kent*. Chapel Hill: University of North Carolina Press.

Lewis, Ph. 1976. "Defamation: Reputation and Encounter." Pp. 271–284 in L.M. Friedman and M. Rehbinder (eds.). *Zur Soziologie des Gerichtsverfahren (Jahrbuch für Rechtssoziologie und Rechtstheorie*, vol. 4). Opladen: Westdeutscher Verlag.

Lichtenberg, G. Ch. 1983. "Sudelbücher (1765–1799)." Pp. 63–526 in G. Ch. Lichtenberg. *Schriften und Briefe*, vol. 1. Frankfurt: Insel Verlag.

Lomer, G. 1913. "Über den Klatsch: Eine psychologische Studie." *Psychiatrisch-neurologische Wochenschrift*. 15:171–175.

Lopate, C. 1978. "Jackie!" Pp. 130–140 in G.A. Tuchman et al. (eds.). *Hearth and Home: Images of Women in the Mass Media*. New York: Oxford University Press.

Loudon, J.B. 1961. "Kinship and Crisis in South Wales." *British Journal of Sociology* 12:333–350.

Luckmann, Th. 1981. "Zum hermeneutischen Problem der Handlungs- wissenschaften." Pp. 513–523 in M. Fuhrmann et al. (eds.). *Text und Applikation (Poetik und Hermeneutik*, vol. IX). Munich: W. Fink.

———. 1986. "Grundformen der gesellschaftlichen Vermittlung des Wissens: Kommunikative Gattungen." Pp. 191- 211 in F. Neidhardt et al. (eds.). *Kultur und Gesellschaft* (Special Issue 27 of the *Kölner Zeitschrift für Soziologie und Sozialpsychologie*). Opladen: Westdeutscher Verlag.

Luckmann, Th. and J.R. Bergmann. 1982. "Bibliographie: Mündliche Gattungen alltäglicher Kommunikation." Manuscript, University of Konstanz.

Luhmann, N. 1962. "Der neue Chef." *Verwaltungsarchiv* 53:11–24.

———. 1964/1976. *Funktionen und Folgen formaler Organisation*. Berlin: Duncker und Humblot.

Lumley, F.E. 1925. "Gossip." Pp. 211–236 in F.E. Lumley. *Means of Social Control*. New York: The Century Co.

Lutz, G. 1954. "Sitte und Infamie: Untersuchungen zur rechtlichen Volkskunde am Phänomen des Verrufs." Dissertation, University of Würzburg.

Malinowski, B. 1922/1960. *Argonauts of the Western Pacific*. New York: Dutton.

———. 1923/1946. "The Problem of Meaning in Primitive Languages." Pp. 296–336 in C.K. Ogden and I. A. Richards (eds.). *The Meaning of Meaning*. London: Routledge & Kegan Paul.

———. 1926. *Crime and Custom in Savage Society*. New York: Harcourt, Brace & Co.

———. 1929. *The Sexual Life of Savages in North-Western Melanesia*. New York: Halcyon House.

Marcus, G.E. and D. Cushman. 1982. "Ethnographies as Texts." *Annual Review of Anthropology* 11:25–69.

Marquard, O. 1973. "Beitrag zur Philosphie der Geschichte des Abschieds von der Philosophie der Geschichte." Pp. 241–250 in R. Koselleck and W.-D. Stempel (eds.). *Geschichte— Ereignis und Erzählung (Poetik und Hermeneutik,* vol. V). Munich: W. Fink.

————. 1981. "Die Frage nach der Frage, auf die die Hermeneutik die Antwort ist." Pp. 117–146 in O. Marquard. *Abschied vom Prinzipiellen.* Stuttgart: Reclam.

Martens, W. 1968. *Die Botschaft der Tugend: Die Aufklärung im Spiegel der deutschen Moralischen Wochenschriften.* Stuttgart: Metzler.

Matthes, J. 1983. "Die Soziologen und ihre Zukunft." Pp. 19–124 in J. Matthes (ed.). *Krise der Arbeitsgesellschaft? Verhandlungen des 21. Deutschen Soziologentages in Bamberg 1982.* Frankfurt: Campus Verlag.

Mauss, M. 1925/1978. "Die Gabe." Pp. 9–144 in M. Mauss. *Soziologie und Anthropologie,* vol. II. Frankfurt: Ullstein.

Mauthner, F. 1906/1982. *Beiträge zu einer Kritik der Sprache,* vol. 1. Frankfurt: Ullstein.

McCarthy, M. 1962. "The Fact of Fiction." Pp. 249–270 in M. McCarthy. *On the Contrary: Articles on Beliefs.* New York: Noonday Press.

McFarlane, G. 1977. "Gossip and Social Relationships in a Northern Irish Community." Pp. 95–118 in M. Stuchlik (ed.). *The Queen's University Papers in Social Anthropology,* vol. 2: *Goals and Behavior.* Belfast: Queen's University of Belfast Department of Social Anthropology.

Mead, G.H. 1934. *Mind, Self, and Society.* Chicago: University of Chicago Press.

Mead, M. 1949/1958. *Male and Female: A Study of the Sexes in a Changing World.* New York: Morrow.

Medini, G. and E.H. Rosenberg. 1976. "Gossip and Psychotherapy." *American Journal of Psychotherapy* 30:452–462.

Merry, S.E. 1981. *Urban Danger: Life in a Neighborhood of Strangers.* Philadelphia: Temple University Press.

————. 1984. "Rethinking Gossip and Scandal." Pp. 271–302 in D. Black (ed.). *Toward a General Theory of Social Control,* vol. 1. Orlando, Fla.: Academic Press.

Merton, R.K. 1968. "Continuities in the Theory of Reference Groups and Social Structure." Pp. 335–440 in R.K. Merton. *Social Theory and Social Structure.* New York: The Free Press.

Mettetal, G. 1978. "Fantasy, Gossip, and Self-Disclosure: Children's Conversations with Friends." Pp. 717–736 in R. Bostrom (ed.). *Communication Yearbook,* vol. 7. Beverly Hills, California: International Communication Association.

Meuli, K. 1953. "Charivari." Pp. 231–243 in H. Kusch (ed.). *Festschrift Franz Dornseiff.* Leipzig: Bibliographisches Institut.

Mitchell, J.C. 1973. "Networks, Norms, and Institutions." Pp. 15- 35 in J. Boissevain and J.C. Mitchell (eds.). *Network Analysis: Studies in Human Interaction.* The Hague: Mouton.

Mitscherlich, A. 1963. "Kurze Apologie des Klatsches." Pp. 327- 329 in A. Mitscherlich. *Auf dem Wege zur vaterlosen Gesellschaft.* Munich: R. Piper.

Moerman, M. 1973. "The Use of Precedent in Natural Conversation: A Study in Practical Legal Reasoning." *Semiotica* 9:193–218.

Müller, H. 1981. *Dienstbare Geister: Leben und Arbeitswelt städtischer Dienstboten.* (*Schriften des Museums für Deutsche Volkskunde*, vol. 6). Berlin: Reimer.

Müller, K.E. 1984. *Die bessere und die schlechtere Hälfte: Ethnologie des Geschlechterkonflikts.* Frankfurt: Campus Verlag.

Müller-Staats, D. 1983. "Klagen über Dienstboten: Eine Untersuchung zum Verhältnis von Herschaften and Dienstboten, mit besonderer Berücksichtigung Hamburgs im 19. Jahrhundert." Dissertation, University of Hamburg.

Mulkay, M. and G.N. Gilbert 1982. "Joking Apart: Some Recommendations Concerning the Analysis of Scientific Culture." *Social Studies of Science* 12:585–613.

Murphy, M.D. 1985. "Rumors of Identity: Gossip and Rapport in Ethnographic Research." *Human Organization* 44:132–137.

Murphy, Y. and R.F. Murphy. 1974. *Women of the Forest.* New York: Columbia University Press

Naish, J. 1978. "Désirade: A Negative Case." Pp. 238–258 in P. Caplan and J.M. Burja (eds.). *Women United, Women Divided: Cross-Cultural Perspectives on Female Solidarity.* London: Tavistock Publications.

Nathe, P.A. 1976. "Prickly Pear Coffee House: The Hangout." *Urban Life* 5:75–104.

Nelson, C. 1974. "Public and Private Politics: Women in the Middle Eastern World." *American Ethnologist* 1:551–563.

Nietzsche, F. 1878/1968. "Menschliches, Allzumenschliches: Ein Buch für freie Geister." In F. Nietzsche. *Studienausgabe in vier Bänden*, vol. 2. Frankfurt: Fischer-Bücherei.

Oevermann, U. 1983. "Zur Sache: Die Bedeutung Adornos methodologischem Selbstverständnis für die Begründung einer materialen soziologischen Strukturanalyse." Pp. 234–289 in L. von Friedburg and J. Habermas (eds.). *Adorno-Konferenz 1983.* Frankfurt: Suhrkamp Verlag.

Oevermann, U. et al. 1979. "Die Methodologie einer 'objektiven Hermeneutik' und ihre allgemeine forschungslogische Bedeutung in den Sozialwissenschaften." Pp. 352–434 in H.-G. Soeffner (ed.). *Interpretive Verfahren in den Sozial- und Textwissenschaften.* Stuttgart: Metzler.

Ogburn, W.F. and M.F. Nimkoff. 1950. *Sociology.* Boston: Houghton Mifflin.

Olinick, S.L. 1980. "The Gossiping Psychoanalyst." *International Review of Psychoanalysis* 7:439–445.

O'Neill, J. 1981. "The Literary Production of Natural and Social Science Inquiry: Issues and Applications in the Social Organization of Science." *Canadian Journal of Sociology* 6:105–120.

Paine, R. 1967. "What is Gossip About? An Alternative Hypothesis." *Man* 2:278–285.

———. 1968. "Gossip and Transaction." *Man* (N.S.) 3:305–308.

———. 1970. "Informal Communication and Information Management." *Canadian Revue of Sociology and Anthropology* 7:172–188.

Park, R.E. 1915. "Suggestions for the Investigation of Human Behavior in the City Environment." *American Journal of Sociology* 20:577–612.

Parsons, E.C. 1936. "Town Gossip." Pp. 386–478 in E.C. Parsons. *Mitla: Town of the Souls and Other Zapoteco-Speaking Pueblos of Oaxaca Mexico*. Chicago: University of Chicago Press.

Paul, J. 1801/1975. "Das heimliche Klaglied der jetzigen Männer." Pp. 1087–1120 in J. Paul. *Werke in zwölf Bänden*, vol. 8. Munich: Hanser.

Pavel, T.G. 1978. "Literary Criticism and Methodology." *Disposition* 3:145–156.

Peckham, M. 1972. "Romanticism, Science, and Gossip." *Shenandoah* 23(4):81–89.

Perrot, M. 1981. "Rebellische Weiber: Die Frau in der französichen Stadt des 19. Jahrhunderts." Pp. 71–98 in C. Honegger and B. Heinz (eds.). *Listen der Ohnmacht: Zur Sozialgeschichte weiblicher Widerstandsformen*. Frankfurt: Europäische Verlagsanstalt.

Peters, E.L. 1972. "Aspects of the Control of Moral Ambiguities: A Comparative Analysis of Two Culturally Disparate Modes of Social Control." Pp. 109–162 in M. Gluckman (ed.). *The Allocation of Responsibility*. Manchester: Manchester University Press.

Phillips, G. 1860. "Über den Ursprung der Katzenmusiken: Eine canonistisch-mythologische Abhandlung." Pp. 26–92 in G. Phillips. *Vermischte Schriften*. Vienna: W. Braumüller.

Pitt-Rivers, J.A. 1954/1971. *The People of the Sierra*. Chicago: University of Chicago Press.

Platt, J. 1983. "The Development of the 'Participant Observation' Method in Sociology: Origin Myth and History." *Journal of the History of the Behavioral Sciences* 19:379–393.

Plessner, H. 1924/1972. *Grenzen der Gemeinschaft: Eine Kritik des sozialen Radikalismus*. Bonn: Bouvier.

Pomerantz, A. 1980. "Telling My Side: 'Limited Access' as a 'Fishing' Device." *Sociological Inquiry* 50:186–198.

———. 1984. "Agreeing and Disagreeing with Assessments: Some Features of Preferred/Dispreferred Turn Shapes." Pp. 57–101 in J.M. Atkinson and J. Heritage (eds.). *Structures of Social Action: Studies in Conversation Analysis*. Cambridge: Cambridge University Press.

Popitz, H. 1968. *Über die Präventivwirkung des Nichtwissens*. Tübingen: J.C.B. Mohr.

Pouillon, J. and P. Maranda (eds.). 1970. *Éhange et communications. Mélanges offerts à Claude Lévi-Strauss, à l'occasion de son 60ème anniversaire*. vol. 1. The Hague and Paris: Mouton.

Preisendanz, W. 1984. "Zur Ästhetizität des Gesprächs bei Fontane." Pp. 473–487 in K. Stierle and R. Warning (eds.). *Das Gespräch (Poetik und Hermeneutik, vol. XI)*. Munich: W. Fink.

Radin, P. 1927/1957. *Primitive Man as Philosopher*. New York: Dover.

Ranulf, S. 1938. *Moral Indignation and Middle Class Psychology: A Sociological Reader*. Copenhagen: Levin & Munksgaard.

Reichenau, Ch. von 1936. "Die Übertreibung." Pp. 202–217 in G. Albrecht ,(ed.). *Reine und angewandte Soziologie (Festschrift für Ferdinand Tönnies)*. Leipzig: Buske.

Riegelhaupt, J.F. 1967. "Saloio Women: An Analysis of Informal and Formal Political and Economic Roles of Portuguese Peasant Women." *Anthropological Quarterly* 40:109–126.

Riemann, G. 1977. "Stigma, formelle soziale Kontrolle, das Leben mit den anderen: Eine empirische Untersuchung zu drei Gegenstandsbereichen des Alltagswissen von Obdachlosen." Dissertation, University of Bielefeld.

Riesman, D. and J. Watson. 1964. "The Sociability Project: A Chronicle of Frustration and Achievement." Pp. 235–321 in P.E. Hammond (ed.). *Sociologists at Work*. Garden City, New York: Doubleday.

Riesman, D., R.J. Potter, and J. Watson. 1965. "Sociability, Permissiveness, and Equality." Pp. 185–212 in D. Riesmann. *Abundance for What?* Garden City, N.Y.: Doubleday.

Riviere, P. 1970. "Factions and Exclusions in Two South American Village Systems." Pp. 245–255 in M. Douglas (ed.). *Witchcraft Confessions and Accusations*. London: Tavistock Publications.

Roberts, J.M. 1964. "The Self-Management of Cultures." Pp. 433- 454 in W.H. Goodenough. *Explorations in Cultural Anthropology*. New York: McGraw-Hill.

Rogers, S.C. 1975. "Female Forms of Power and the Myth of Male Dominance: A Model of Female/Male Interaction in Peasant Society." *American Ethnologist* 2:727–756.

Rohr, R. 1979. "Auf Abruf bereit: Lokaljournalisten bei der Arbeit." Pp. 76–96 in H.M. Kepplinger (ed.). *Angepaßte Außenseiter: Wie Journalisten denken und wie sie arbeiten*. Freiburg: K. Alber.

Rose, A.M. 1956/1965. *Sociology: The Study of Human Relations*. New York: Knopf.

Rosenbaum, J.B. and M. Subrin. 1963. "The Psychology of Gossip." *Journal of the American Psychoanalytic Association* 11:158–163.

Rosnow, R.L. 1977. "Gossip and Marketplace Psychology." *Journal of Communication* 27:158–163.

Rosnow, R.L. and G.A. Fine. 1976. *Rumor and Gossip: The Social Psychology of Hearsay*. New York: Elsevier.

Ross, E.A. 1901/1929. *Social Control: A Survey of the Foundations of Order*. New York: Macmillan.

Roth, E.W. 1927. *Die materiellrechtliche und prozessuale Bedeutung des Indiskretionsdelikts*. Breslau: Schletter'sche Buchhandlung.

Rotzoll, C. 1982. "Klatsch: Ein Kulturgut." *Frankfurter Allgemeine Zeitung*, Aug. 21.

Rouček, J.S. 1947/1956. *Social Control*. New York: Van Nostrand.

Roy, D.F. 1960. "'Banana Time': Job Satisfaction and Informal Interaction." *Human Organization* 18(4):158–168.

Rubinstein, J. 1973. *City Police*. New York: Farrar, Strauss & Giroux.

Ruesch, J. and G. Bateson. 1951. *Communication: The Social Matrix of Psychiatry*. New York: Norton.

Ryave, A.L. 1978. "On the Achievement of a Series of Stories." Pp. 113–132 in J. Schenkein (ed.). *Studies in the Organization of Conversational Interaction*. New York: Academic Press.

Ryle, G. 1949. *The Concept of Mind*. New York: Barnes & Noble.

Rysman, A. 1977. "How Gossip Became a Woman." *Journal of Communication* 27:176–180.

Sabini, J. and M. Silver. 1982. "A Plea for Gossip." Pp. 89–106 in J. Sabini and M. Silver. *Moralities of Everyday Life*. Oxford: Oxford University Press.

Sacks, H. 1971. "Das Erzählen von Geschichten innerhalb von Unterhaltungen." Pp. 307–314 in R. Kjolseth and F. Sack (eds.). *Zur Soziologie der Sprache*. Opladen: Westdeutscher Verlag.

———. 1972. "On the Analyzability of Stories by Children." Pp. 325–345 in J.J. Gumperz and D. Hymes (eds.). *Directions in Sociolinguistics: The Ethnography of Communication*. New York: Basil Blackwell.

———. 1974. "An Analysis of the Course of a Joke's Telling in Conversation." Pp. 337–353 in R. Bauman and J. Scherzer (eds.). *Explorations in the Ethnography of Speaking*. London: Cambridge University Press.

Sacks, H. and E. Schegloff. 1979. "Two Preferences in the Organization of Reference to Persons in Conversation and Their Interaction." Pp. 15–21 in G. Psathas (ed.). *Everyday Language: Studies in Ethnomethodology*. New York: Irvington Publishers.

Sansom, B. 1972. "When Witches Are Not Named." Pp. 193–226 in M. Gluckman (ed.). *The Allocation of Responsibility*. Manchester: Manchester University Press.

Schäfer-Elmayer, N. and D. Schäfer-Elmayer. 1969. *Der neue Elmayer: Gutes Benehmen immer gefragt*. Vienna: P. Zsolnay.

Scharfe, M. 1966. "Rügebräuche." Pp. 196–266 in H. Bausinger et al. (eds.). *Dörfliche Fasnacht zwischen Neckar und Bodensee*. Tübingen: Vereinigung für Volkskunde.

Schegloff, E. 1968. "Sequencing in Conversational Openings." *American Anthropologist* 70:1075–1095.

———. 1972. "Notes on a Conversational Practice: Formulating Place." Pp. 75–119 in D. Sudnow (ed.). *Studies in Social Interaction*. New York: The Free Press.

———. 1979. "Identification and Recognition in Telephone Conversation Openings." Pp. 23–78 in G. Psathas (ed.). *Everyday Language: Studies in Ethnomethodology*. New York: Irvington Publishers.

Schegloff, E. and H. Sacks. 1973. "Opening Up Closings." *Semiotics* 8:289–327.

Scheler, M. 1925/1961. *Ressentiment*. New York: The Free Press.

Schenk, M. 1983. "Das Konzept des sozialen Netzwerks." Pp. 88–104 in F. Neidhardt (ed.). *Gruppensoziologie*, (Special Issue 25 of the *Kölner Zeitschrift für Soziologie und Sozialpsychologie*). Opladen: Westdeutscher Verlag.

Schenkein, J.N. 1978. "Identity Negotiations in Conversation." Pp. 57–78 in J.N. Schenkein (ed.). *Studies in the Organization of Conversational Interaction*. New York: Academic Press.

Schiffauer, W. 1985. "Weltbild und Selbstverständnis der Bauern von Subay: Eine Ethnographie." Dissertation, Free University of Berlin.

Schiffrin, D. 1980. "Meta-Talk: Organizational and Evaluative Brackets in Discourse." *Sociological Inquiry* 50:199–236.

Schivelbusch, W. 1980. *Das Paradies, der Geschmack und die Vernunft: Eine Geschichte der Genußmittel*. Munich: Hanser.

Schleiermacher, F.E.D. 1799/1927. "Versuch einer Theorie des geselligen Betragens." Pp. 1–31 in F.E.D. Schleiermacher. *Auswahl in vier Bänden*, vol. II. Leipzig: Felix Meiner Verlag.

Schmölders, C. (ed.). 1979. *Die Kunst des Gesprächs: Texte zur Geschichte der europäischen Konversationstheorie*. Munich: Deutscher Taschenbuch Verlag.

Schönfeldt, S.G. 1983. "Was ist noch schöner als Klatsch?" *Zeit Magazine*, Sept. 23.

Schott, R. 1968. "Das Geschichtsbewußtsein schriftloser Völker." *Archiv für Begriffsgeschichte* 12:166–205.

Schulte, R. 1978. "Dienstmädchen in herrschaftlichen Haushalt: Zur Genese ihrer Sozialpsychologie." *Zeitschrift für bayerische Landesgeschichte* 41:879–920.

Schuster, I.M.G. 1979. *New Women of Lusaka*. Palo Alto, California: Stanford University Press.

Schütz, A. 1932/1967. *The Phenomenology of the Social World*. Evanston, Ill.: Northwestern University Press.

———. 1946/1976. "The Well-Informed Citizen: An Essay on the Social Distribution of Knowledge." Pp. 120–134 in A. Schütz. *Collected Papers*, vol. II. The Hague: Martinus Nijhoff.

———. 1954/1973. "Concept and Theory Formation in the Social Sciences." Pp. 48–66 in A. Schütz. *Collected Papers*, vol. I. The Hague: Martinus Nijhoff.

Schütz, A. and Th. Luckmann. 1973. *Structures of the Life-World*. Evanston, Ill.: Northwestern University Press.

———. 1984. *Strukturen der Lebenswelt*,vol. 2. Frankfurt: Suhrkamp Verlag.

Schütze, F. 1977. "Exkurs über Klatschkommunikation in der Ortsgesellschaft." Pp.19–22 in F. Schütze. "Die Technik des narrativen Interviews in Interaktionsfeldstudien— dargestellt an einem Projekt zur Erforschung von kommunalen Machtstrukturen." University of Bielefeld, Department of Sociology, *Arbeitsberichte und Forschungsmaterialen*, No. 1.

Selby, H.A. 1974. *Zapoteco Deviance: The Convergence of Folk and Modern Sociology*. Austin: University of Texas Press.

Shibutani, T. 1966. *Improvised News: A Sociological Study of Rumor*. Indianapolis: Bobbs-Merrill.

Silbermann, A. 1974. "Systematische Inhaltsanalyse." Pp. 253–339 in R. König (ed.). *Handbuch der empirischen Sozialforschung*,vol. 4. Stuttgart: Ferdinand Enke Verlag.

Silverman, S. 1975. *Three Bells of Civilization: The Life of an Italian Hill Town*. New York: Columbia University Press.

Simmel, G. 1908/1968a. "Exkurs über den schriftlichen Verkehr." Pp. 287–288 in G. Simmel. *Soziologie: Untersuchungen über die Formen der Vergesellschaftung*. Berlin: Duncker & Humblot.

———. 1908/1968b. "Das Geheimnis und die geheime Gesellschaft." Pp. 256–304 in G. Simmel. *Soziologie: Untersuchungen über die Formen der Vergesellschaftung*. Berlin: Duncker & Humblot.

———. 1908/1968c. *Soziologie: Untersuchungen über die Formen der Vergesellschaftung*. Berlin: Duncker & Humblot.

———. 1917/1970. "Die Geselligkeit (Beispiel der reinen oder formalen Soziologie)." Pp. 48–68 in G. Simmel. *Grundfragen der Soziologie*. Berlin: Walter de Gruyter Verlag.

Skinner, B.F. 1948. *Walden Two*. New York: Macmillan.

Smith, Th. V. 1937. "Custom, Gossip, Legislation." *Social Forces* 16:24–34.

Soeffner, H.-G. 1982. "Statt einer Einleitung: Prämissen einer sozialwissenschaftlichen Hermeneutik." Pp. 9–48 in H.-G. Soeffner. *Beiträge zu einer empirischen Sprachsoziologie*. Tübingen: Narr.

———. 1984. "Hermeneutik—Zur Genese einer wissenschaftlichen Einstellung durch die Praxis der Auslegung." Pp. 9–52 in H.-G. Soeffner (ed.). *Beiträge zu einer Soziologie der Interaktion*. Frankfurt: Campus Verlag.

———. 1985. "Anmerkungen zu gemeinsamen Standards standardisierter und nicht-standardisierter Verfahren in der Sozialforschung." Pp. 109–126 in M. Kaase and M. Küchler (eds.). *Herausforderungen der Empirischen Sozialforschung*. Mannheim: Zentrum für Umfragen, Methoden und Analysen.

Spacks, P.M. 1982. "In Praise of Gossip." *The Hudson Review* 25:19–38.

———. 1985. *Gossip*. New York: Knopf.

Srinivas, M.N. 1976. *The Remembered Village*. Berkeley: University of California Press.

Stein, M.R. 1960/1972. *The Eclipse of Community: An Interpretation of American Studies*. Princeton: Princeton University Press.

Stempel, W.-D. 1983. "Fiktion in konversationellen Erzählungen." Pp. 331–356 in D. Henrich and W. Iser (eds.). *Funktionen der Fiktion* (*Poetik und Hermeneutik* vol. X). Munich: W. Fink.

———. 1984. "Bemerkungen zur Kommunikation im Alltagsgespräch." Pp. 151–169 in K. Stierle and R. Warning (eds.). *Das Gespräch* (*Poetik und Hermeneutik* vol. XI). Munich: W. Fink.

Sternberg, M. 1982. "Proteus in Quotation-Land: Mimesis and the Forms of Reported Discourse." *Poetics Today* 3:107–156.

Stirling, R.B. 1956. "Some Psychological Mechanisms Operative in Gossip." *Social Forces* 34:262–267.

Stok, W. 1929. *Geheimnis, Lüge und Mißverständnis: Eine beziehungswissenschaftliche Untersuchung* (*Beiträge zur Beziehungslehre*, Issue II). Munich: Duncker & Humblot.

Streck, B. 1985. "Netzwerk: Der transaktionale Einspruch gegen das Paradigma der struktural-funktionalistischen Ethnologie." *Anthropos* 80:569–586.

Streeck, J. 1988. "Seniorinnengelächter." Pp. 54–77 in H. Kotthoff (ed.). *Das Gelächter der Geschlechter: Humor und Macht in Gesprächen von Frauen und Männern*. Frankfurt: Fischer.

Sudnow, S. 1967/1973. *Passing On*. Englewood Cliffs, N.J.: Prentice-Hall.

Suls, J.M. 1977. "Gossip as Social Comparison." *Journal of Communication* 27:164–168.

Sulzberger, C.F. 1953. "Why Is It Hard to Keep Secrets." *Psychoanalysis* 2:37–43.

Sutton, H. and L.W. Porter. 1968. "A Study of the Grapevine in a Governmental Organization." *Personnel Psychology* 21:223–230.

Szwed, J. 1966. "Gossip, Drinking, and Social Control: Consensus and Communication in a Newfoundland Parish." *Ethnology* 5:434–441.

Tanner, R.E.S. 1964. "Conflict within Small European Communities in Tanganyika." *Human Organization* 23:319–327.

Tenbruck, F.H. 1962. "Soziale Kontrolle." Pp. 226–231 in *Staatslexikon der Görresgesellschaft*, vol. 7. Freiburg: K. Alber.

Tentori, T. 1976. "Social Class and Family in a Southern Italian Town." Pp. 273–285 in J.G. Peristiany (ed.). *Mediterranean Family Structures*. Cambridge: Cambridge University Press.

Terasaki, A.K. 1976. "Pre-Announcement Sequences in Conversation." *Social Science Working Papers* No. 99. Irvine: University of California.

Theophrastus. 1953. *The Characters of Theophrastus*. Cambridge, Mass.: Harvard University Press.

Thiel, K. 1905. *Iniuria und Beleidigung: Eine Vorarbeit zur Bestimmung des Begriffes der Beleidigung*. Breslau: Schletter.

Thiele-Dohrmann, K. 1975. *Unter dem Siegel der Verschwiegenheit: Die Psychologie des Klatsches*. Düsseldorf: E. Kabel.

Thomas, W.I. 1928/1969. *The Unadjusted Girl*. Montclair, N.J.: Patterson Smith.

Thomas, W.I. and F. Znaniecki. 1919/1958. *The Polish Peasant in Europe and America*. New York: Dover.

Thomasius, Ch. 1710/1979. "Von der Klugheit, sich in täglicher Konversation wohl aufzuführen." Pp. 183–186 in C. Schmölders (ed.). *Die Kunst des Gesprächs: Texte zur Geschichte der europäischen Konversationstheorie*. Munich: Deutscher Taschenbuch Verlag.

Tiger, L. and R. Fox. 1971. *The Imperial Animal*. New York: Holt, Rinehart and Winston.

Tolstoy, L. 1871–76/1931. *Anna Karenina*. New York: Grosset & Dunlap.

Treiber, H. 1986. "Obertanen: Gesellschaftsklatsch—ein Zugang zur geschlossenen Gesellschaft der Prestige-Oberschicht." *Journal für Sozialforschung* 26:140–159.

Trublet, N. 1735/1979. "Gedanken über die Konversation." Pp. 194–198 in C. Schmölders (ed.). *Die Kunst des Gesprächs: Texte zur Geschichte der europäischen Konversationstheorie*. Munich: Deutscher Taschenbuch Verlag.

Turner, R. 1968. "Talk and Troubles: Contact Problems of Former Mental Patients." Dissertation, University of California, Berkeley.

Vedel, V. 1901. *By og Borger i Middelalderen*. Copenhagen: Nordiske Forlag.

Vidich, A.J. and J. Bensman. 1958. *Small Town in Mass Society: Class, Power, and Religion in a Rural Community*. Princeton: Princeton University Press.

Viebig, C. 1925. *Das tägliche Brot*. Berlin: E. Fleischel.

Vološinov, V.N. 1929/1973. *Marxism and the Philosophy of Language*. New York: Seminar Press.

Vossler, K. 1923. "Die Grenzen der Sprachsoziologie." Pp. 210–260 in K. Vossler. *Gesammelte Aufsätze zur Sprachphilosophie*. Munich: K. Hueber.

Wahrig (Brockhaus-Wahrig). *Deutsches Wöterbuch*, 6 vols. Wiesbaden/Stuttgart: Brockhaus/Deutsche Verlagsanstalt.

Waliullah, A.-M. 1982. "Potiches ou moulins à paroles: Réflexions sur le bavardage—Qui bavarde? De quoi? Pourquoi?" *Langage et Société* 21:93–99.

Waller, W. 1961. *The Sociology of Teaching*. New York: Russell & Russell.

Walser, K. 1985, "Prostitutionsverdacht und Geschlechterforschung: Das Beispiel der Dienstmädchen um 1900." *Geschichte und Gesellschaft* 11:99–111.

Weber, M. 1904/1968. "Die 'Objektivität' sozialwissenschaftlicher und sozialpolitischer Erkenntnis." Pp. 1–64 in M. Weber. *Methodologische Schriften*. Frankfurt: S. Fischer.

———. 1921–22/1978. *Economy and Society*. Berkeley: University of California Press.

Weigle, M. 1978. "Women as Verbal Artists: Reclaiming the Sisters of Enheduanna." *Frontiers* III(3):1–9.

Wenglinsky, M. 1973. "Errands." Pp. 83–100 in A. Birenbaum and E. Sagarin (eds.). *People in Places*. New York: Praeger.

Werbner, R.P. 1984. "The Manchester School in South-Central Africa." *Annual Review of Anthropology* 13:157–185.

Wesel, U. 1985. *Frühformen des Rechts in vorstaatlichen Gesellschaften*. Frankfurt: Suhrkamp Verlag.

West, J. 1945. *Plainville U.S.A.*. New York: Columbia University Press.

Whiting, B.B. 1950. *Paiute Society* New York: Viking Fund Publications in Anthropology 15.

Whyte, W.H. 1956. *The Organization Man*. New York: Simon and Schuster.

Wiese, L. von. 1924–28/1955. *System der Allgemeinen Soziologie als Lehre von den sozialen Prozessen und den sozialen Gebilden der Menschen (Beziehungslehre)*. Berlin: Duncker & Humblot.

Wiese, L. von (ed.). 1928. *Das Dorf als soziales Gebilde* (Issue 1 of the *Beiträge zur Beziehungslehre*). Munich/Leipzig: Duncker & Humblot.

Wikan, U. 1980. *Life among the Poor in Cairo*. London and New York: Tavistock Publications.

Williams, W.M. 1956. *The Sociology of an English Village: Gosforth*. London: Routledge & Kegan Paul.

Wilson, P.J. 1973. *Crab Antics: The Social Anthropology of English-Speaking Negro Societies of the Caribbean*. New Haven: Yale University Press.

———. 1974. "Filcher of Good Names: An Enquiry into Anthropology and Gossip." *Man* 9:93–102.

Wolf, E. 1984, "Klatsch—Balsam für die Seele." *Journal für die Frau* 16:131–132.

Wolf, M. 1972. *Women and the Family in Rural Taiwan*. Stanford, California: Stanford University Press.

Wolter, I. N.d. *Benimm-Brevier für junge Menschen*. Wiesbaden: Falken Verlag

Wunderlich, H. 1894. *Unsere Umgangssprache in der Eigenart ihrer Satzfügung*. Weimar: E. Felber.

Wylie, L. 1957. *Village in the Vaucluse*. Cambridge, Mass.: Harvard University Press.

Yerkovich, S.M. 1976. "Gossiping: Or, the Creation of Fictional Lives, Being a Study of the Subject in an Urban American Setting Drawing upon Vignettes from Upper Middle Class Lives." Dissertation, University of Pennsylvania.

———. 1977. "Gossiping as a Way of Speaking." *Journal of Communication* 27:192–196.

Zeitlin, S.J. 1979. "Pop Lore: The Aesthetic Principles in Celebrity Gossip." *Journal of American Culture* 2:186–192.

Zinzendorf, N.L. Graf. 1723/1979. "Gedanken vom Reden und Gebrauch der Worte." Pp. 187–193 in C. Schmölders (ed.). *Die Kunst des Gesprächs: Texte zur Geschichte der europäischen Konversationstheorie*. Munich: Deutscher Taschenbuch Verlag.

Zorbaugh, H.W. 1929. *The Golden Coast and the Slum: A Sociological Study of Chicago's Near North Side*. Chicago: University of Chicago Press.

Index